The Knowledge Economy

Resources for the Knowledge-Based Economy

THE KNOWLEDGE ECONOMY
Dale Neef

KNOWLEDGE IN ORGANIZATIONS
Laurence Prusak

KNOWLEDGE MANAGEMENT AND ORGANIZATIONAL DESIGN
Paul S. Myers

KNOWLEDGE MANAGEMENT TOOLS
Rudy L. Ruggles, III

THE STRATEGIC MANAGEMENT OF INTELLECTUAL CAPITAL
David A. Klein

The Knowledge Economy

Dale Neef
Editor

Butterworth-Heinemann
Boston Oxford Johannesburg Melbourne New Delhi Singapore

Recognizing the importance of preserving what has been written, Butterworth–Heinemann prints its books on acid-free paper whenever possible.

Butterworth–Heinemann supports the efforts of American Forests and the Global ReLeaf program in its campaign for the betterment of trees, forests, and our environment.

Library of Congress Cataloging-in-Publication Data
The knowledge economy / Dale Neef, editor.
p. cm. — (Resources for the knowledge-based economy)
Includes bibliographical references and index.
ISBN 0-7506-9936-1 (alk. paper)
1. Information technology—Economic aspects. 2. Information resources—Economic aspects. 3. Information services industry. 4. Telecommunication. I. Neef, Dale, 1959– . II. Series.
HC79.I55K57 1997
330.9—dc21 97-34241
CIP

British Library Cataloguing-in-Publication Data
A catalogue record for this book is available from the British Library.

The publisher offers special discounts on bulk orders of this book.
For information, please contact:
Manager of Special Sales
Butterworth–Heinemann
225 Wildwood Avenue
Woburn, MA 01801-2041
Tel: 617-928-2500
Fax: 617-928-2620

For information on all Butterworth–Heinemann books available, contact our World Wide Web home page at: http://www.bh.com

10 9 8 7 6 5 4 3 2 1

Printed in the United States of America

Table of Contents

Acknowledgments

The Ernst & Young Center for Business Innovation[SM] provided support for this project, and Suzanne Connolly, particularly, provided valuable assistance in securing permissions for reprint of the selections.

Introduction to Series—
Why Knowledge, Why Now?

Why is there such an upsurge of interest in knowledge? In 1996 there were at least six major conferences on the subject; three new journals focusing on knowledge (sometimes loosely called intellectual capital or organizational learning) were published; and many major firms in the United States and Europe added positions such as chief knowledge officer, organizational learning officer, and even a few vice presidents for intellectual capital!

Why the focus on a subject that, at some levels, has been around since the pre-Socratic philosophers? Is it yet another one of the multitudinous management enthusiasms that seem to come and go with the frequency of some random natural phenomena? We don't think so! Many of us doing research on this subject have seen the rise and fall of many of these varied nostrums—all of which attempted to offer firms a new road to achieving a sustainable competitive advantage. However, when much of the shouting dies down, we conclude that, excluding monopolistic policies and other market irregularities, there is no sustainable advantage other than what a firm knows, how it can utilize what it knows, and how fast it can learn something new!

However, this still does not answer the questions why knowledge, why now? Let us list some very broad trends that seem to be playing a significant role in the current development of knowledge:

A) The globalization of the economy, which is putting terrific pressure on firms for increased adaptability, innovation, and process speed.

B) The awareness of the value of specialized knowledge, as embedded in organizational processes and routines, in coping with the pressures of globalization.

C) The awareness of knowledge as a distinct factor of production and its role in the growing book value to market value ratios within knowledge-based industries.

D) Cheap networked computing, which is at last giving us a tool for working with and learning from each other.

While many can argue for and against the significance of these trends, we feel that the preponderance of evidence points to the increasing substitution of brain for brawn within our organizations and our social lives. Yet we have developed few conceptional tools to better work with "wetware."

It is with these forces in mind that we offer the following volume to you. While there are, as yet, few agreed-upon standards and analytic frames and definitions, there are enough serious articles and books to help managers get some real traction in dealing with the crucial yet elusive subject of knowledge.

After all, we have had about 500 years of thought concerning the other major factors of production, for example, land, labor, and capital. Let these volumes start the process of codifying knowledge about knowledge in order for us to better manage in the twenty-first century.

Laurence Prusak,
Series Editor

1

The Knowledge Economy: An Introduction

Dale Neef

How often in the past months have we heard or seen the phrase "the knowledge-based economy"? Was it in a political campaign, or in an article from a popular business weekly? Its use has become almost commonplace in American business circles, and yet its context varies enormously. The phrase has been used enthusiastically to describe a new interconnected economy and the positive effect of newly emerging technologies in the workplace and home. Equally, it has been used to lament the effect of downsizing on the blue-collar sectors of the labor force. For some, "knowledge-based economy" describes the ever-increasing proportion of the nation's GNP dedicated to computerization and high-technology electronics industries. For others, it is the impetus behind "knowledge management"—adaptation of traditional organizational structures in a way that better accommodates the highly skilled "knowledge workers" who populate the high-performance workplace and provide complex problem-solving services. The knowledge-based economy is a phrase that has been used to describe both a coming age of global prosperity and a coming economic apocalypse.

So what is this knowledge-based economy? Is it really new or unique? What are its effects, and what does it mean to us? To help answer these questions, this anthology has been compiled with the support of Ernst & Young's Center for Business Innovation as a means of providing answers for anyone in business or public-policy-making fields who would like to know what academics and economists are talking about when they refer to the knowledge-based economy. The anthology is a collection of articles that deal with the most important developing themes in this area: computing, telecommunications, globalization, and the interconnected economy; the shift in employment from "brawn to brains"; organizational changes brought about by the new breed of knowledge workers functioning in the new high-performance workplace; and the effect that "knowledge elitism" may have on public policy concerning education and training, wealth disparity, and social exclusion. Using seminal articles from a variety of sources, this volume is intended to be a primer for introducing the reader to all aspects of the knowledge-based economy.

The basic thesis behind the emergence of a knowledge-based economy is that during the past five years there has been a unique combination of focused market incentives that have led to immense technical progress in the areas of computing, biotechnology, telecommunications, and transportation (to name only a few) and which have begun to foster dramatic changes in the way in which economies, organizations, and governments will function in the future. Indeed, there is now compelling evidence that the sudden and ever-accelerating burst of growth in high-technology and high-skill services and in the new products and service structure they are creating may bring about some of the most profound and unexpected changes to the way in which we live and work witnessed since the nineteenth-century transition from an agricultural to an industrial society.

How can we tell that this economic transition is occurring? There are many indicators, but the most obvious signals can be seen in the changing nature of the workplace in all major developed economies. During the past several years there has been a marked shift from goods-based production to high-skill, high-technology, service-based growth. Low-skill, blue-collar positions have been disappearing at an alarming rate in developed economies as labor-based production has been shifted to lower-cost areas throughout the world. An increasing percentage of the GNP of developed economies is now derived from high-skill services. Knowledge in the form of complex problem solving, technological innovation, creative exploitation of new markets, and the development of new product or service offerings is central to success in these areas.

Organization for Economic Cooperation and Development (OECD) statistics reflect this remarkable transition. Since the 1960s, service prices have increased more than three times as rapidly as industrial prices, and the percentage of the American GNP dedicated to services (a typical OECD national example) has risen from just over 50% to more than 80%.[1] Of these services, 63% are considered to be in high-skill categories. According to the World Bank, 64% of the world's wealth now consists of "human capital," and a recent study by McKinsey concluded that, by the turn of the millennium, more than 80% of all jobs in America will be "cerebral" in nature.[2]

Beyond just statistics, the relative impact of this trend on the global economy is brought even more sharply into focus when we consider the extent to which output from high-skill, knowledge-based services contributes to our everyday lives. Unlike earlier years in which a good proportion of employment consisted of low- to medium-skill work in blue-collar manufacturing or farm work, today's "knowledge work" includes fields such as education, advertising, architecture, research and development, media production, selling, filmmaking, accountancy, law, theater, computer software development, consultancy services, photography, the greater portion of health care, social work, publishing, management, banking, the realm of the church, real estate, and most government work. Although often intangible (unmeasurable by predictable quantity or price) in the traditional sense, this knowledge-based work increasingly represents the bulk of wealth creation and employment in modern economies.

Nor has the growth of knowledge-based work been confined to the services sector alone. The extent to which knowledge work has risen, even in the shrinking manufacturing and goods production sector, is remarkable. Unlike the 1950-to-1980 boom years in which most work required only medium- or low-level production or transport ("make or move") skills that were easily learned and endlessly repeated, today's modern production enterprise is dominated by knowledge work. Even the assembly line is shifting toward higher-skilled employees. Today more than 15% of factory-line workers have some college education, and nearly 30% of precision production or craft workers are college graduates.[3] Output of functions such as customer service, strategic planning, marketing and sales, research and development, finance and accounting, and human resources provides the impetus for growth and change, and these positions are largely dominated by college graduates, who often have advanced degrees. New technology and human-based productivity techniques involving empowerment, teams, and lower-level decision responsibilities for operational line workers all require a more highly skilled workforce. Enterprises in the new knowledge-based economy can no longer ensure growth through duplication of commodities at ever-increasing levels with low-skill, low-wage employees. Enterprise growth today depends on innovation, and innovation depends on knowledge.

As a result, it is becoming obvious that individuals (and organizations) who are best able to leverage their knowledge advantage will increasingly account for a greater portion of total output. They will also become the recipients of a consistently greater portion of relative earnings. In short, for developed economies, knowledge work—activities that involve complex problem identification, problem solution, or high-technology design and that result in innovative new products or services or create new ways of exploiting markets—has quickly become the focus for economic growth and individual and organizational prosperity. This change will have profound effects on our way of life at both organizational and national levels.

A second important indicator of this knowledge-based transition is the increasing globalization of firms. As the emphasis of computing technology in the past five years has shifted from accounting to high-speed communications, convergent developments, particularly in transport, computing, and telecommunications capabilities, have created a potentially unbounded economic framework in which both a global market and a global labor pool are emerging. In many instances, this electronic corporate globalization is already occurring. More than 100 American firms, for example, outsource their software "code cutting" to sites in India, where the work is completed and returned overnight electronically by highly skilled programmers at only a fraction of the labor costs demanded in the US. In fact, it is estimated that as many as 4 million "virtual aliens" are employed directly in the American workforce—residing outside the nation's borders, undercutting traditional labor markets, paying no taxes—connected only through electronic telecommunications networks.[4]

These new technologies, combined with growing market saturation domestically, have necessitated global extension and have pushed corporations well beyond the realm of multinationalism toward the development of the "non-national" organization, in which cross-border operations extend increasingly into complex, loose alliance networks of vendors, outsourcing agents, and distribution channels worldwide.

The first part of this anthology explores the dramatic changes occurring in today's global economy and, by contrasting ideas of leading economic and management thinkers, begins to develop a blueprint of the coming global economic network. Part One begins, appropriately, with one of the most influential management theorists of the past 25 years—Peter F. Drucker, who first previewed the coming of the knowledge-based society in the 1980s. His essay, "From Capitalism to Knowledge Society," is an explanation of the broad, worldwide shift from "brawn to brains-based economies" set in a historical context. In "The Rise of the Virtual State," Richard Rosecrance, Professor of Political Science at the University of California, Los Angeles, describes the effect that the exponential growth of knowledge-based industries is having on the traditional global-political framework. He argues that innovations in communications, computing, and transport have led to a global marketplace that will eventually bring into question our very notion of national sovereignty and the role of individual domestic governments. Part One concludes with a short essay, "From High Volume to High Value," by Robert Reich, former Secretary of Labor and Harvard University Professor, who, as one of the most vocal exponents of the theme, argues that America needs to rethink its traditional organizational structures and strategies in light of this dramatic shift in the global economy.

With an ever-increasing proportion of advanced economies being devoted to knowledge-based services, a new economic theory is beginning to emerge, which suggests that the ability to exploit markets and to innovate, in turn, has replaced production efficiency (and therefore the concept of cost-reduction productivity) as the major driver of growth in the international economy. Similarly, there are indications that domestic growth arises not through expansion or replenishment of market share (particularly in the near-saturation domestic market of developed economies), but through the introduction of entirely new technologies or problem-solving services that create new markets. Increasingly, the knowledge skills needed to create these technologies and services, whether on an individual, organizational, or national level, may be the key to economic growth and prosperity.

But, as we learn from Drucker's essay, knowledge has been a factor of growth throughout history, and key economic milestones such as the development of the sail, the printing press, the steam engine, electricity, or the telephone were all evolutionary steps that helped shape and change the world economy. Despite the many innovations during the past two centuries, Adam Smith's basic economic framework has remained intact. Why should we believe that today's concentration of knowledge services and high technology will result in any more profound a change in economic principles than the development of penicillin or the splitting of the atom did before? The response seems to be that never before have we had so many knowledge workers, nor the tools and infrastructure born of high-technology computing by which to spread their knowledge so quickly and in such quantity. Nor, more important, in the past have there ever been the personal profit incentives or collaborative organizational designs that would allow knowledge workers to collectively gather and develop innovative ideas. The combined effect seems almost to create a force of its own. When focused and given the proper incentives, knowledge and the technology it spawns seem to be irrepressible—creating products, services, and markets at a rapid and unpredictable rate.

As might be expected, technology-based knowledge as an economic force today seems to behave contrary to many aspects of neo-classical economic theory, particularly in an unbounded, global-market setting. Unlike traditional goods production, which seems inevitably to shrink under competitive forces, knowledge seems to grow under its own effect, creating markets that never before existed, attracting and producing more innovation, and thereby "increasing returns." Problem-solving services soon follow, focusing on modest needs and creating from these needs new areas for growth and expansion. Traditional forces of production—land, labor, capital, and, indeed, monetary and fiscal policy—are less relevant when seen in the context of a knowledge-based economy. Similarly, as organizations increasingly become part of the interconnected global economy, traditional models of comparative advantage and perfect competition are brought into question. It may well be that the classical force behind economic growth described by Adam Smith as "the invisible hand," by Marx as the "dialectic of change," and by Schumpeter as "the gale of creative destruction" needs to be rethought in terms of the force of knowledge.

Part Two, "Knowledge as the Economic Force of Growth and Change," explores the many ways in which knowledge as a force requires us to rethink our traditional view of economics. It begins with an essay by David S. Landes, entitled "Homo Faber, Homo Sapiens." Landes provides a broad and accessible mixture of economic theory and historical anecdote concerning the effect that technology and knowledge have had on economic growth in the past. Next, in a fascinating thesis that demonstrates just one of the many differences exhibited by knowledge-based work, W. Brian Arthur, Professor of Economics and Population Studies at Stanford, explains how the shift from goods production to ideas-based services has turned one of the most long-held assumptions of economic thought—that of diminishing returns—on its head. In his essay "Increasing Returns and the New World of Business," Arthur argues that knowledge-based work behaves in a different way than traditional goods-based production, exhibiting the tendency for organizations or nations that lead in a particular ideas-based market to derive an ever-increasing advantage over their competition—essentially benefiting from a progressive learning curve, which provides them ever-increasing returns. Finally, Candice Stevens, Head of the Science and Technology Policy Division of the OECD, provides a good overview of the entire debate in her essay "The Knowledge-Driven Economy."

As seen in Part One, as communications technology combines with true global marketing, it will no longer be possible for large-scale enterprises to remain wholly domestic in either production or sales. Although such an evolution may be positive in some ways (e.g., traditional growth-stifling retreat into tariffs, economic isolationism, or nationalistic fervor may become less likely), competing openly on the global market necessitates a critical rethinking of our traditional view of economics. But in order to understand economic performance it is necessary to understand how to measure productivity and output. This is becoming increasingly difficult in the knowledge-based economy.

Already some 20% of the production of US companies now takes place abroad. Multinational companies such as Nestlé (headquartered in Switzerland) have as much as 98% of their production capacity outside their host nation.[5] A typical example of modern global production networking is cited by Robert Reich: "Precision ice hockey equipment is designed in Sweden, financed in Canada, and assembled in Cleveland and Denmark for distribution in North America and Europe, respectively, out of alloys whose molecular structure was researched and patented in Delaware and fabricated in Japan. An advertising campaign is conceived in Britain; film footage for it is shot in Canada, dubbed in Britain, and edited in New York." What portion of this product is American? What portion is foreign?[6]

This increasingly common scenario creates an obvious nightmare for economists, statisticians, and accountants who are trying to track national growth and productivity levels, especially when they use traditional accounting methods that reflect only hard assets and make no provision for measuring the typical "intangible" outputs of the knowledge-based economy. National accounting models were designed to track the production of physical products, not to value or measure the output of ideas that represent a collaborative effort among groups around the world. For example, the national accounts system still creates production figures for steel output and corn yields but makes no provision for tracking the ideas-based output of areas such as telecommunications, software development, entertainment, or financial services.

To make things more complicated, even when an effort to estimate knowledge-based output is made (e.g., in education or health care), from a traditional accounting standpoint, productivity gains are cited not as improvement but as lowered output. Knowledge-based work often does not result in greater volumes of anything; instead, it results in intangible but no less valuable outputs such as improved quality, time savings, or increased customer satisfaction. The results then, are widely disparate book value to market value ratios (Microsoft, for example, has an accounting book value of $5 billion dollars but a market value of $102 billion) and an inaccurate understanding of national economic performance.

Accordingly, Part Three, "Measuring and Managing the Intangibles of Knowledge," focuses on one of the most compelling issues associated with understanding knowledge as an economic force—how to create a system by which knowledge can be made visible, be assigned a value, and be declared on a standardized basis for comparison among firms. The need for valuation and measurement of human capital has been recognized for a number of years, for although we know that a growing percentage of the US GNP is dedicated to high-skilled service-provision work in which the only real assets are intangible (i.e., dependent on what the employee "knows), knowledge and its effects are not easy to measure precisely and therefore do not appear on any balance sheet and are not reflected in figures for national economic growth.

Peter Howitt, Professor of Economics at the University of Western Ontario, begins Part Three with an essay entitled "On Some Problems in Measuring Knowledge-Based Growth," in which he explores the many difficulties one encounters when trying to develop a system that can account for knowledge on a standardized basis. Many suggest that because fewer company assets are now "measurable," the present asset-based accounting systems used for investment analysis, taxation, and the like are increasingly inappropriate for accurately valuing income-earning potential for human-capital-based companies. They suggest that a new national accounts taxonomy is necessary to help take accurate account of knowledge-based assets—at both organizational and national levels. In "The Management of Intellectual Assets: A New Corporate Perspective," Professor Richard Hall, Chair of Operations and Procurement Strategy at Durham University, looks at the nature of assets from both an accountancy and an operations perspective, exploring the growing demand for measuring and managing the "products" of a knowledge-based economy: patents, trade marks, registered designs, copyright, goodwill, and other forms of intellectual property, and suggesting that organizations need to incorporate these aspects directly into their corporate strategies. Finally, in "Measuring and Managing Technological Knowledge," Roger E. Bohn, from the University of California, San Diego, suggests a framework for valuing and measuring knowledge in its several stages that extends from tacit to explicit.

On the enterprise level, a knowledge-based economy means that the transformation continues away from complex organizations with strictly governed employees doing simple work to that of simple organizations with highly trusted individuals doing complex work. If knowledge is the key to long-term competitive advantage, it is incumbent upon organizations to help their employees to apply their knowledge and skills to best effect. For that reason, "knowledge management"—the ability to capture and leverage what employees know in order to exploit new markets or create innovative new products or services—is becoming a critical management-science focus.

Knowledge management theory asserts that in order to prosper in the knowledge-based economy, organizations will need to change their traditional ways of doing things. They will need to focus increasingly on high-value service opportunities and to optimize the way they utilize (and pay for) their most creative knowledge workers.

Part Four, "Learning Organizations in the Global Knowledge-Based Economy," examines changes that successful organizations must make between now and the millennium in order to succeed in the knowledge-based economy. First, they must become "learning organizations," recruiting highly skilled employees and providing a culture in which increasingly responsible knowledge workers can flourish. As the need for instant, accurate information grows, organizations must invest in technical architectures that distribute, on demand, both internal and external information to the knowledge workers.

In an ever-increasing information jungle, a key corporate responsibility will be to organize that information coherently so that it can be readily accessed. Information must be "maintained" to be accurate and current. Often, for any true benefit to decision makers, raw or complex information must be analyzed first by one or more experts in order to be put into proper context. Increasingly, learning organizations will turn to sophisticated and integrated IT solutions to capture performance and accounting information on an enterprise-wide basis and will seek to shed noncore and low-skill functions through (often global) outsourcing policies, maintaining only loose electronic alliances. Universally, those organizations that are best able to capture and leverage the ever-growing volume of information necessary to monitor the true performance of their firms, to create new products or develop unique methods for exploiting appropriate markets, and that can provide this information in a readily accessible form to their key decision makers will prosper.

As larger enterprises continue to evolve toward the transnational corporation by expanding globally through start-ups, mergers, or acquisitions, internal communication, cooperation, and knowledge-sharing will be even more important. Within the framework of international mergers and acquisitions, a better method for understanding the value of the human capital being acquired (and the likelihood of retaining it) will be crucial. Despite recent downsizing trends, in the knowledge-based economy, cost reduction and shedding of human/knowledge assets will not be a prescription for growth or success.

In "The Coming of Knowledge-Based Business," Stan Davis, author, lecturer, and a Fellow at Ernst & Young's Center for Business Innovation, and Jim Botkin, president of InterClass and a Fellow at the University of Texas at Austin, look at the growing "interconnected economy" and explore how knowledge-based products will begin to reshape the way businesses view the products and services they design. In the knowledge-based economy, flexibility, adaptation, and innovation will be seen as critical attributes for a successful firm. In "Organisational Foundations of the Knowledge-Based Economy," John Mathews of the University of South Wales looks at how different companies have viewed organizational learning in Australia, Japan, Korea, and Chinese Taipei—all with differing approaches and degrees of success.

How do organizations know where to invest in education and training if they don't know what knowledge they have or what their employees need to know? In "Investing in Human Capital," Riel Miller and Gregory Wurzburg from the OECD discuss the broad issues surrounding the failure of traditional education and training structures to consider human capital—what workers know—and question how organizations today can develop effective education and training programs without first developing a method for understanding what their employees know, what they need to know, and what learning/teaching methods are most appropriate for that knowledge transfer to take place.

Part Five, "Society and Public Policy: Government, Education, and Training in the Knowledge-Based Economy," focuses on the effect that the shift to a knowledge-based economy is already having on national economies and public policy making, and which reflects a more malevolent side of the force of knowledge. In a society that is structured around competition and meritocracy, many believe that the disparity between the incomes of the knowledge elite and traditional low- or medium-skilled workers is growing at a frightening pace. Unlike the low- and medium-skill labor markets that prevailed for years (pre-1990s), inclusion in the highly skilled labor force of the knowledge-based economy is unlikely to be automatic or universal. Because knowledge is now the basis for wealth creation, economies are beginning to see increasing income disparity in favor of those individuals (and, similarly, organizations and nations) who are well-educated and thus capable of contributing to these high-skill areas. Wealth will increasingly be concentrated in the hands of those actively participating in the knowledge sector, and although "a rising tide lifts all boats," aggregate growth will continue to remain subdued. As labor-based manufacturing continues to be "shed" or outsourced globally, incomes of low- to medium-skilled workers will continue to see a relative decline, and unemployment among the least-able and lowest-skilled within the labor workforce will remain persistently high.

This trend toward polarization of earnings has become increasingly visible in most prosperous Western economies since the mid-1980s and will have an enormous impact on national economic growth, on the function and scope of modern business, and on individual prosperity in the next few years. Never before the 1990s has the US economy experienced broad, real-wage reductions among the majority of its workforce—even while the economy continued to grow. The hardest hit have been people with low levels of education or skills, those blue-collar workers who between 1973 and 1993 found real hourly wages dropping between 15% and 19%.[7] The percentage of Americans who fell below the poverty level ($13,000 for a family of four) rose by 50% between 1979 and 1992. Where is the money going? To a large extent, it is going to the new breed of knowledge workers who make up some 20% of the population and who earn more than the remaining four-fifths of the workforce combined. This polarization effect will be further aggravated by continued globalization of business assets and growing competition from modern new economies (particularly in the Pacific Rim), which boast an increasingly highly educated, highly skilled workforce without correspondingly high wage expectations.[8]

Thus, the unbounded global economy combined with the dramatic shift toward demand for knowledge-based skills place a renewed importance on a nation's education and training regime. Unfortunately, in the US and Britain, particularly, there are clear indications that the education and training infrastructure necessary to provide these knowledge-based skills broadly throughout the population is becoming both inadequate and inappropriate for the knowledge-based economy.

One problem is that, although the knowledge elite usually do well, the US and British educational systems tend to provide a progressive and structured path for only the most scholastically successful. Those who probably need education most—the vast majority who do not enroll in full-time education after high school—find that society provides little formal structure or guidance. That 50% to 75% of Americans are essentially turned loose into the world at age 17 without any further program structure (such as that found in four-year college series of classes, university-sponsored career counseling, and collaborative university-business job interviews) upon which to develop key knowledge and skills.[9] At best, there exists ample opportunity to return to the formal education cycle in the future (through extensive junior college or night programs). At worst, they are left to enter the job market with their potential underdeveloped, beginning with low-skill jobs and falling into the downward learning spiral where random courses are begun and abandoned because of the pressures of work.

What of training in the workplace? OECD surveys indicate that much of the training traditionally provided within industries has been curtailed or focused on those in management positions who already have broad knowledge and skills. (Unfortunately, surveys also indicate that employees with the lowest levels of performance are too often unappreciative of their own education needs and, in any case, are powerless to insist on a second chance for education provided at their employers' expense.) This is particularly true among small and medium-sized enterprises, which have a smaller capacity for education and training budgets. Cost concerns, an inability to measure the results of training, and the potential of expensively trained employees being "poached" (taking their knowledge out the door) have all contributed to the belief that firm-based education is more a perk than an ongoing learning experience.

This kind of education and training structure was acceptable in an industrial goods-based society in which average skills and education still promised a strong and sustainable income. But in the knowledge-based economy, individuals and organizations will be confronted more and more with the need to create a system that fosters high-skill development among a greater number of the population, or else see a great proportion of citizens face the prospect of decreasing earnings and increased job insecurity. Although the performance of America's knowledge elite will remain high, without a change in current policies, an enormous proportion of the working population may well become increasingly economically disenfranchised because of a poor education and training infrastructure.

Not only are we neglecting continuing education for a good portion of our population after the age of 17, but America's traditional primary and secondary schools are beginning to fall well behind the standards of other developed nations. Worryingly, just as the demand for high-skilled knowledge workers is growing, statistics indicate clearly that by virtually any indicator (test scores, enrollment, completion rates, funding, etc.) the US, particularly, is falling well behind emerging nations in terms of average educational attainment. Unable to contribute to the knowledge-based growth sector of the economy, these future workers will be entering a globally competitive job market in which an increasing proportion of the traditional medium- and low-skill jobs that provided prosperity to their parents have long since been eliminated through downsizing or global outsourcing.

This complex and compelling area of concern has recently spawned a number of thoughtful essays. Part Five begins with former Dean of MIT's Sloan School of Management Lester C. Thurow's article "An Era of Man-Made Brainpower Industries," in which he explores the rapid development of "brainpower industries" and provides a sweeping inventory of the changes in skills, technologies, and values that the shift to a knowledge-based economy demands of America. Hedrick Smith, famous for his seminal book *The Russians,* has deftly turned his hand to the problems of education in the US, where the education system is failing the "mid-kids"—that majority of students who do not go on to full-time college education. In "High School—The Neglected Majority: Whose Mid-Kids Are on Track for the Global Economy?" Smith provides an interesting comparison of three high-school-aged students—one in the US, one in Germany, and one in Japan—and explores the relative merits and disadvantages of the various national educational systems in preparing their population to compete in the knowledge-based economy. In chapter 16, Danielle Colardyn and Marianne Durand-Drouhin, both from the Education and Training Division of the OECD in Paris, provide a brief but thorough summary of the changing demands on training and education in an environment of technological innovation, economic restructuring, and keener global competition in their essay "Recognizing Skills and Qualifications." In the last chapter, "Human Resource Development in the Knowledge-Based Economy," David Stern, of the OECD's Centre for Educational Research, contends that the knowledge-based economy requires faster and continuous learning, which means that knowledge and skills developed outside the workplace (at traditional schools or universities) are increasingly likely to become obsolete before they can be put to use. In this chapter Stern looks at how firms, schools, and governments in nations as diverse as Sweden, Korea, France, and Australia are successfully implementing collaborative programs of work-based learning.

Those, then, are the opportunities and challenges we are now facing with the onset of the global knowledge-based economy. It is an area of complex and often inaccessible debate, in which compelling arguments can easily be lost within dense academic prose—or worse, become mere soundbites in popular business weeklies. The sixteen essays collected in this volume represent a broad range of thought from prominent academic and public-policy-making sources selected in order to highlight the impact that this dramatic shift toward the knowledge-based economy will have in the coming decade on ourselves, our families, businesses, and the national economy as a whole.

NOTES

1. *The Economist,* July 6, 1996, p. 68
2. Richard Rosecrance, "The Rise of the Virtual State," *Foreign Affairs,* July/August 1996, p. 50; and "The Knowledge-based Economy," OECD Publications, Paris 1996.
3. John Holusha, "First to College, Then to the Mill," *New York Times,* August 22, 1995, p. D1; cited by Lester Thurow in *The Future of Capitalism* (New York: William Morrow, 1996), p. 76.
4. Don Tapscott, "The Digital Economy," *The Economist,* "Survey: The Software Industry," May 25, 1996, p. 6.
5. Rosecrance, p. 52.

6. Robert Reich, *The Work of Nations* (New York: Knopf, 1991), p. 112.
7. Council of Economic Advisers, *Economic Report of the President 1995*, pp. 276, 311, 326; cited by Thurow, p. 24.
8. Daniel Feenberg and James Poterba, "Income Inequality and the Incomes of Very High Income Taxpayers," NBER Working Paper no. 4229, December 1992, p. 31; cited by Thurow, p. 2 and Jeremy Rifkin, *The End of Work* (New York: Putnam 1995), pp. 172–180.
9. Hedrick Smith, *Rethinking America* (New York, Random House, 1995), p. 127.

Part One

The Changing Economic Landscape

2

From Capitalism to Knowledge Society

Peter F. Drucker

Within 150 years, from 1750 to 1900, capitalism and technology conquered the globe and created a world civilization. Neither capitalism nor technical innovations were new; both had been common, recurrent phenomena throughout the ages, both in West and East. What was brand new was their speed of diffusion and their global reach across cultures, classes and geography. And it was this, their speed and scope, that converted capitalism into "Capitalism" and into a "system." It converted technical advances into the "Industrial Revolution."

This transformation was driven by a radical change in the meaning of knowledge. In both West and East knowledge had always been seen as applying to *being*. Almost overnight, it came to be applied to *doing*. It became a resource and a utility. Knowledge had always been a private good. Almost overnight it became a public good.

For a hundred years—in the first phase—knowledge was applied to *tools, processes, products*. This created the Industrial Revolution. But it also created what Marx called "alienation" and new classes and class war, and with it Communism. In its second phase, beginning around 1880 and culminating around World War II, knowledge in its new meaning came to be applied to *work*. This ushered in the *Productivity Revolution* which in 75 years converted the proletarian into a middle-class bourgeois with near-upper-class income. The Productivity Revolution thus defeated class war and Communism. The last phase began after World War II. Knowledge is being applied to *knowledge* itself. This is the *Management Revolution*. Knowledge is now fast becoming the *one* factor of production, sidelining both capital and labour. It may be premature (and certainly would be presumptuous) to call ours a "knowledge society"—so far we only have a knowledge economy. But our society is surely "post-capitalist."

Capitalism, in one form or another, has occurred and recurred many times throughout the ages, and in the Orient as well as in the West. And there have been many earlier periods of rapid technical invention and innovation, again in the Orient as well as in the West, many of them producing technical changes fully as radical as any in the late eighteenth or early nineteenth centuries.[1] What is unprecedented and unique about the developments of the last 250 years is their speed and scope. Instead of being one element in society as all earlier capitalism had been, Capitalism—with a capital C—became society. Instead of being confined, as always before, to a narrow locality, Capitalism—again with a capital C—took over all of Western and Northern Europe, in a short 100 years from 1750 to 1850. Then within another 50 years it took over the entire inhabited world.

All earlier capitalism had been confined to small narrow groups in society. Nobles, land-owners and the military, peasants, professionals, craftsmen, even labourers, were almost untouched by it. Capitalism with a capital C soon permeated and transformed all groups in society wherever it spread.

From earliest times in the Old World new tools, new processes, new materials, new crops, new techniques—what we now call "technology"—diffused swiftly.

Few modern inventions, for instance, spread as fast as a thirteenth-century one; eyeglasses. Derived from the optical experiments of an English Franciscan friar, Roger Bacon (died 1292 or 1294) around 1270, reading glasses for the elderly were in use at the Papal Court of Avignon by 1290, at the Sultan's Court in Cairo by 1300 and at the Court of the Mongol Emperor of China no later than 1310. Only the sewing machine and the telephone, fastest-spreading of all nineteenth-century inventions, moved as quickly.

But earlier technological change, almost without exception, remained confined to one craft or one application. It took another 200 years—until the early 1500s—before Bacon's invention had its second application: eyeglasses to correct nearsightedness. The potter's wheel was in full use in the Mediterranean by 1500 BC. Pots to cook, and to store water and food, were used in every household. Yet the principle underlying the potter's wheel was not applied until AD 1000 to women's work—spinning.

Similarly, the redesign of the windmill around the year AD 800 which converted it from the toy it had been in Antiquity into a true machine—and a fully "automated" one at that—was not applied to ships for more than 300 years, that is, until after 1100. Until then, ships were oared; if wind was used at all to propel them, it was an auxiliary and only if it blew in the right direction. The sail to drive a ship works in exactly the same way as the sail that drives the windmill. The need for a sail that would enable a ship to sail cross-wind and against the wind had been known for a long time. The windmill was redesigned in Northern France or in the Low Countries, that is, in regions thoroughly familiar with ships and navigation. Yet it did not occur to anyone for several hundred years to apply something invented to pump water and to grind corn, that is, for use on land, to use offshore.

The inventions of the Industrial Revolution, however, were immediately applied across the board, and across all conceivable crafts and industries. They were immediately seen as *technology.*

James Watt's (1736–1819) redesign of the steam engine between 1765 and 1776 made it into a cost-effective provider of power. Watt himself throughout his own productive life focused on one use only: to pump water out of a mine—the use for which the steam engine had first been designed by Newcomen in the early years of the eighteenth century. But one of England's leading iron masters immediately saw that the redesigned steam engine could also be used to blow air into a blast furnace and bid for the second engine Watt had built. And Watt's partner, Matthew Boulton (1728–1809), right away promoted the steam engine as a provider of power for all kinds of industrial processes, especially, of course, for the then largest of all manufacturing industries, textiles. Thirty-five years later, an American, Robert Fulton (1765–1815), floated the first steamship on New York's Hudson River. Another 20 years later the steam engine was put on wheels and the locomotive was born. And by 1840—at the latest by 1850—the steam engine had transformed every single manufacturing process—from glass making to printing. It had transformed long-distance transportation on land and sea, and it was beginning to transform farming. By then, it had penetrated almost the entire world—with Tibet, Nepal and the interior of tropical Africa the only exceptions.

The nineteenth century believed—and most people still do—that the Industrial Revolution was the first time a change in the "mode of production" (to use Karl Marx's term) changed social structure and created new classes, the capitalist and the proletarian. But this belief too is not valid. Between AD 700 and 1000 two brand-new classes were created in Europe by technological change: the feudal knight and the urban craftsman. The knight was created by the invention of the stirrup—an invention coming out of Central Asia around the year AD 700; the craftsman by the redesign of water wheel and windmill into true machines which, for the first time, used inanimate forces—water and wind—as motive power rather than human muscle as Antiquity had done.

The stirrup made it possible to fight on horseback; without it a rider wielding a lance, sword or heavy bow would immediately have been thrown off the horse by the force of Newton's Second Law: "To every action there is a reaction." For several hundred years the knight was an invincible "fighting machine." But this machine had to be supported by a "military-agricultural complex"—something quite new in history. Germans until this century called it a *Rittergut,* a knight's estate endowed with legal status and with economic and political privileges, and containing at least 50 peasant families or 200 people to produce the food needed to support the fighting machine: the knight, his squire, his three horses and his twelve to fifteen grooms. The stirrup, in other words, created feudalism.

The craftsman of Antiquity had been a slave. The craftsman of the first "machine age," the craftsman of Europe's Middle Ages, became the urban ruling class, the "burgher," who then created Europe's unique city, and both the Gothic and the Renaissance.

The technical innovations—stirrup, water wheel and windmill—traveled throughout the entire Old World, and fast. But the classes of the earlier industrial revolution remained European phenomena on the whole. Only Japan evolved around AD 1100 proud and independent craftsmen who enjoyed high esteem and, until 1600, considerable power. But while the Japanese adopted the stirrup for riding they continued to fight on foot. The rulers in rural Japan were the commanders of foot soldiers—the *daimyo*. They levied taxes on the peasantry but had no feudal estates. In China, in India, in the world of Islam, the new technologies had no social impact whatever. Craftsmen in China remained serfs without social status. The military did not become land-owners but remained, as in Europe's Antiquity, professional mercenaries. Even in Europe the social changes generated by this early industrial revolution took almost 400 years to have a full effect.

By contrast, the social transformation of society brought about by Capitalism and Industrial Revolution took less than a hundred years to become fully effective in Western Europe. In 1750 capitalists and proletarians were still marginal groups. In fact, proletarians in the nineteenth-century meaning of the term (that is, factory workers) hardly existed at all. By 1850 capitalists and proletarians were the dynamic classes of Western Europe, and were on the offensive. They rapidly became the dominant classes wherever capitalism and modern technology penetrated. In Japan the transformation took less than 30 years, from the Meiji Restoration in 1867 to the war with China in 1894. It took not much longer in Shanghai and Hong Kong, Calcutta and Bombay, or in the Tsar's Russia.

Capitalism and the Industrial Revolution—because of their speed and of their scope—created a world civilization.[2]

THE NEW MEANING OF KNOWLEDGE

Unlike those "terrible simplifiers," the nineteenth-century ideologues such as Hegel and Marx, we now know that major historical events rarely have just one cause and just one explanation. They typically result from the convergence of a good many separate and independent developments.

One example of how history works is the genesis of the computer. Its earliest root is the binary system, that is, the realization of a seventeenth-century mathematician-philosopher, the German Gottfried Leibnitz (1646–1716), that all numbers can be represented by just two: 0 and 1. The second root is the discovery of a nineteenth-century English inventor, Charles Babbage (1792–1871), that toothed wheels (that is, mechanics) could represent the arithmetic functions: addition, subtraction, multiplication and division—the discovery of a genuine "computing machine." Then in the early years of this century, two English logicians, Alfred North Whitehead (1861–1947) and Bertrand Russell (1872–1970), in their *Principia Mathematica,* showed that any concept if presented in rigorously logical form can be expressed mathematically. From this discovery an Austro-American, Otto Neurath (flourished 1915–1930), working as statistician for the US War Production Board of World War I, derived "data," that is, the idea, then brand-new and heretical, that all information from any area, whether anatomy or astronomy, economics, history, or zoology, is exactly the same when quantified, and can be treated and presented the same way (the idea, by the way, that also underlies modern statistics). A little earlier, just before World War I, an American, Lee de Forest (1873–1961), invented the audion tube to convert electronic impulses into sound waves, thus making possible the broadcasting of speech and music. Twenty years later it occurred to engineers working at a medium-sized punch-card manufacturer called IBM that the audion tube could be used to switch electronically from 0 to 1 and back again. If any of these elements had been missing there would have been no computer. And no one can say which of these was *the* element. With all of them in place, however, the computer became virtually inevitable. It was then pure accident, however, that it became an American development—the accident of World War II which made the American military willing to spend enormous sums on developing (quite unsuccessfully, by the way, until well after World War II) machines to calculate at high speed the position of fast-moving aircraft overhead and of fast-moving enemy ships. Otherwise the computer would probably have become a British development. Indeed, an English company, the food producer and restaurant owner J. Lyons & Co., in the 1940s actually developed the first computer for commercial purpose that really worked, the "*Leo*"—Lyons just couldn't raise the money to compete with the Pentagon and had to abandon its working and successful (and very much cheaper) machine.

Similarly, many separate developments—most of them probably quite unconnected with each other—went into making capitalism into Capitalism and technical advance into the Industrial Revolution. The best-known theory—that Capitalism was the child of the "Protestant Ethic"— expounded in the opening years of this century by the German sociologist Max Weber (1864–1920)—has, however, been largely discredited. There just is not enough evidence for it. There is only a little more evidence to support Karl Marx's earlier thesis that the steam engine, the new prime mover, required such enormous capital investment that craftsmen could no longer finance their "means of production," and had to cede control to the capitalist. There is one critical element, however, without which well-known phenomena, i.e. capitalism and technical advance, could not possibly have turned into a social and worldwide pandemic. It is the radical change in the *meaning of knowledge* that occurred in Europe around the year 1700, or shortly thereafter.[3]

There are as many theories as to what we can know and how we can know it as there have been metaphysicians from Plato in 400 BC to Ludwig Wittgenstein (1889–1951) and Karl Popper (1902–) in our days. But since Plato's days there have only been two theories in the West—and since somewhat the same time, two theories in the East—regarding the meaning and function of knowledge. Plato's spokesman, the wise Socrates, holds that the only function of knowledge is self-knowledge, that is, the intellectual, moral and spiritual growth of the person. His ablest opponent, the brilliant and learned Protagoras, holds, however, that the purpose of knowledge is to make the holder effective by enabling him to know what to say and how to say it. For Protagoras knowledge meant logic, grammar and rhetoric—later to become the *trivium,* the core of learning in the Middle Ages—and still very much what we mean by a "liberal education" or what the Germans mean by *Allgemeine Bildung*. In the East there were pretty much the same two theories of knowledge. Knowledge for the Confucian was knowing what to say and how to say it and the way to advancement and earthly success. Knowledge for the Taoist and the Zen monk was self-knowledge and the road to enlightenment and wisdom. But while the two sides thus sharply disagreed about what knowledge means, they were in total agreement as to what it did –*not* mean. It did not mean *ability to do*. It did *not* mean *utility.* Utility was not knowledge; it was *skill*—the Greek word is *téchne.*

Unlike their Far Eastern contemporaries, the Chinese Confucians with their infinite contempt for anything but book learning, both Socrates and Protagoras respected *téchne.*

In fact, in the West contempt for skill was unknown until England's eighteenth-century "gentleman." And this contempt which reached such heights in Victorian England was surely little but a futile last-ditch defense against the gentleman's being replaced as society's ruling group by capitalist and technologist.

But even to Socrates and Protagoras, *téchne,* however commendable, was not knowledge. It was confined to one specific application and had no general principles. What the shipmaster knew about navigating from Greece to Sicily could not be applied to anything else. Furthermore, the only way to learn a *téchne* was through apprenticeship and experience. A *téchne* could not be explained in words, whether spoken or written. It could only be demonstrated. As late as 1700, or even later, the English did not speak of "crafts." They spoke of "mysteries"—and not only because the possessor of a craft skill was sworn to secrecy but also because a craft, by definition, was inaccessible to anyone who had not been apprenticed to a master and had thus been taught by example.

THE INDUSTRIAL REVOLUTION

Then, beginning after 1700—and within an incredibly short 50 years—technology was invented. The very word is a manifesto in that it combined *téchne,* that is, the mystery of a craft skill, with *logy,* that is, organized, systematic, purposeful knowledge. The first engineering school, the French *Ecole des Ponts et Chaussées,* was founded in 1747, followed around 1770 in Germany by the first School of Agriculture and in 1776 by the first School of Mining. In 1794 the first technical university, the French *Ecole Polytechnique,* was founded, and with it, the profession of engineer. Shortly thereafter, between 1820 and 1850, medical education and medical practice were reorganized as a systematic technology.

In a parallel development, Britain, between 1750 and 1800, shifted from patents being monopolies to enrich royal favorites to patents being granted to encourage the application of knowledge to tools, products and processes, and to reward inventors provided they publish their inventions. This not only triggered a century of feverish mechanical invention in Britain; it finished craft mystery and secretiveness.

The great document of this dramatic shift from skill to technology—one of the most important books in history—was the *Encyclopédie,* edited between 1751 and 1772 by Denis Diderot (1713–1784) and Jean d'Alembert (1717–1783). This famous work attempted to bring together in organized and systematic form the knowledge of all crafts, and in such a way that the non-apprentice could learn to be a "technologist." It was by no means accidental that articles in the *Encyclopédie* that describe an individual craft (e.g. spinning or weaving) were not written by craftsmen. They were written by "information specialists": people trained as analysts, as mathematicians, as logicians—both Voltaire and Rousseau were contributors. The underlying thesis of the *Encyclopédie* was that effective results in the material universe—in tools, processes and products—are produced by systematic analysis, and by systematic, purposeful application of knowledge.

But the *Encyclopédie* also preached that principles which produced results in one craft would produce results in any other. That was anathema, however, to both the traditional man of knowledge and the traditional craftsman.

None of the technical schools of the eighteenth century aimed at producing *new* knowledge—nor did the *Encyclopédie*. None even talked of the application of *science* to tools, processes and products, that is, to technology. This idea had to wait for another hundred years until 1840 or so, when a German chemist, Justus Liebig (1803–1873), applied science to invent first, artificial fertilizers and then a way to preserve animal protein, the meat extract. What the early technical schools and the *Encyclopédie* did was, however, more important perhaps. They brought together, codified and *published* the *téchne,* the craft mystery, as it had been developed over millennia. They converted experience into knowledge, apprenticeship into textbook, secrecy into methodology, doing into applied knowledge. These are the essentials of what we have come to call the "Industrial Revolution," i.e. the transformation by technology of society and civilization worldwide.

It is this change in the meaning of knowledge which then made modern Capitalism inevitable and dominant. The speed of technical change created demand for capital way beyond anything the craftsman could possibly supply. The new technology also required concentration of production, that is, the shift to the factory. Knowledge could not be applied in thousands and tens of thousands of small individual workshops and in the cottage industries of the rural village. It required concentration of production under one roof.

The new technology also required large-scale energy, whether water power or steam power, which could not be decentralized. But, though important, these energy needs were secondary. The central point was that production almost overnight moved from being craft based to being technology based. As a result, the capitalist moved almost overnight into the center of economy and society. Before, he had always been "supporting cast."

As late as 1750, large-scale enterprise was governmental rather than private. The earliest and for many centuries the greatest of all manufacturing enterprises in the Old World was the famous arsenal owned and run by the government of Venice. And the eighteenth-century "manufactories" such as the porcelain works of Meissen and Sèvres were still government-owned. But by 1830 large-scale private capitalist enterprise dominated in the West. Another 50 years later, by the time Karl Marx died in 1883, private capitalist enterprise had penetrated everywhere except to such remote corners of the world as Tibet or the Empty Quarter of Arabia.

There was resistance, of course, both to technology and to capitalism. There were riots, in England for instance, or in German Silesia. But these were local, lasted a few weeks or at most a few months, and did not even slow down the speed and spread of Capitalism.

The Industrial Revolution, that is, the machine and the factory system, spread equally fast and equally without meeting much resistance, if any.

Adam Smith's (1723–1790) *Wealth of Nations* appeared in the same year (1776) in which James Watt patented the perfected steam engine. Yet the *Wealth of Nations* pays practically no attention to machines or factories or industrial production altogether. The production it describes is still craft based. Even 40 years later after the Napoleonic Wars, factories and machines were not yet seen as central even by acute social observers. They play practically no role in the economics of David Ricardo (1772–1832). Even more surprising, neither factory nor factory workers nor bankers can be found in the books of Jane Austen (1775–1817), England's most perceptive social critic. Her society (as has often been said) is thoroughly "bourgeois." But it is still totally pre-industrial, a society of squires and tenants, parsons and naval officers, lawyers, craftsmen and shopkeepers. Only in far-away America did Alexander Hamilton (1757–1809) see very early that machine-based manufacturing was fast becoming the central economic activity. But few even among his followers paid much attention to his 1791 *Report on Manufactures* until long after his death.

By the 1830s, however, Honoré de Balzac (1799–1850) was turning out best-selling novel after best-selling novel depicting a capitalist France whose society was dominated by bankers and by the stock exchange. And another 15 years later, capitalism, the factory system, the machine, are central in the mature works of Charles Dickens (1812–1870), and so are the new classes, the capitalists and the proletarians.

In *Bleak House* (1852) the new society and its tensions form the sub-plot in the contrast between two able brothers, both sons of the squire's housekeeper. One becomes a great industrialist in the North who plans to get himself elected to Parliament to fight the land-owners and break their power. The other chooses to remain a loyal retainer of the broken, defeated, ineffectual (but pre-capitalist) "gentleman." And Dickens's *Hard Times* (1854) is the first and by far the most powerful industrial novel, the story of a bitter strike in a cotton mill and of class war at its starkest.

This unheard of speed with which society was transformed created the social tensions and conflicts of the new order. We now know that there is no truth in the all but universal belief that factory workers in the early nineteenth century were worse off and were treated more harshly then they had been as landless labourers in the pre-industrial countryside. They were badly off, no doubt, and harshly treated. But they flocked to the factory precisely because they were still better off than they were at the bottom of a static, tyrannical and starving rural society. They still experienced a much better "quality of life."

We should have known this all along, by the way. In the factory town infant mortality immediately went down and life expectancies immediately went up, thus triggering the enormous population growth of industrializing Europe. But now, that is, since World War II, we also have the example of the Third-World countries. Brazilians and Peruvians stream into the *favelas* and *barrios* of Rio de Janeiro and Lima. However hard, life there is better than in the impoverished *Noreste* of Brazil or on Peru's *Altiplano*. Indians today say: "The poorest beggar in Bombay still eats better than the farm hand in the village." "England's green and pleasant land" which William Blake (1757–1827) in his famous poem on the "New Jerusalem" hoped to liberate from the new "satanic mills" was in reality one vast rural slum.

But while industrialization thus, from the beginning, meant material improvement rather than Marx's famous "immiseration," the speed of change was so breathtaking as to be deeply traumatic. The new class, the "proletarians," became "alienated," to use the term Marx coined. Their alienation, Marx predicted, would make inevitable their exploitation. For they were becoming totally dependent for their livelihood on access to the "means of production" which were owned and controlled by the capitalist. This then, Marx predicted, would increasingly concentrate ownership in fewer and bigger hands and increasingly impoverish a powerless proletariat—until the day on which the system would collapse under its own weight, with the few remaining capitalists being overthrown by proletarians who "had nothing to lose but their chains."

We now know that Marx was a false prophet—the very opposite of what he predicted has in fact happened. But this is hindsight. Most of his contemporaries shared his view of capitalism even if they did not necessarily share his prediction of the outcome. Even anti-Marxists accepted Marx's analysis of the "inherent contradictions of capitalism." Some were confident that the military would keep the proletarian rabble in check as was apparently the greatest of nineteenth-century capitalists, the American banker J. P. Morgan (1837–1913). Liberals of all stripes believed that somehow there could be reform and amelioration. But the conviction that capitalist society was a society of inevitable class conflict, practically every thinking person of the late nineteenth-century shared with Marx—and in fact by 1910 most "thinking people," at least in Europe (but also in Japan), were inclining towards Socialism. The greatest of nineteenth-century Conservatives, Benjamin Disraeli (1804–1881), saw capitalist society very much as Marx did. So did his conservative counterpart on the Continent, Otto von Bismarck (1815–1898); it motivated him, after 1880, to enact the social legislation that produced ultimately the twentieth-century Welfare State. The conservative social critic, the American novelist Henry James (1843–1916), chronicler of American wealth and European aristocracy, was so obsessed by class war and by the fear of class war that he made it the theme of his most haunting novel *The Princess Casamassima*. He wrote it in 1883, the very year of Marx's death.

THE PRODUCTIVITY REVOLUTION

What then defeated Marx and Marxism? By 1950 a good many of us already knew that Marxism had failed both morally and economically (I had said so already in 1939 in my book *The End of Economic Man*). But Marxism was still the one coherent ideology for most of the world. And for most of the world it looked invincible. There were "anti-Marxists" galore, but, as yet, few "non-Marxists," that is, people who thought that Marxism had become irrelevant—as most of the world now knows. Even those bitterly opposed to Socialism were still convinced that it was in the ascendant.

The father of Neo-conservatism throughout the Western world, the Anglo-Austrian economist Friedrich von Hayek (1899–1992), in his 1944 book *The Road to Serfdom* argued that Socialism would inevitably mean enslavement. There is, Hayek then said, no such thing as "Democratic Socialism"; there is only "Totalitarian Socialism." But Hayek did not argue in 1944 that Marxism *could* not work. On the contrary, he was very much afraid that it could and would work. But his last book, *The Fatal Conceit* (University of Chicago Press, 1988), written 40 years later, argues that Marxism could never have worked. And by the time he published this book almost everybody—and especially almost everybody in the Communist countries—had already come to the same conclusion.

What then overcame the "inevitable contradictions of capitalism," the "alienation" and "immiseration" of the proletarians and with it the "proletarian" altogether?

The answer is the *Productivity Revolution.*

When knowledge changed its meaning 250 years ago it began to be applied to tools, processes and products. This is still what "technology" means to most people and what is being taught in engineering schools. But two years before Marx's death the Productivity Revolution had begun. In 1881 an American, Frederick Winslow Taylor (1856–1915), first applied knowledge to the study of *work,* the analysis of work and the engineering of work.

Work has been around as long as man. All animals in fact have to work for their living. And in the West the dignity of work has been paid lip service for a long time.

The second oldest Greek text, following the Homeric epics by only a hundred years or so, is a poem by Hesiod (eighth century BC) entitled *Works and Days,* which sings of the work of the farmer. One of the finest Roman poems is Virgil's (70–19 BC) *Georgics,* a cycle of songs about the work of the farmer. Although there is no such concern with work in the Eastern literary tradition, the Emperor of China once a year touched a plough to celebrate rice planting.

But both in the West and in the East, these were purely symbolic gestures. Neither Hesiod nor Virgil actually looked at what a farmer *does.* Nor did anybody else throughout most of recorded history.[4] Work was beneath the attention of educated people, of well-to-do people, of people of authority. Work is what slaves did. "Everybody knew" that the only way a worker could produce more was by working longer hours or by working harder. Marx too shared this belief with every other nineteenth-century economist or engineer.

It was pure accident that Frederick Winslow Taylor, a well-to-do, educated man, became a worker. Poor eyesight forced him to give up going to Harvard and to take instead a worker's job in an iron foundry. Being extremely gifted, Taylor very soon rose to be one of the bosses. And his metal-working inventions made him a rich man very early. What then got Taylor to start on the study of work was his shock at the mutual and growing hatred between capitalists and workers, which had come to dominate the late nineteenth century. Taylor, in other words, saw what Marx saw and Disraeli and Bismarck and Henry James. But he also saw what they failed to see: the conflict was unnecessary. He set out to make workers productive so that they would earn decent money.

Taylor's motivation was not efficiency. It was not the creation of profits for the owners. To his very death he maintained that the major beneficiary of the fruits of productivity had to be the worker and not the owner. His main motivation was the creation of a society in which owners and workers, capitalists and proletarians had a common interest in productivity and could build a relationship of harmony on the application of knowledge to work. The ones who have come closest to understanding this so far are Japan's post-World War II employers and Japan's post-World War II unions.

Few figures in intellectual history have had greater impact than Taylor. And few have been so wilfully misunderstood and so assiduously misquoted.[5] In part, Taylor has suffered because history has proven him right and the intellectuals wrong. In part, Taylor is ignored because contempt for work still lingers, above all among the intellectuals. Surely shovelling sand—the most publicized of Taylor's analyses—is not something an "educated man" would appreciate let alone consider important.

In much larger part, however, Taylor's reputation has suffered precisely because he applied knowledge to the study of work. This was anathema to the labour unions of his day; and they mounted against Taylor one of the most vicious campaigns of character assassination in American history.

Taylor's crime, in the eyes of the unions, was his assertion that there is no "skilled work." In manual operations there is only "work." All can be analysed the same way. Any worker who is then willing to do the work the way analysis shows it should be done is a "first-class man," deserving a "first-class wage"—that is, as much or more than the skilled worker got with his long years of apprenticeship.

But the unions that were respected and powerful in Taylor's America were the unions in the government-owned arsenals and shipyards in which, prior to World War I, all peace-time defence production was done in the United States. These unions were craft monopolies. Membership of them was restricted to sons or relatives of members. They required an apprenticeship of five to seven years but had no systematic training or work study. Nothing was allowed ever to be written down. There were not even blueprints or any other drawings of the work to be done. The members were sworn to secrecy and were not permitted to discuss their work with non-members. Taylor's assertion that work could be studied, could be analysed, could be divided into a series of simple repetitive motions each of which had to be done in its one right way, its own best time, and with its own right tools was indeed a frontal attack on them. And so they vilified him and succeeded in having Congress ban task study in government arsenals and shipyards, a ban that prevailed until after World War II.

Taylor did not improve matters by offending the owners of his day as much as he offended the unions. While he had little use for unions he was contemptuously hostile to the owners; his favorite epithet for them was "hogs." And then there was his insistence that the workers rather than the owners should get the lion's share of the revenue gains scientific management produced. To add insult to injury: his "Fourth Principle" demanded that work study be done in consultation, if not in partnership, with the worker. Finally, Taylor held that authority in the plant must not be based on ownership. It could be based only on superior knowledge. He demanded, in other words, what we now call "professional management"—and that was anathema and "radical heresy" to nineteenth-century capitalists. He was bitterly attacked by them as a "trouble-maker" and a "socialist." (Some of his closest disciples and associates, especially Karl Barth, Taylor's right-hand man, were indeed open and avowed "leftists" and strongly anti-capitalist.)

Taylor's axiom that all manual work, skilled or unskilled, could be analysed and organized by the application of knowledge seemed preposterous to his contemporaries. And that there is a mystique to craft skill was universally accepted for many, many years.

This belief still encouraged Hitler in 1941 to declare war on the United States. For the latter to field an effective force in Europe would require a large fleet to transport troops. America at that time had almost no merchant marine and no destroyers to protect it. Modern war, Hitler further argued, required precision optics and in large quantities; and there were no skilled optical workers in America.

Hitler was absolutely right. The United States did not have much of a merchant marine and its destroyers were few and ludicrously obsolete. It also had almost no optical industry. But by applying Taylor's "task study" the United States learned how to train totally unskilled workers, many of them former sharecroppers raised in a pre-industrial environment, and converted them in 60 or 90 days into first-rate welders and shipbuilders. The United States equally trained within a few months the same kind of people to turn out precision optics of better quality than the Germans ever did—and on an assembly line to boot.

Altogether, where Taylor had the greatest impact was probably in training.

Adam Smith, only a hundred years earlier, had taken for granted that it takes at least 50 years of experience (and more likely a full century) until a country or a region has acquired the necessary skills to turn out high-quality products—his examples were the production of musical instruments in Bohemia and Saxony, and of silk fabrics in Scotland. Seventy years later, around 1840, a German, August Borsig (1804–1854)—one of the first people outside England to build a steam locomotive—invented what is still the German system of apprenticeship which combines practical plant experience under a master with theoretical grounding in school. It is still the foundation of Germany's industrial productivity. But even Borsig's apprenticeship took three to five years. Then, first in World War I but especially in World War II, the United States systematically applied Taylor's approach to training "first-class men" in a few months. This, more than any other factor, explains why the United States could mount the war production which ultimately defeated both Japan and Germany.

All earlier economic powers in modern history—England, the United States, Germany—emerged through leadership in new technology. The post-World War II economic powers—first Japan, then South Korea, Taiwan, Hong Kong, Singapore—all owe their rise to Taylor's training. It enabled them to endow a still largely pre-industrial and therefore still low-wage workforce with world-class productivity in practically no time. In the post-World War II decades Taylor-based training became the one truly effective engine of economic development.

The application of knowledge to work explosively increased productivity.[6] For hundreds of years there had been no increase in the ability of workers to turn out goods or to move goods. Machines created greater capacity. But workers themselves were no more productive than they had been in the workshops of ancient Greece, in building the roads of Imperial Rome or in producing the highly prized woollen cloth which gave Renaissance Florence its wealth.

But within a few years after Taylor began to apply knowledge to work, productivity began to rise at a rate of 3½–4% compound a year—which means doubling every 18 years or so. Since Taylor began, productivity has increased some fiftyfold in all advanced countries. On this unprecedented expansion rest all the increases in both standard of living and in the quality of life in developed countries.

Half of this additional productivity has been taken in the form of increased purchasing power, that is, in a higher standard of living. But between one-third and one-half has been taken in the form of increased leisure. As late as 1910 workers in developed countries still worked as much as they had ever worked before, that is, at least 3000 hours a year. By now even the Japanese work 2000 hours a year, the Americans around 1850, the Germans, at most, 1600—and they all produce fifty times as much per hour as 80 years ago. Other substantial shares of the increased productivity have been taken in the form of health care, which has grown from something like 0% of Gross National Product (GNP) to 8–12% in developed countries, and in the form of education, which has grown from around 2% of GNP to 10% or more.

And most of this increase—as Taylor predicted—has been taken by the workers, that is, by Marx's proletarians. Henry Ford (1863–1947) brought out the first cheap car, the Model T in 1907. It was "cheap," however, only by comparison with all other cars on the market which, in terms of average incomes, cost as much as a two-engine private plane today. At $750 Henry Ford's Model T cost what a fully employed industrial worker in the United States earned in three to four years—for then 80 cents was a good day's wage and, of course, there were no "benefits." Even an American physician in those days rarely earned more than $500 a year. Today, a unionized car worker in the United States, Japan or Germany, working only 40 hours a week, earns $50,000 in wages and benefits—$45,000 after taxes—which is roughly eight times what a cheap new car in the United States costs today.

By 1930 Taylor's Scientific Management—despite resistance by unions and by intellectuals—had swept the developed world. As a result Marx's "proletarian" became a "bourgeois." The blue-collar worker in manufacturing industry, the "proletarian," rather than the "capitalist," became the true beneficiary of Capitalism and the Industrial Revolution. This explains the total failure of Marxism in the highly developed countries for which Marx had predicted "revolution" by 1900. It explains why, after 1918, there was no "Proletarian Revolution" even in the defeated countries of Central Europe in which there was misery, hunger and unemployment. It explains why the Great Depression did not lead to a Communist Revolution, as Lenin and Stalin—and practically all Marxists—had confidently expected. By that time, Marx's proletarians had not yet become "affluent." But they had already become middle class. They had become productive.

"Darwin, Marx, Freud" is the trinity often cited as the "makers of the modern world." Marx would be taken out and replaced by Taylor if there were any justice in the world. But that Taylor is not given his due is a minor matter. It *is* a serious matter, however, that far too few people realize that it is the application of knowledge to work which created developed economies by setting off the productivity explosion of the last hundred years. Technologists give the credit to machines, economists to capital investment. But both were as copious in the first hundred years of the capitalist age, that is, before 1880, as they have been since. In respect to technology or to capital, the second hundred years differed little from the first hundred. But there was absolutely no increase in worker productivity in the first hundred years—and consequently also little increase in workers' real incomes or any decrease in their working hours. What made the second hundred years so critically different can only be explained as the result of *applying knowledge to work.*

The productivity of the new classes, the classes of the post-capitalist society, can be increased *only* by applying knowledge to work. Neither machines nor capital can do it—indeed if applied alone they are likely to impede rather than to create productivity.

When Taylor started, nine out of every ten working people did manual work, making or moving *things*; in manufacturing, in farming, in mining, in transportation. The productivity of people engaged in making and moving things is still going up at the historical rate of 3½–4%—and in American and French agriculture even faster. But the *Productivity Revolution* is over. Forty years ago, in the 1950s, people who engaged in work to make or to move things were still a majority in all developed countries. By 1990 they had shrunk to one-fifth of the workforce. By 2010 they will be no more than one-tenth. Increasing the productivity of manual workers in manufacturing, in farming, in mining, in transportation can no longer by itself create wealth. The productivity revolution has become a victim of its own success. From now on what matters is the productivity of non-manual workers. And that requires *applying knowledge to knowledge.*

THE MANAGEMENT REVOLUTION

When I decided in 1926 not to go to college but to go to work after finishing secondary school, my father was quite distressed; ours had long been a family of lawyers and doctors. But he did not call me a "drop-out." He did not try to change my mind. And he did not prophesy that I would never amount to anything. I was a responsible adult wanting to work as an adult.[7]

Thirty years later, when my son reached age 18, I practically forced him to go to college. Like his father, he wanted to be an adult among adults. Like his father, he felt that in 12 years of sitting on a school bench he had learned little, and that his chances to learn much by spending four more years on a school bench were not particularly great. Like his father at that age, he was action-focused and not learning-focused.

And yet by 1958, 31 years after I had moved from being a high-school graduate to being a trainee in an export firm, the college degree had become a necessity. It had become the passport to practically all careers. Not to go to college in 1958 was "dropping out" for an American boy who had grown up in a well-to-do family and who had done well in school. My father did not have the slightest difficulty in finding a trainee job for me in a reputable merchant house. Thirty years later such firms would not have accepted a high-school graduate as a trainee. They would all have said "go to college for four years—and then you probably should go on to graduate school."

In my father's generation—he was born in 1876—going to college was either for the sons of the wealthy or for a very small number of poor but exceptionally brilliant youngsters (such as he had been).

Of all the American business successes of the nineteenth century, only one went to college: J. P. Morgan went to Göttingen to study mathematics but dropped out after one year. Few of the others even attended high school let alone graduated from it. In the novels of Edith Wharton, the chronicler of American society around 1910 to 1920, the sons of the old and rich New York families do go to Harvard and to Harvard Law School. But practically none of them then practices law. Higher education was a luxury and an ornament and a pleasant way to spend one's early adulthood.

By my time, going to college was already desirable. It gave social status. But it was by no means necessary nor very much of a help in one's life and career. When I did the first study of a major business corporation, General Motors,[8] the Public Relations Department at the company tried very hard to conceal the fact that a good many of their top executives had gone to college. The proper thing then was to start as a machinist and work one's way up.[9] As late as 1950 or 1960, the quickest way to middle-class income—in the United States, in Britain, in Germany (though already no longer in Japan)—was *not* to go to college. It was to go to work at age 16 in one of the unionized mass-production industries. There one earned a middle-class income after a few months—the result of the productivity explosion. These opportunities are practically gone. Now there is practically no access to middle-class income without a formal degree which certifies to the acquisition of knowledge that can only be obtained systematically and in a school.

The change in the meaning of knowledge that began 250 years ago has transformed society and economy. Formal knowledge is seen as both the key personal resource and the key economic resource. *Knowledge is the only meaningful resource today.* The traditional "factors of production"—land (i.e. natural resources), labor and capital—have not disappeared. But they have become secondary. They can be obtained, and obtained easily, provided there is knowledge. And knowledge in this new meaning is knowledge as a utility, knowledge as the means to obtain social and economic results.

These developments, whether desirable or not, are responses to an irreversible change: *knowledge is now being applied to knowledge.* This is the third and perhaps the ultimate step in the transformation of knowledge. Supplying knowledge to find out how existing knowledge can best be applied to produce results is, in effect, what we mean by *management.* But knowledge is now also being applied systematically and purposefully to define what *new* knowledge is needed, whether it is feasible and what has to be done to make knowledge effective. It is being applied, in other words, to Systematic Innovation.[10]

This third change in the dynamics of knowledge can be called the *Management Revolution.* Like its two predecessors—knowledge applied to tools, processes and products, and knowledge applied to human work—the Management Revolution has swept the Earth. It took a hundred years, from the middle of the eighteenth century to the middle of the nineteenth for the Industrial Revolution to become dominant and worldwide. It took some 70 years, from 1880 to the end of World War II, for the Productivity Revolution to become dominant and worldwide. It has taken less than 50 years—from 1945 to 1990—for the Management Revolution to become dominant and worldwide.

Most people, when they hear the word "management," still hear "business management." Management did first emerge in its present form in large-scale business organizations. When I first began to work on management some 50 years ago I too concentrated on business management.[11] But we soon learned that management is needed in all modern organizations, whether businesses or non-businesses. In fact, we soon learned that it is needed even *more* in organizations that are not businesses, whether not-for-profit but non-governmental organizations (what I have called the "Social Sector") or government agencies. These organizations need management the most precisely because they lack the discipline of the "bottom line" under which business stands. That management is not confined to business was recognized first in the United States. But it is now becoming accepted in all developed countries (as witness the receptivity in Western Europe, Japan and Brazil to my 1990 book *Managing the Non Profit Organization*).

We now know that management is a generic function of all organizations, whatever their specific mission. It is the generic organ of the knowledge society.

Management has been around for a very long time. I am often asked whom I consider the best or the greatest executive. My answer is always "the man who conceived, designed and built the first Egyptian Pyramid more than 4000 years ago—and it still stands." But management as a specific kind of work was not seen until after World War I—and then by a handful of people only. Management as a discipline only emerged after World War II. As late as 1950 when the World Bank began to lend money for economic development, the word "management" was not even in its vocabulary. In fact, while management was *invented* thousands of years ago it was not discovered until after World War II.

One reason for its discovery was the experience of World War II itself and especially the performance of American industry. But perhaps equally important to the general acceptance of management has been the performance of Japan since 1950. Japan was not an "underdeveloped" country after World War II. But its industry and economy were almost totally destroyed; and it had practically no domestic technology. The nation's main resource was its willingness to adopt and to adapt the management which the Americans had developed during World War II (and especially training). Within 20 years, from the 1950s, when the American occupation of Japan ended, to the 1970s, Japan became the world's second economic power and a technology leader.

When the Korean War ended in the early 1950s South Korea was destroyed even more than Japan had been seven years earlier. And it had never been anything but a backward country, especially as the Japanese systematically suppressed Korean enterprise and Korean higher education during their 35 years of occupation. But by using the colleges and universities of the United States to educate their able young people, and by importing and applying management South Korea became a highly developed country within 25 years.

With this powerful expansion of management came a growing understanding of what management really is. When I first began to study management, during and immediately after World War II,[12] a manager was defined as "someone who is responsible for the work of subordinates." A manager, in other words, was a "boss," and management was rank and power. This is probably still the definition a good many people have in mind when they speak of managers and management.

But by the early 1950s, the definition had already changed to "a manager is responsible for the performance of people." Now we know that this also is too narrow a definition. The right definition is "*a manager is responsible for the application and performance of knowledge.*"

This change means that we now see knowledge as the essential resource. Land, labour and capital are chiefly important as restraints. Without them even knowledge cannot produce. Without them even management cannot perform. Where there is effective management, that is, application of knowledge to knowledge, we can always obtain the other resources.

That knowledge has become *the* resource, rather than *a* resource is what makes our society "post-capitalist." It changes, and fundamentally, the structure of society. It creates new social dynamics. It creates new economic dynamics. It creates new politics.

FROM KNOWLEDGE TO KNOWLEDGES

Underlying all three phases in the shift to knowledge—the Industrial Revolution, the Productivity Revolution, the Management Revolution—is a fundamental change in the meaning of knowledge. We have moved from knowledge to knowledges.

Traditional knowledge was general. What we now consider knowledge is, of necessity, highly specialized. We never before spoke of a man or woman "of knowledge." We spoke of an "educated person." Educated persons were generalists. They knew enough to talk or write about a good many things, enough to understand a good many things. But they did not know enough to *do* any one thing. As an old saying has it: you would want an educated person as a guest at your dinner table, but you would not want him or her alone with you on a desert island where you need somebody who knows how to do things. In fact, in today's university the traditional "educated persons" are not considered "educated persons" at all. They are looked down upon as dilettantes.

In *A Connecticut Yankee in King Arthur's Court* the hero of the 1889 book by Mark Twain (1833–1910) was not an educated person. He surely knew neither Latin nor Greek, had probably never read Shakespeare and did not even know the Bible well. But he knew how to *do* everything mechanical, up to and including generating electricity and building telephones.

The purpose of knowledge for Socrates was self-knowledge and self-development. Results were internal. For his antagonist, Protagoras, the result was the ability to know what to say and to say it well. It was "image," to use a contemporary term. For more than 2000 years Protagoras' concept of knowledge dominated Western learning and defined knowledge. The medieval *trivium,* the educational system that up to this day underlies what we call a "liberal education," consisted of Grammar, Logic and Rhetoric—the tools needed to decide what to say and how to say it. They are not tools for deciding what to *do* and how to do it. The Zen concept of knowledge and the Confucian concept of knowledge—the two concepts that dominated Eastern learning and Eastern culture for thousands of years—were similar. The first focused on self-knowledge, the second—like the medieval *trivium*—on the Chinese equivalents of Grammar, Logic and Rhetoric.

The knowledge we *now* consider knowledge proves itself in *action.* What we now mean by knowledge is information effective in action, information focused on results. Results are *outside* the person, in society and economy, or in the advancement of knowledge itself.

To accomplish anything this knowledge has to be highly specialized. This was the reason why the tradition—beginning with the ancients but still persisting in what we call "liberal education"—relegated it to the status of *téchne* or craft. It could neither be learned nor taught. Nor did it imply any general principle whatever. It was specific and specialized. It was experience rather than learning, training rather than schooling. But today we do not speak of these specialized knowledges as "crafts." We speak of "disciplines." This is as great a change in intellectual history as any ever recorded.

A discipline converts a "craft" into a methodology—such as engineering, the scientific method, the quantitative method or the physician's differential diagnosis. Each of these methodologies converts *ad hoc* experience into system. Each converts anecdote into information. Each converts skill into something that can be taught and learned.

The shift from knowledge and knowledges has given knowledge the power to create a new society. But this society has to be structured on the basis of knowledge being specialized and of knowledge people being specialists. This gives them their power. But it also raises basic questions—of values, of vision, of beliefs, that is of all the things that hold society together and give meaning to life.

NOTES

1. The best discussion of capitalism as a recurrent and fairly frequent phenomenon are two books by the great French economic historian, Fernand Braudel: *The Mediterranean* (2 vols) (first published in France in 1949; English translation New York: Harper & Row, 1972); and *Civilization & Capitalism* (3 vols) (first published in France in 1979, English translation New York: Harper & Row, 1981). The best discussions of earlier "industrial revolutions" are *Medieval Technology and Social Change* by Lynn White Jr (Oxford University Press, 1962); *The Medieval Machine; The Industrial Revolution of the Middle Ages* by Jean Gimpel (first published in France in 1975; English translation New York: Holt Rinehart & Winston, 1976); and the monumental *Science & Civilization in China* by the British biochemist, orientalist and historian Joseph Needham (Cambridge University Press), publication of which began in 1954 with half of the planned 25 parts yet to appear. What Needham has published so far has, however, already completely changed our knowledge of early technology. For earlier "industrial revolutions" see also my book *Technology Management & Society* (London: Heinemann, 1973), especially Chapters 3, 7 and 11.
2. The best history of this development is *Prometheus Unbound* by the Harvard historian David S. Landes (Cambridge University Press, 1969).
3. This change is explored in some depth in my 1961 essay: "The Technological Revolution; Notes on the Relationship of Technology, Science and Culture," reprinted in my 1973 essay volume *Technology, Management and Society* (London: Heinemann) and in my 1992 essay volume *The Ecological Vision* (New Brunswick, NJ: Transaction Publishers.)
4. And there still is no history of work—but then also, despite all the philosophizing about knowledge, there is no history of knowledge either. Both should become important areas of study within the next decades or at least within the next century.
5. In fact, no factually reliable biography was published until 1991, when *Frederick W. Taylor; Myth and Reality* by Charles D. Wrege and Ronald J. Greenwood appeared (Homewood, Illinois: Irwin).
6. The term itself was unknown in Taylor's time. In fact, it was still unknown until before World War II, when it first began to be used in the United States. As late as 1950 the most authoritative English dictionary, the *Concise Oxford,* still did not list the term "productivity" in its present meaning.
7. That I then also got a doctorate on the side had more to do with my trying to annoy my father than with any belief on my part that it would make any difference to my life and career.
8. Published in my book *Concept of the Corporation* (1946).

9. The story is told in the chapter "Alfred P. Sloan" in my book *Adventures of a Bystander* (1980, reissued 1991).
10. On this, see my book *Innovation and Entrepreneurship* (1985).
11. In my book *The Practice of Management,* which first established management as a discipline and which appeared in 1954, most of the discussion is of business management, and so are most examples.
12. On this, see my 1946 book, *Concept of the Corporation.*

3
The Rise of the Virtual State

Richard Rosecrance

TERRITORY BECOMES PASSÉ

Amid the supposed clamor of contending cultures and civilizations, a new reality is emerging. The nation-state is becoming a tighter, more vigorous unit capable of sustaining the pressures of worldwide competition. Developed states are putting aside military, political, and territorial ambitions as they struggle not for cultural dominance but for a greater share of world output. Countries are not uniting as civilizations and girding for conflict with one another. Instead, they are downsizing—in function if not in geographic form. Today and for the foreseeable future, the only international civilization worthy of the name is the governing economic culture of the world market. Despite the view of some contemporary observers, the forces of globalization have successfully resisted partition into cultural camps.

Yet the world's attention continues to be mistakenly focused on military and political struggles for territory. In beleaguered Bosnia, Serbian leaders sought to create an independent province with an allegiance to Belgrade. A few years ago Iraqi leader Saddam Hussein aimed to corner the world oil market through military aggression against Kuwait and, in all probability, Saudi Arabia; oil, a product of land, represented the supreme embodiment of his ambitions. In Kashmir, India and Pakistan are vying for territorial dominance over a population that neither may be fully able to control. Similar rivalries beset Rwanda and Burundi and the factions in Liberia.

These examples, however, look to the past. Less developed countries, still producing goods that are derived from land, continue to covet territory. In economies where capital, labor, and information are mobile and have risen to predominance, no land fetish remains. Developed countries would rather plumb the world market than acquire territory. The virtual state—a state that has downsized its territorially based production capability—is the logical consequence of this emancipation from the land.

In recent years the rise of the economic analogue of the virtual state—the virtual corporation—has been widely discussed. Firms have discovered the advantages of locating their production facilities wherever it is most profitable. Increasingly, this is not in the same location as corporate headquarters. Parts of a corporation are dispersed globally according to their specialties. But the more important development is the political one, the rise of the virtual state, the political counterpart of the virtual corporation.

The ascent of the trading state preceded that of the virtual state. After World War II, led by Japan and Germany, the most advanced nations shifted their efforts from controlling territory to augmenting their share of world trade. In that period, goods were more mobile than capital or labor, and selling abroad became the name of the game. As capital has become increasingly mobile, advanced nations have come to recognize that exporting is no longer the only means to economic growth; one can instead produce goods overseas for the foreign market.

As more production by domestic industries takes place abroad and land becomes less valuable than technology, knowledge, and direct investment, the function of the state is being further redefined. The state no longer commands resources as it did in mercantilist yesteryear; it negotiates with foreign and domestic capital and labor to lure them into its own economic sphere and stimulate its growth. A nation's economic strategy is now at least as important as its military strategy; its ambassadors have become foreign trade and investment representatives. Major foreign trade and investment deals command executive attention as political and military issues did two decades ago. The frantic two weeks in December 1994 when the White House outmaneuvered the French to secure for Raytheon Company a deal worth over $1 billion for the management of rainforests and air traffic in Brazil exemplifies the new international crisis.

Timeworn methods of augmenting national power and wealth are no longer effective. Like the headquarters of a virtual corporation, the virtual state determines overall strategy and invests in its people rather than amassing expensive production capacity. It contracts out other functions to states that specialize in or need them. Imperial Great Britain may have been the model for the nineteenth century, but Hong Kong will be the model for the 21st.

The virtual state is a country whose economy is reliant on mobile factors of production. Of course it houses virtual corporations and presides over foreign direct investment by its enterprises. But more than this, it encourages, stimulates, and to a degree even coordinates such activities. In formulating economic strategy, the virtual state recognizes that its own production does not have to take place at home; equally, it may play host to the capital and labor of other nations. Unlike imperial Germany, czarist Russia, and the United States of the Gilded Age—which aimed at nineteenth-century omnicompetence—it does not seek to combine or excel in all economic functions, from mining and agriculture to production and distribution. The virtual state specializes in modern technical and research services and derives its income not just from high-value manufacturing, but from product design, marketing, and financing. The rationale for its economy is efficiency attained through productive downsizing. Size no longer determines economic potential. Virtual nations hold the competitive key to greater wealth in the 21st century. They will likely supersede the continent-sized and self-sufficient units that prevailed in the past. Productive specialization will dominate internationally just as the reduced instruction set, or "RISC," computer chip has outmoded its more versatile but slower predecessors.

THE TRADING STATE

In the past, states were obsessed with land. The international system with its intermittent wars was founded on the assumption that land was the major factor in both production and power. States could improve their position by building empires or invading other nations to seize territory. To acquire land was a boon: a conquered province contained peasants and grain supplies, and its inhabitants rendered tribute to the new sovereign. Before the age of nationalism, a captured principality willingly obeyed its new ruler. Hence the Hapsburg monarchy, Spain, France, and Russia could become major powers through territorial expansion in Europe between the sixteenth and nineteenth centuries.

With the Industrial Revolution, however, capital and labor assumed new importance. Unlike land, they were mobile ingredients of productive strength. Great Britain innovated in discovering sophisticated uses for the new factors. Natural resources—especially coal, iron, and, later, oil—were still economically vital. Agricultural and mineral resources were critical to the development of the United States and other fledgling industrial nations like Australia, Canada, South Africa, and New Zealand in the nineteenth century. Not until late in the twentieth century did mobile factors of production become paramount.

By that time, land had declined in relative value and become harder for nations to hold. Colonial revolutions in the Third World since World War II have shown that nationalist mobilization of the population in developing societies impedes an imperialist or invader trying to extract resources. A nation may expend the effort to occupy new territory without gaining proportionate economic benefits.

In time, nationalist resistance and the shift in the basis of production should have an impact on the frequency of war. Land, which is fixed, can be physically captured, but labor, capital, and information are mobile and cannot be definitively seized; after an attack, these resources can slip away like quicksilver. Saddam Hussein ransacked the computers in downtown Kuwait City in August 1990 only to find that the cash in bank accounts had already been electronically transferred. Even though it had abandoned its territory, the Kuwaiti government could continue to spend billions of dollars to resist Hussein's conquest.

Today, for the wealthiest industrial countries such as Germany, the United States, and Japan, investment in land no longer pays the same dividends. Since mid-century, commodity prices have fallen nearly 40 percent relative to prices of manufactured goods.[1] The returns from the manufacturing trade greatly exceed those from agricultural exports. As a result, the terms of trade for many developing nations have been deteriorating, and in recent years the rise in prices of international services has outpaced that for manufactured products. Land prices have been steeply discounted.

Amid this decline, the 1970s and 1980s brought a new political prototype: the trading state. Rather than territorial expansion, the trading state held trade to be its fundamental purpose. This shift in national strategy was driven by the declining value of fixed productive assets. Smaller states—those for which, initially at any rate, a military-territorial strategy was not feasible—also adopted trade-oriented strategies. Along with small European and East Asian states, Japan and West Germany moved strongly in a trading direction after World War II.

Countries tend to imitate those that are most powerful. Many states followed in the wake of Great Britain in the nineteenth century; in recent decades, numerous states seeking to improve their lot in the world have emulated Japan. Under Mikhail Gorbachev in the 1980s, even the Soviet Union sought to move away from its emphasis on military spending and territorial expansion.

In recent years, however, a further stimulus has hastened this change. Faced with enhanced international competition in the late 1980s and early 1990s, corporations have opted for pervasive downsizing. They have trimmed the ratio of production workers to output, saving on costs. In some cases productivity increases resulted from pruning of the work force; in others output increased. These improvements have been highly effective; according to economist Stephen Roach in a 1994 paper published by the investment banking firm Morgan Stanley, they have nearly closed the widely noted productivity gap between services and manufacturing. The gap that remains is most likely due to measurement problems. The most efficient corporations are those that can maintain or increase output with a steady or declining amount of labor. Such corporations grew on a worldwide basis.

Meanwhile, corporations in Silicon Valley recognized that cost-cutting, productivity, and competitiveness could be enhanced still further by using the production lines of another company. The typical American plant at the time, such as Ford Motor Company's Willow Run factory in Michigan, was fully integrated, with headquarters, design offices, production workers, and factories located on substantial tracts of land. This comprehensive structure was expensive to maintain and operate, hence a firm that could employ someone else's production line could cut costs dramatically. Land and machines did not have to be bought, labor did not have to be hired, medical benefits did not have to be provided. These advantages could result from what are called economies of scope, with a firm turning out different products on the same production line or quality circle.

Or they might be the result of small, specialized firms' ability to perform exacting operations, such as the surface mounting of miniaturized components directly on circuit boards without the need for soldering or conventional wiring. In either case, the original equipment manufacturer would contract out its production to other firms. SCI Systems, Solectron, Merix, Flextronics, Smartflex, and

Sanmina turn out products for Digital Equipment, Hewlett-Packard, and IBM. In addition, AT&T, Apple, IBM, Motorola, MCI, and Corning meet part of their production needs through other suppliers. TelePad, a company that makes pen-based computers, was launched with no manufacturing capability at all. Compaq's latest midrange computer is to be produced on another company's production line.

Thus was born the virtual corporation, an entity with research, development, design, marketing, financing, legal, and other headquarters functions, but few or no manufacturing facilities: a company with a head but no body. It represents the ultimate achievement of corporate downsizing, and the model is spreading rapidly from firm to firm. It is not surprising that the virtual corporation should catch on. "Concept" or "head" corporations can design new products for a range of different production facilities. Strategic alliances between firms, which increase specialization, are also very profitable. According to the October 2, 1995, *Financial Times,* firms that actively pursue strategic alliances are 50 percent more profitable than those that do not.

TOWARD THE VIRTUAL STATE

In a setting where the economic functions of the trading state have displaced the territorial functions of the expansionist nation, the newly pruned corporation has led to the emerging phenomenon of the virtual state. Downsizing has become an index of corporate efficiency and productivity gains. Now the national economy is also being downsized. Among the most efficient economies are those that possess limited production capacity. The archetype is Hong Kong, whose production facilities are now largely situated in southern China. This arrangement may change after 1997 with Hong Kong's reversion to the mainland, but it may not. It is just as probable that Hong Kong will continue to govern parts of the mainland economically as it is that Beijing will dictate to Hong Kong politically. The one country–two systems formula will likely prevail. In this context, it is important to remember that Britain governed Hong Kong politically and legally for 150 years, but it did not dictate its economics. Nor did this arrangement prevent Hong Kong Chinese from extending economic and quasi-political controls to areas outside their country.

The model of the virtual state suggests that political as well as economic strategy push toward a downsizing and relocation of production capabilities. The trend can be observed in Singapore as well. The successors of Lee Kuan Yew keep the country on a tight political rein but still depend economically on the inflow of foreign factors of production. Singapore's investment in China, Malaysia, and elsewhere is within others' jurisdictions. The virtual state is in this sense a negotiating entity. It depends as much or more on economic access abroad as it does on economic control at home. Despite its past reliance on domestic production, Korea no longer manufactures everything at home, and Japanese production (given the high yen) is now increasingly lodged abroad. In Europe, Switzerland is the leading virtual nation; as much as 98 percent of Nestlé's production capacity, for instance, is located abroad. Holland now produces most of its goods outside its borders. England is also moving in tandem with the worldwide trend; according to the Belgian economic historian Paul Bairoch in 1994, Britain's foreign direct investment abroad was almost as large as America's. A remarkable 20 percent of the production of U.S. corporations now takes place outside the United States.

A reflection of how far these tendencies have gone is the growing portion of GDP consisting of high-value-added services, such as concept, design, consulting, and financial services. Services already constitute 70 percent of American GDP. Of the total, 63 percent are in the high-value category. Of course manufacturing matters, but it matters much less than it once did. As a proportion of foreign direct investment, service exports have grown strikingly in most highly industrialized economies. According to a 1994 World Bank report, *Liberalizing International Transactions in Services,* "The reorientation of [foreign direct investment] towards the services sector has occurred in almost all developed market economies, the principal exporters of services capital: in the most important among them, the share of the services sector is around 40 percent of the stock of outward FDI, and that share is rising."

Manufacturing, for these nations, will continue to decline in importance. If services productivity increases as much as it has in recent years, it will greatly strengthen U.S. competitiveness abroad. But it can no longer be assumed that services face no international competition. Efficient high-value services will be as important to a nation as the manufacturing of automobiles and electrical equipment once were.[2] Since 1959, services prices have increased more than three times as rapidly as industrial prices. This means that many nations will be able to prosper without major manufacturing capabilities.

Australia is an interesting example. Still reliant on the production of sheep and raw materials (both related to land), Australia has little or no industrial sector. Its largest export to the United States is meat for hamburgers. On the other hand, its service industries of media, finance, and telecommunications—represented most notably by the media magnate Rupert Murdoch—are the envy of the world. Canada represents a similar amalgam of raw materials and powerful service industries in newspapers, broadcast media, and telecommunications.

As a result of these trends, the world may increasingly become divided into "head" and "body" nations, or nations representing some combination of those two functions. While Australia and Canada stress the headquarters or head functions, China will be the 21st-century model of a body nation. Although China does not innately or immediately know what to produce for the world market, it has found success in joint ventures with foreign corporations. China will be an attractive place to produce manufactured goods, but only because sophisticated enterprises from other countries design, market, and finance the products China makes. At present China cannot chart its own industrial future.

Neither can Russia. Focusing on the products of land, the Russians are still prisoners of territorial fetishism. Their commercial laws do not yet permit the delicate and sophisticated arrangements that ensure that "body" manufacturers deliver quality goods for their foreign "head." Russia's transportation network is also primitive. These, however, are temporary obstacles. In time Russia, with China and India, will serve as an important locus of the world's production plant.

THE VESTIGES OF SERFDOM

The world is embarked on a progressive emancipation from land as a determinant of production and power. For the Third World, the past unchangeable strictures of comparative advantage can be overcome through the acquisition of a highly trained labor force. Africa and Latin America may not have to rely on the exporting of raw materials or agricultural products; through education, they can capitalize on an educated labor force, as India has in Bangalore and Ireland in Dublin. Investing in human capital can substitute for trying to foresee the vagaries of the commodities markets and avoid the constant threat of overproduction. Meanwhile, land continues to decline in value. Recent studies of 180 countries show that as population density rises, per capita GDP falls. In a new study, economist Deepak Lal notes that investment as well as growth is inversely related to land holdings.[3]

These findings are a dramatic reversal of past theories of power in international politics. In the 1930s the standard international relations textbook would have ranked the great powers in terms of key natural resources: oil, iron ore, coal, bauxite, copper, tungsten, and manganese. Analysts presumed that the state with the largest stock of raw materials and goods derived from land would prevail. CIA estimates during the Cold War were based on such conclusions. It turns out, however, that the most prosperous countries often have a negligible endowment of natural resources. For instance, Japan has shut down its coal industry and has no iron ore, bauxite, or oil. Except for most of its rice, it imports much of its food. Japan is richly endowed with human capital, however, and that makes all the difference.

The implications for the United States are equally striking. As capital, labor, and knowledge become more important than land in charting economic success, America can influence and possibly even reshape its pattern of comparative advantage. The "new trade theory," articulated clearly by the economist Paul Krugman, focuses on path dependence, the so-called QWERTY effect of past choices. The QWERTY keyboard was not the arrangement of letter-coded keys that produced the fastest typing, except perhaps for left-handers. But, as the VHS videotape format became the standard for video recording even though other formats were technically better, the QWERTY keyboard became the standard for the typewriter (and computer) industry, and everyone else had to adapt to it. Nations that invested from the start in production facilities for the 16-kilobyte computer memory chip also had great advantages down the line in 4- and 16-megabyte chips. Intervention at an early point in the chain of development can influence results later on, which suggests that the United States and other nations can and should deliberately alter their pattern of comparative advantage and choose their economic activity.

American college and graduate education, for example, has supported the decisive U.S. role in the international services industry in research and development, consulting, design, packaging, financing, and the marketing of new products. Mergers and acquisitions are American subspecialties that draw on the skills of financial analysts and attorneys. The American failure, rather, has been in the first 12 years of education. Unlike that of Germany and Japan (or even Taiwan, Korea, and Singapore), American elementary and secondary education falls well below the world standard.

Economics teaches that products should be valued according to their economic importance. For a long period, education was undervalued, socially and economically speaking, despite productivity studies by Edward Denison and others that showed its long-term importance to U.S. growth and innovation. Recent studies have underscored this importance. According to the World Bank, 64 percent of the world's wealth consists of human capital. But the social and economic valuation of kindergarten through 12th-grade education has still not appreciably increased. Educators, psychologists, and school boards debate how education should be structured, but Americans do not invest more money in it. Corporations have sought to upgrade the standards of teaching and learning in their regions, but localities and states have lagged behind, as has the federal government. Elementary and high school teachers should be rewarded as patient creators of high-value capital in the United States and elsewhere. In Switzerland, elementary school teachers are paid around $70,000 per year, about the salary of a starting lawyer at a New York firm. In international economic competition, human capital has turned out to be at least as important as other varieties of capital. In spite of their reduced functions, states liberated from the confines of their geography have been able, with appropriate education, to transform their industrial and economic futures.

THE REDUCED DANGER OF CONFLICT

As nations turn to the cultivation of human capital, what will a world of virtual states be like? Production for one company or country can now take place in many parts of the world. In the process of downsizing, corporations and nation-states will have to get used to reliance on others. Virtual corporations need other corporations' production facilities. Virtual nations need other states' production capabilities. As a result, economic relations between states will come to resemble nerves connecting heads in one place to bodies somewhere else. Naturally, producer nations will be working quickly to become the brains behind emerging industries elsewhere. But in time, few nations will have within their borders all the components of a technically advanced economic existence.

To sever the connections between states would undermine the organic unit. States joined in this way are therefore less likely to engage in conflict. In the past, international norms underlying the balance of power, the Concert of Europe, or even rule by the British Raj helped specify appropriate courses of action for parties in dispute. The international economy also rested partially on normative agreement. Free trade, open domestic economies, and, more recently, freedom of movement for capital were normative notions. In addition to specifying conditions for borrowing, the International Monetary Fund is a norm-setting agency that inculcates market economics in nations not fully ready to accept their international obligations.

Like national commercial strategies, these norms have been largely abstracted from the practices of successful nations. In the nineteenth century many countries emulated Great Britain and its precepts. In the British pantheon of virtues, free trade was a norm that could be extended to other nations without self-defeat. Success for one nation did not undermine the prospects for others. But the acquisition of empire did cause congestion for other nations on the paths to industrialization and growth. Once imperial Britain had taken the lion's share, there was little left for others. The inability of all nations to live up to the norms Britain established fomented conflict between them.

In a similar vein, Japan's current trading strategy could be emulated by many other countries. Its pacific principles and dependence on world markets and raw materials supplies have engendered greater economic cooperation among other countries. At the same time, Japan's insistence on maintaining a quasi-closed domestic economy and a foreign trade surplus cannot be successfully imitated by everyone; if some achieve the desired result, others necessarily will not. In this respect, Japan's recent practices and norms stand athwart progress and emulation by other nations.

President Clinton rightly argues that the newly capitalist developmental states, such as Korea and Taiwan, have simply modeled themselves on restrictionist Japan. If this precedent were extended to China, the results would endanger the long-term stability of the world economic and financial system. Accordingly, new norms calling for greater openness in trade, finance, and the movement of factors of production will be necessary to stabilize the international system. Appropriate norms reinforce economic incentives to reduce conflict between differentiated international units.

DEFUSING THE POPULATION BOMB

So long as the international system of nation-states lasts, there will be conflict among its members. States see events from different perspectives, and competition and struggle between them are endemic. The question is how far conflicts will proceed. Within a domestic system, conflicts between individuals need not escalate to the use of physical force. Law and settlement procedures usually reduce outbreaks of hostility. In international relations, however, no sovereign, regnant authority can discipline feuding states. International law sets a standard, but it is not always obeyed. The great powers constitute the executive committee of nation-states and can intervene from time to time to set things right. But, as Bosnia shows, they often do not, and they virtually never intervene in the absence of shared norms and ideologies.

In these circumstances, the economic substructure of international relations becomes exceedingly important. That structure can either impel or retard conflicts between nation-states. When land is the major factor of production, the temptation to strike another nation is great. When the key elements of production are less tangible, the situation changes. The taking of real estate does not result in the acquisition of knowledge, and aggressors cannot seize the needed capital. Workers may flee from an invader. Wars of aggression and wars of punishment are losing their impact and justification.

Eventually, however, contend critics such as Paul Ehrlich, author of *The Population Bomb,* land will become important once again. Oil supplies will be depleted; the quantity of fertile land will decline; water will run dry. Population will rise relative to the supply of natural resources and food. This process, it is claimed, could return the world to the eighteenth and nineteenth centuries, with clashes over territory once again the engine of conflict. The natural resources on which the world currently relies may one day run out, but, as before, there will be substitutes. One sometimes forgets that in the 1840s whale oil, which was the most common fuel for lighting, became unavailable. The harnessing of global energy and the production of food does not depend on particular bits of fluid, soil, or rock. The question, rather, is how to release the energy contained in abundant matter.

But suppose the productive value of land does rise. Whether that rise would augur a return to territorial competition would depend on whether the value of land rises relative to financial capital, human capital, and information. Given the rapid technological development of recent years, the primacy of the latter seems more likely. Few perturbing trends have altered the historical tendency toward the growing intangibility of value in social and economic terms. In the 21st century it seems scarcely possible that this process would suddenly reverse itself, and land would yield a better return than knowledge.

Diminishing their command of real estate and productive assets, nations are downsizing, in functional if not in geographic terms. Small nations have attained peak efficiency and competitiveness, and even large nations have begun to think small. If durable access to assets elsewhere can be assured, the need to physically possess them diminishes. Norms are potent reinforcements of such arrangements. Free movement of capital and goods, substantial international and domestic investment, and high levels of technical education have been the recipe for success in the industrial world of the late twentieth century. Those who depended on others did better than those who depended only on themselves. Can the result be different in the future? Virtual states, corporate alliances, and essential trading relationships augur peaceful times. They may not solve domestic problems, but the economic bonds that link virtual and other nations will help ease security concerns.

THE CIVIC CRISIS

Though peaceful in its international implications, the rise of the virtual state portends a crisis for democratic politics. Western democracies have traditionally believed that political reform, extension of suffrage, and economic restructuring could solve their problems. In the 21st century none of these measures can fully succeed. Domestic political change does not suffice because it has insufficient jurisdiction to deal with global problems. The people in a particular state cannot determine international outcomes by holding an election. Economic restructuring in one state does not necessarily affect others. And the political state is growing smaller, not larger.

If ethnic movements are victorious in Canada, Mexico, and elsewhere, they will divide the state into smaller entities. Even the powers of existing states are becoming circumscribed. In the United States, if Congress has its way, the federal government will lose authority. In response to such changes, the market fills the vacuum, gaining power.

As states downsize, malaise among working people is bound to spread. Employment may fluctuate and generally decline. President Clinton observed last year that the American public has fallen into a funk. The economy may temporarily be prosperous, but there is no guarantee that favorable conditions will last. The flow of international factors of production—technology, capital, and labor—will swamp the stock of economic power at home. The state will become just one of many players in the international marketplace and will have to negotiate directly with foreign factors of production to solve domestic economic problems. Countries must induce foreign capital to enter their domain. To keep such investment, national economic authorities will need to maintain low inflation, rising productivity, a strong currency, and a flexible and trained labor force. These demands will sometimes conflict with domestic interests that want more government spending, larger budget deficits, and more benefits. That conflict will result in continued domestic insecurity over jobs, welfare, and medical care. Unlike the remedies applied in the insulated and partly closed economies of the past, purely domestic policies can no longer solve these problems.

THE NECESSITY OF INTERNATIONALIZATION

The state can compensate for its deficient jurisdiction by seeking to influence economic factors abroad. The domestic state therefore must not only become a negotiating state but must also be internationalized. This is a lesson already learned in Europe, and well on the way to codification in East Asia. Among the world's major economies and polities, only the United States remains, despite its potent economic sector, essentially introverted politically and culturally. Compared with their counterparts in other nations, citizens born in the United States know fewer foreign languages, understand less about foreign cultures, and live abroad reluctantly, if at all. In recent years, many English industrial workers who could not find jobs migrated to Germany, learning the language to work there. They had few American imitators.

The virtual state is an agile entity operating in twin jurisdictions: abroad and at home. It is as prepared to mine gains overseas as in the domestic economy. But in large countries, internationalization operates differentially. Political and economic decision-makers have begun to recast their horizons, but middle managers and workers lag behind. They expect too much and give and learn too little. That is why the dawn of the virtual state must also be the sunrise of international education and training. The virtual state cannot satisfy all its citizens. The possibility of commanding economic power in the sense of effective state control has greatly declined. Displaced workers and businesspeople must be willing to look abroad for opportunities. In the United States, they can do this only if American education prepares the way.

NOTES

1. See, for example, Enzo R. Grilli and Maw Cheng Yang, "Primary Commodity Prices, Manufactured Goods Prices, and the Terms of Trade of Developing Countries: What the Long Run Shows," *The World Bank Economic Review,* 1988, Vol. 2, No. 1, pp. 1–47.
2. See José Ripoll, "The Future of Trade in International Services," Center for International Relations Working Paper, UCLA, January 1996.
3. Daniel Garstka, "Land and Economic Prowess" (unpublished mimeograph), UCLA, 1995; Deepak Lal, "Factor Endowments, Culture and Politics: On Economic Performance in the Long Run" (unpublished mimeograph), UCLA, 1996.

4
From High Volume to High Value

Robert Reich

The modern corporation at the close of the twentieth century bears only a superficial resemblance to its midcentury counterpart. The names and logos of America's core corporations are still emblematic of the American economy—General Electric, AT&T, General Motors, Ford, IBM, Kodak, American Can, Sears, Caterpillar Tractor, TWA, and so on, including even a few new giants virtually unknown at midcentury, like Texas Instruments, McDonald's, Xerox, and American Express. They still conjure up images of vast wealth and control over the wheels of commerce. They are still headquartered in formidable glass-and-steel buildings, as before, and their top executives still hobnob with politicians and celebrities, and write autobiographies congratulating themselves on their wisdom and daring.

But underneath, all is changing. America's core corporation no longer plans and implements the production of a large volume of goods and services; it no longer owns or invests in a vast array of factories, machinery, laboratories, warehouses, and other tangible assets; it no longer employs armies of production workers and middle-level managers; it no longer serves as gateway to the American middle class. In fact, the core corporation is no longer even American. It is, increasingly, a façade, behind which teems an array of decentralized groups and subgroups continuously contracting with similarly diffuse working units all over the world.

The transformation has been less than smooth. No longer able to generate large earnings from high-volume production of standard commodities—and unable to restore profits by protecting the American market, cutting prices, or rearranging assets—America's core corporations are gradually, often painfully, turning toward serving the unique needs of particular customers. By trial and error, by fits and starts, often under great stress, and usually without much awareness of what they are doing or why, the firms that are surviving and succeeding are shifting from high volume to high value. A similar transformation is occurring in other national economies which have traditionally been organized around high-volume production.

A few illustrations will help make the point. In the United States, as in other leading areas of the world economy, the fastest-growing and most profitable part of steelmaking is no longer in mammoth 5,000-employee integrated mills producing long runs of steel ingots. It is in steels intended for particular uses: corrosion-resistant steels (hot-dipped galvanized or electrogalvanized) produced for specific automobiles, trucks, and appliances; iron powder that can be packed and forged into lightweight and precisely balanced parts used in crankshafts and other high-stressed parts of engines; alloys comprising steel mixed with silicon, nickel, or cobalt, for turbine and compressor disks, spacers, seals, and other high-temperature components of aircraft (McDonnell Douglas now buys composite helicopter blades comprising seventeen different materials, for $50,000 each); and mini-mills, using electric-arc furnaces and scrap metal to serve particular customers. A similar transformation is occurring in plastics, where high earnings no longer flow from large batches of basic polymers like polystyrene, but from special polymers created from unique combinations of molecules which can withstand varying degrees of stress and temperature and can be molded into intricate parts (like those found in cellular telephones or computers). In chemicals, the biggest profits likewise lie in specialty chemicals designed and produced for particular industrial uses.

Whether the industry is old or new, mature or high-tech, the pattern is similar. Leading tool and die casters make precision castings out of aluminum and zinc for computer frames, inserts, housings, and disk-drive components. The most profitable textile businesses produce specially coated and finished fabrics for automobiles, office furniture, rain gear, and wall coverings. The fastest-growing and most profitable semiconductor firms make specialized microprocessors and customized chips tailored to the particular needs of buyers. As computers with standard operating systems become commodities, the largest profits lie in the software that links computers to particular user needs. (In 1984, 80 percent of the cost of a computer was in its hardware, 20 percent in software; by 1990, the proportions were just the reverse.)

Traditional services are experiencing the same transformation. The highest profits in telecommunications derive from customized long-distance services like voice, video, and information processing; from "smart buildings" connecting office telephones, computers, and facsimile machines; and from specialized telecommunications networks linking employees in different locations. The fastest-growing trucking, rail, and air freight businesses meet shippers' needs for specialized pickups and deliveries, unique containers, and worldwide integration of different modes of transportation. The most profitable financial businesses offer a wide range of services (linking banking, insurance, and investment) tailored to the specific needs of individuals and businesses. As news becomes a commodity available on twenty-four-hour television, the fastest-growing news and wire service businesses similarly assemble unique packages of information tailored to subscribers' needs (customized newsletters, video news release services, eventually even home-computer-customized "videotext" newspapers). Again, from high volume to high value.

These businesses are profitable both because customers are willing to pay a premium for goods or services that exactly meet their needs and because these high-value businesses cannot easily be duplicated by high-volume competitors around the world. While competition among high-volume producers continues to compress profits on everything that is uniform, routine, and standard—that is, on anything that can be made, reproduced, or extracted in volume almost anywhere on the globe—successful businesses in advanced nations are moving to a higher ground based on specially tailored products and services. The new barrier to entry is not volume or price; it is skill in finding the right fit between particular technologies and particular markets. Core corporations no longer focus on products as such; their business strategies increasingly center upon specialized knowledge.

Look closely at these high-value businesses and you see three different but related skills that drive them forward. Here, precisely, is where the value resides. First are the problem-solving skills required to put things together in unique ways (be they alloys, molecules, semiconductor chips, software codes, movie scripts, pension portfolios, or information). Problem-solvers must have intimate knowledge of what such things might be able to do when reassembled, and then must turn that knowledge into designs and instructions for creating such outcomes. Unlike the researchers and designers whose prototypes emerged fully formed from the laboratory or drafting table ready for high-volume production, these people are involved in a continuing search for new applications, combinations, and refinements capable of solving all sorts of emerging problems.

Next are the skills required to help customers understand their needs and how those needs can best be met by customized products. In contrast to selling and marketing standardized goods—which requires persuading many customers of the virtues of one particular product, taking lots of orders for it, and thus meeting sales quotas—selling and marketing customized products requires having an intimate knowledge of a customer's business, where competitive advantage may lie, and how it can be achieved. The key is to identify new problems and possibilities to which the customized product might be applicable. The art of persuasion is replaced by the identification of opportunity.

Third are the skills needed to link problem-solvers and problem-identifiers. People in such roles must understand enough about specific technologies and markets to see the potential for new products, raise whatever money is necessary to launch the project, and assemble the right problem-solvers and -identifiers to carry it out. Those occupying this position in the new economy were typically called "executives" or "entrepreneurs" in the old, but neither term fully connotes their role in high-value enterprise. Rather than controlling organizations, founding businesses, or inventing things, such people are continuously engaged in managing ideas. They play the role of strategic broker.

In the high-value enterprise, profits derive not from scale and volume but from continuous discovery of new linkages between solutions and needs. The distinction that used to be drawn between "goods" and "services" is meaningless, because so much of the value provided by the successful enterprise—in fact, the only value that cannot easily be replicated worldwide—entails services: the specialized research, engineering, and design services necessary to solve problems; the specialized sales, marketing, and consulting services necessary to identify problems; and the specialized strategic, financial, and management services for brokering the first two. Every high-value enterprise is in the business of providing such services.

Steelmaking is becoming a service business, for example. When a new alloy is molded to a specific weight and tolerance, services account for a significant part of the value of the resulting product. Steel service centers help customers choose the steels and alloys they need, and then inspect, slit, coat, store, and deliver the materials. Computer manufacturers are likewise in the service business, where a larger and larger portion of every consumer dollar goes toward customizing software and then integrating and installing systems around it. IBM is a service company, although it appears annually on the list of the nation's largest industrial firms. In 1990 more than one-third of its profits came from designing software, up from 18 percent in the mid-1980s, and more than 20 percent came from integrating computer systems. Much of the rest was related to what it calls "sales and support," which involves helping customers define their data-processing needs, choose appropriate hardware and software, get it up and running, and then working out the bugs. Less than 20,000 of IBM's 400,000 employees were classified as production workers engaged in traditional manufacturing. The immensely successful IBM personal computer itself comprises a collection of services—research, design, engineering, sales, service; only 10 percent of its purchase price is for the physical manufacture of the machine.

America's arcane system of national accounting still has separate categories for manufacturing and services—classifying, for example, computer software as a service (although it is reproduced like a manufactured item) and a computer as a manufactured good (although an ever-larger portion of the cost of a computer lies in computer services). The pharmaceutical industry is classified under "manufacturing," although a drug's production costs actually represent only a tiny fraction of the total costs, which mostly involve services like research and development, clinical trials, patent applications and regulatory clearances, drug detailing, and distribution. We are told, repeatedly, that nearly 80 percent of the new jobs created in the 1980s were in services, and that some 70 percent of private-sector employees now work in service businesses. But as the lines begin to blur between services and goods, such numbers are increasingly meaningless in terms of what is actually occurring in the economy and where the real value lies.

Part Two

Knowledge as the Economic Force of Growth and Change

5

Homo Faber, Homo Sapiens: Knowledge, Technology, Growth, and Development

David S. Landes

But this rich. Rich *is just a sound. What is* rich? Rich *is education . . . expertise . . . technology.* Rich *is knowing. We have money, yes. But we are not* rich. *We are like the child who inherits money from the father he never knew. He has not been brought up to spend it. He has it in his hands; he doesn't know how to use it. If you do not know how to spend money, you are not* rich. *We are not rich.*

Without this knowledge, this understanding, we are nothing. We import everything. *The bricks to make houses, we import. The men who build them, we import. You go to the market, what is there that is made by Arabs? Nothing. It is Chinese, French, American . . . it is not Arab. Is a country rich that cannot make a brick, or a motorcar, or a book? It is not rich, I think.*

—Mohammed Mannei,
merchant banker in the Persian Gulf.[1]

THEIR NATION SAVED, KUWAITIS NOW WAIT FOR SOMEONE TO FIX IT; MANY OF THEM, MEANWHILE, PLAN A SUMMER IN LONDON, AS DECISIONS GO UNMADE

—Headline, *Wall Street Journal*[2]

From *Contention,* Volume 1, Number 3, Spring 1992. Reprinted by permission of the University of California, Los Angeles Department of History.

If you don't upgrade your technological base and only stay in the same product range and move it offshore, that doesn't solve your problem. That's [the] American disease—move everything offshore but don't move up. For success in the next ten years, we have to become more Japanese.

—T. J. Huang, business executive, Taiwan[3]

A number of scholars have made it a point to distinguish between growth with and without technological progress. Eric Jones, for example, in a recent book entitled *Growth Recurring* (1988), argues that what matters is not so much technical innovation as "intensive growth," that is, growth in product or income per head; and that while technology no doubt contributes mightily to such growth, it is not necessary to it.[4] On that he is surely right: per capita economic growth can and does take place in the absence of technological advance. A favorable change in prices, for example, can enhance substantially the value of product; the best illustration from our own time is the oil shock of 1973, which brought fabulous wealth to oil-producing nations.

And yet I disagree with Mr. Jones. What I would call windfall growth, that is, growth that is not based on gains in productivity derived from advances in technique and organization, is intrinsically precarious and ephemeral.[5] Such opportunistic and often adventitious gains in product per head cannot long endure, and this, because of dynamic market response. For one thing, the victims of such gains (because someone has to pay) will react by finding ways of reducing the bill. These will typically take the form of substituting one factor for another, of replacing increasingly costly materials by cheaper ones for example, or of economizing material by using more thrifty labor, or of installing better, material-saving or energy-saving equipment. For another, the beneficiaries of these windfall gains will be pressed by this response to sustain their margins by reducing costs. The sellers must change, for the buyers will, especially if—as is often the case—they come from advanced industrial societies. If the beneficiaries do not improve, growth will quickly run out of steam. This is obviously true when that growth is based on the discovery and exploitation of wasting assets such as mineral wealth. Deposits give out, and even before that happens, other sources will be sought, found, and put to use. Meanwhile there are always potential substitutes, too expensive perhaps before, but now commercially useful, not only because of the shift in relative prices, but also because of technological advances by the users. But even with a reproducible product, the initial impetus of a favorable shift in demand, for example, will lose force as buyers adjust.[6]

A good example of the difference of growth with and without technological change is furnished by the history of the textile manufacture during the Industrial Revolution: a tale of two countries. In the period 1500–1750, the indigenous manufacture of cotton cloth in India received a huge impulse from access to an almost insatiable European market: consumers could not get enough of these fine fabrics, which surpassed anything that Europe could make. The great East Indian trading companies built much of their wealth on this import trade. To meet this expanded demand, the Indians had recourse to additional spinners and weavers. This was growth without technological progress.

Meanwhile the British, seeking to protect the domestic woolen manufacture against this flood of low-cost goods, passed at the turn of the seventeenth century a number of protectionist calico acts; and behind this barrier, their rural cottage industry learned to turn out lighter, cheaper woolens and worsteds, mixed woolen-linens (fustians and linsey-woolseys), and more and more cottons (but this was only a beginning) for growing home and foreign markets. The British initially reacted to this swelling demand as the Indians before them: they simply devoted more resources to manufacture, pulling in more labor from farther afield. This too was growth without technological progress. But in the long run, the British could not persist along these lines, for the simple reason that the supply of labor was far less elastic than in India. As labor costs rose, especially in the spinning branch of the industry, manufacturers and inventors sought to build machines to replace people. The success of this technology, first in spinning, then in weaving, first in cotton, then in other fibers, inaugurated a process of ramifying technological change. Thus was born a new mode of production, what Marx called modern industry—that is, mechanized manufacture under supervision, what contemporaries called the factory system.[7] This new machine-spun yarn finished by destroying Indian hand spinning, and it was not until factories were built in India beginning in the mid-19th century that the manufacture of cotton yarn was revived.

Meanwhile, what of growth-without-progress? The beneficiaries will have more money to spend, and if they do not invest in technical improvement, there is every likelihood that they will consume it, waste it, or sink it in private and public monuments. The Egypt of the cotton boom of the 1860s is an excellent example of the dissipation of windfall wealth. For a while, Egypt was a happy-hunting-ground for ambitious projectors, drawn by the sharp increase in national income and government revenues; while the government itself capitalized its income prospects in the form of large international loans, whose proceeds went to pay mostly for pomp and circumstance. In the end, even the best of the state's investments, the shares it acquired voluntarily and not so voluntarily in the Suez Canal Company, had to be sold to meet onerous credit obligations assumed in more prosperous times.[8] The oil-producing nations of today have tried to do better, if only because they know something about the past. Even so, most of them are liable to see their wells dry up before they can convert growth into development.[9]

One might even argue a moralistic position, that growth without technological advance is not good for you; that it represents short-run advantage that will be paid for in long-run retardation. The historical examples are numerous: the most important is Spain's response to the windfall wealth transferred in the form of bullion and specie from the Americas in the 16th and 17th centuries. The Spanish spent most of the money on war and imports of food and manufactures from workshop countries to the north (notably England and the Low Countries) and were foolish enough to rejoice that the rest of the world was working for Spain. This is not to say that there were no observers wise enough to see what was happening; there were just too few of them. One of them, Martin Gonzales de Cellorigo, wrote in 1600: "If Spain has neither money nor gold nor silver, it is because it has these things, and if it is poor, it is because it is rich . . . One would think that one wanted to make of this republic a republic of enchanted people living outside the natural order."[10] One can find similar orgies of destructive self-indulgence among the oil-rich countries of the late 20th century.

The combination of growth *cum* technological change (or, as the causal sequence often runs, technological change *cum* growth) is in many ways a natural process: that is the way things work; that is "doin' what comes naturally." Adam Smith saw it clearly when he propounded the link between the size of the market, division of labor, and the gains to specialization: the division of labor is a function of the size of the market; the larger the market, the greater the degree of specialization and the simpler the tasks, with consequent gains to experience in both skill and proficiency; and simplification is both opportunity for and inspiration to technical improvement. The whole makes possible a self-confirming upward spiral.[11]

Technology, of course, is applied, routinized knowledge and as such transferable. (For the purpose of this discussion, I include in technology both software and hardware, process innovations [of course] and product innovations, organizational gains as well as new methods.) Indeed, it is this process of knowledge transfer that is at the heart of technological diffusion. This diffusion in turn has been the history of modern industrialization: a complex of technological changes, concentrated initially (18th century) in England, were imitated and emulated abroad, first in nearby areas of Continental Europe, then in more distant (peripheral) areas and in overseas extensions of Europe, eventually in non-Western countries beginning with Japan.

To be sure, this process of emulation was never the same, for it varied with time and place. For one thing, the content of the pool of technology was ever changing as new techniques were invented and old ones improved; for another, the usefulness (marginal product) of given technologies necessarily varied with the circumstances of the follower-imitator (particularly with relative factor costs); so that no country's path of development was the same as any other's. To infer from this diversity, however, that the British industrial revolution was not seen as a lesson and challenge in technological possibilities is simply wrong. The point is not whether one had to clone the British way; but rather whether the interrelated complex of British innovations—machines, power, a new ferrous metallurgy, the factory—was not the essence of a new mode of production. European and American statesmen and businessmen and economists of that day understood perfectly well what was at stake: British industrial superiority threatened national autonomy and parity. So they set about copying, importing, learning, stealing, borrowing, and instilling the new industrial knowledge.[12]

Looking at the spread of these technologies, it seems clear that the principal agent of diffusion has been the human carrier of skill and knowledge. One can buy the equipment, but learning how to work it is another matter; and to make it, adapt it, improve it, quite another. This primary reliance on the human medium was more important at the beginning, when the modes of communication and instruction were rudimentary, when hardware was less standardized, maintenance less routinized. We do a lot better today.

A few thoughts about equipment: equipment is from one point of view nothing but embodied knowledge and technique; and equipment usually comes accompanied by instructions. But as anyone knows who has tried to make unassisted use of complex electronic devices, instruction manuals are a snare and delusion; hence the rise of a thriving industry producing instruction manuals to replace and supplement those supplied by the manufacturer. The problem is even more serious when the equipment comes from abroad, for then the instruction manual, if written in the language of the manufacturer, will pose serious, even insoluble problems to users not familiar with the technical idiom. And if written in the language of the customer, it is liable to offer a fascinating exercise in cryptanalysis. (A book could be written on the history of the instruction manual as a case study in incomprehensible communication.) Besides, even if the equipment works, there is so much more to any production process than can be conveyed by plans and the written word—to say nothing of the inevitable hitches and glitches—that nothing less than hands-on experience will do—unless of course time and money are free.

So hardware alone is not enough. Along with it must go the managers and technicians, sometimes invited, sometimes sent by the exporters of hardware to accompany the equipment, maintain it, and teach the foreigners how to use it. David Jeremy tells us in his *Transatlantic Industrial Revolution* that cotton spinning devices found their way to the American colonies in the years following the peace with Britain (1783) but lay idle for want of human know-how. "In New England three Arkwright machines, apparently imperfect models, for carding, roving, and spinning were built by two Scotsmen in 1787 for public exhibition but defied commercial exploitation until Slater arrived three years later."[13] If Jeremy is unable to say, I am certainly not going to venture an opinion about the shortcomings of these machines, but from one point of view, the only thing imperfect about them was the two Scotsmen.

The transfer of knowledge and know-how by human carrier was a source of considerable anxiety to the British of the late 18th and early 19th centuries, who feared the loss of their technological advantage and banned the emigration or seduction of artisans. This prohibition was only partially effective, but it reflected a keen awareness of the stakes. Indeed, the possessors of industrial secrets understood full well that the tools and machines were less important than the men, even within national boundaries. In Britain, mills were built like fortresses, the better to keep workers in and strangers out. Workers were sworn to secrecy; in some places visitors were systematically refused admission; other factories made an occasional exception, but strangers were always to be accompanied. Sometimes the secrecy was selective and was limited to certain equipment or processes, while others were open because already in the public domain.[14] In France and other countries, no industrial worker could leave his job until his employer had signed off in his passbook; and when, toward the end of the 18th century, French manufacturers of clocks and watches were asked by the government to devise a new mode of production based on interchangeable parts by way of offering more effective competition to the watchmakers of Geneva, a recurrent theme of their responses was the careful division of labor and specialization of the work force so that no one worker could know and transmit the full process.[15] A word of caution: even human carriers are not always enough; take them out of their context and they are less than they were. Once the various barriers to export of men and machines were lifted, British manufacturers of textile machinery were only too happy to sell the latest equipment, accompanied by technicians. Even so, few if any customers ever learned to make cottons comparable in fineness and appearance to those of Lancashire. This tells something about the complexity and interrelatedness of these processes, which went from the selection of the raw material to the finishing. Along the way, machines manipulated and processed; but they were only part of the whole.

About human carriers: one has to think of the pains of migration as a continuum. Near and far, moving is moving and invariably entails losses as well as gains. The decision to move, even within one's own country, is never easy; how much harder to go to a strange place of strange tongue. This business of language was an important consideration for those possessors of knowledge who sought to exploit it for better returns at the margin; hence the superior ability of the American colonies and the new American nation to draw British artisans; also their preference for British as against, say, French technology. From the point of view of the British immigrant, America was far away and yet much like home. From the American side, the British visitor was very like those who had preceded him, not only in his speech and manners, but in his pragmatic approach to work and technique.[16]

For the pioneers, the ones who went to strange places before there were other "expats" to receive them, there were often special circumstances of push to reinforce the pull (the prospect of better wages or higher profits). The story I like best is one we owe to John Harris, that indefatigable student of technological diffusion from Britain to France in the 18th century. He tells us about Michael Alcock, to all appearances an important and wealthy hardware manufacturer, who left Birmingham for France in 1755 or 1756 to establish a mill at La Charité on the upper Loire river, on what seemed a suitable natural site but was surely *fin fond de la brousse* (the boondocks) from a French, let alone British, social and cultural point of view. Alcock sought and obtained from the French government a number of exemptions and privileges to encourage his spirit of enterprise, but what seems really to have determined his move, which led to that of a number of British artisans as well, was financial and sentimental difficulties at home. As the documents tell us, he left under a double cloud, not really apparent until after he had gone: he was on the verge of bankruptcy, and when he left, he took with him a thousand pounds sterling (equivalent to twenty years' salary of a skilled worker, say, half a million of today's dollars), leaving his partner to face the music; and he went off with his mistress, the daughter of one of his master workers, much to his wife's chagrin. But Mr. Alcock was a person of uncommon powers of persuasion, and he was soon rejoined by his wife, who was charged with and acquitted of "seducing" other skilled artisans to join her husband in France; and after Mrs. Alcock got to the new home at La Charité, she apparently learned to get along with her rival in what may have been a successful *ménage à trois*. Perhaps the relative isolation of La Charité offered special advantages.[17]

Whatever the reasons for moving (and I have chosen a particularly amusing example), displacement abroad inevitably poses special problems with price attached. It is not easy to leave a familiar national, social, and cultural context to make one's way among people of strange ways and tongue. Expatriate labor is often reluctant labor, so that wage and salary premiums have to be paid; and reluctant labor is also often discontented, troublesome labor, so that its unhappiness affects both sides, both the transmitters and receivers of new ways and new knowledge. Hence a substantial incentive to human import substitution: get free of dependence on the foreigner. One way is to send one's own people abroad to learn, in school or at the bench, openly or in secret. Industrial espionage has a long and distinguished pedigree, going back to the unknown medieval monk who smuggled the silkworm from China to Europe and to tsar Peter of Russia visiting shipyards and forges in the Netherlands and England at the end of the 17th century. It became much more important in the last third of the 18th century, once Continental entrepreneurs realized the character of the British advance and the opportunities it offered.

As noted above, follower countries had good reason to replace imported talent with their own.

The effort to generate one's own skilled labor force depends very much on the nature of the technology. So long as the techniques were closely tied to older artisanal skills, one could build on the existing pool of craftsmen and teach them on the job. This was much the story of technological diffusion in the Industrial Revolution, where most innovations grew out of experience and experiment at the bench, rested in other words on inherited knowledge and know-how.

Machine building offers an excellent example. Powered machines were the heart of the new mode of production, and someone had to learn to operate them; but one also had to learn to build them, and here the skills required were the same as were used in earlier generations to build hand-driven and -operated devices. So when the early British cotton manufacturers looked for technicians to build and maintain their equipment, they found them in older branches such as clock-making; indeed the wheel trains of the early textile machines were known as clockwork. The same for the construction of cotton mills: there was already a profession of millwrights, experienced in the building or installation of corn mills and water wheels, who could apply their know-how in the new branches.

This pre-existence of a pool of skilled craftsmen was a crucial factor in the ability of follower countries to pick up and adapt the new technologies. In western and central Europe, older guild arrangements and standards served as a transmission belt for knowledge from one generation to the next. Ditto for Tokugawa Japan. Even where these artisans could not learn without the help of foreign exemplars, their values and attitudes—the way they thought about work, the standards they set for themselves as well as those set for them—made all the difference. Nothing in the way of intellectual conception, or blueprints and plans for that matter, could replace the conscience and conscientiousness of the craftsman at the bench.

This is an important point. Ian Inkster writes: " . . . any acknowledgement of the frequency of knowledge and machine transfers must cast doubt on arguments which claim that a nation's industrial breakthrough was determined by its own capacity to generate and apply appropriate and systematic knowledge."[18] To be sure; no economy is an island; but conversely, the ability of a society to understand new ideas and work in new ways—to engage in what Robert Brenner calls ongoing emulation—is not to be taken for granted. There may be a large array of knowledge out there, waiting to be learned and used. But not everyone can profit from the opportunity.

One aspect of this learning process is intellectual self-preparation. Legacy alone is not enough, the less so as follower countries are typically in a hurry, determined to pick up new technologies as quickly as possible. This is the function of formal manuals, of how-to books, which go back in Europe to the 16th century and constitute an extraordinary testimony to the precocious openness of knowledge in a world transformed by printing;[19] and of formal schooling, whether in focused vocational schools (schools of mining and civil engineering going back to the early eighteenth century) or general courses in theoretical and applied science. Again, the nations of continental Europe led the way. Whereas Britain continued to rely almost exclusively on the bench training that had made possible the Industrial Revolution, continental Europe invested increasingly in polytechnics, *Gewerbeschulen, écoles professionnelles,* laboratory seminars, and the like.[20]

This emphasis on formal instruction and training in research had (and continues to have) important consequences for the direction and character of industrial development, as the empirical data make clear.[21] For one thing, it facilitated the assimilation of imported knowledge; more important, it promoted the invention of technologies not easily imagined at the bench or furnace. This creative impetus obviously varied from one industry to another. Some of the older branches—textiles, for example, or ceramics, or the building trades—seemed to offer fewer opportunities to new concepts and intellectual constructs. Others, such as the chemical manufacture, long a kind of industrial cuisine, were promising candidates for scientific revolution. But all were touched directly or indirectly by the developing pool of applied scientific knowledge; and here the advantage went to those countries that were producing applied scientists and formally trained technicians. The classic example of the significance of intellectual as well as economic factors for industrial innovation and development is the history of organic chemicals, specifically artificial dyestuffs, where Britain had a superior resource position and the world's biggest market, plus an early lead in invention thanks to William Perkin and aniline mauve (one cannot predict the presence of a creative individual or a lucky discovery, but one can learn to make it a habit), plus a supporting team made up of German technicians (because it was Germany that then offered the best training in chemical analysis and synthesis). Yet in the end Perkin was gone, and the scientist-technicians went back to Germany and laid the foundations of a world-dominating dyestuffs and pharmaceuticals industry.

The tendency over time, then, was to increasingly science-intensive technology based on empirically opaque (testable, applicable, but not sensorially perceptible or experientially understandable) knowledge. This was the story of the so-called Second Industrial Revolution (late 19th and early 20th centuries), which was based on a cluster of energy-saving (electricity, internal combustion motors, fractional-horsepower motors, gaseous and liquid fuels), resource-saving (organic chemicals and artificial materials), time-saving (automobile, airplane, telephone), time-enhancing (cinema, radio) innovations, and so on. These and others depended more and more on the acquisition of esoteric knowledge learned in school; and this new source of technological power gave the advantage to those countries that were best equipped to offer appropriate instruction. The big winners: Germany and the United States; also Switzerland, Scandinavia, and, further on, Japan. The big losers: the old champion, Great Britain, sometime workshop of the world; and the new aspirants and not-yet-aspirants, the poor and backward countries of what we now call the Third World. The day of the workshop was not over. But it was no longer the fountainhead of innovation.

Why were the nations of the Third World losers by this development? The question is interesting theoretically as well empirically. Neoclassical growth models have always assumed that poor countries tend to grow faster than rich because of diminishing returns to capital; and this hypothesis has been reinforced in those extensions of these models that allow for international movement of capital and labor.[22] This assumption, in reverse form, also characterizes the seminal work of Alexander Gerschenkron on the conditions of economic backwardness: his emphasis is not on the falling rate of return to capital (cf. Marx's thesis of a falling rate of profit), but rather on the high rate of return to late starters with access to the large pool of accumulated, available knowledge. In this view, late is great because after is faster.[23]

Unfortunately for theory, this convergence assumption seems to be contradicted by cross-country data, which show the rich growing richer and the poor losing ground.[24] And why should this be so? The answer seems to lie particularly in difficulties of technology transfer and the differential role of human capital: if one holds human capital equal, growth is in fact "substantially negatively related to the initial level of per capita GDP."[25] In other words, convergence would hold if access to and assimilation of knowledge and technology were equal.

They are not. Ideally knowledge should be the freest of the factors of production. Much of it is public; and often (though not always) giving it away does not impoverish the giver—on the contrary, sharing can often be a source of enrichment. And yet effective demand for knowledge falls far short of supply, and this is particularly true for those countries that lack the institutional basis to train people to receive and understand this knowledge.

This incapacity was enormously aggravated by the increasingly esoteric character of scientific and technical knowledge. Hence the relative demotion of the poor countries: they were the least well equipped to impart the new science and technology to their young people.[26] Their facilities for the transmission of knowledge were largely confined to older modes of on-the-job contacts. As a result, their ability to assimilate at home these new bodies of knowledge and make them their own was severely limited. Their best hope was (1) to import foreign enterprise and (2) to send young people to study abroad in the hope that they would come back.

(1) The import of foreign enterprise would seem at first sight advantageous to the receiving country. After all, such firms bring in capital, skilled labor, and above all knowledge. Insofar as they employ native labor, which is often the purpose of the exercise, they necessarily transmit skills; and if the receiving country is sensible and strong-minded, it can insist that training and employment extend to the higher ranks of management and technical expertise. This is what India did with Unilever both before and after independence.[27] The receiving country can even stipulate conditions for and limitations on the repatriation of capital; on the quality and accessibility of the technology employed (state of the art usually); on the security and safety of employment.

And yet technology transfer to poor countries via multinationals has proved less widespread and efficacious than rationality might have led one to expect. For one thing, the supply tends elsewhere: more than three quarters of foreign direct investment has gone to industrial nations, for the simple reason that that's where the money is. Of the remaining quarter, almost half has gone to three recipients: Brazil, Mexico, and Singapore, and one would hardly call the last a Third World country.[28] For another, demand has often been actively discouraged. The admission of foreign enterprises has been widely seen, especially in the Third World, as politically as well as economically problematic. They represent after all a serious competitive threat to local industry (insofar as it exists), not only in the market for finished goods but also (and this has wider ramifications) in the labor market. The point is that these foreign establishments, for all the talk of exploitation (usually implicitly or explicitly defined as paying lower wages than at home), almost invariably pay higher wages than do local employers, and no one is a bigger pain than a competitor who is able to pay higher wages. What's more, these enterprises are motivated by a reprehensible desire to make money and entertain the strange notion that they should be able to keep and repatriate profits. For some, however, especially those who define profit as intrinsically exploitative, such export of gain constitutes a form of compound theft.

As a result, many Third World countries, moved more by ideology than reason (though often by ideology disguised as reason in the form of much that passes as development economics), have so multiplied the obstacles (majority indigenous representation, imposed divulgence of trade secrets, on occasion even to other native firms, prohibitions on repatriation, to say nothing of the high cost of corruption) as to force them into the kind of high-effort, low-profit situation where they prefer to leave or stay away. India has been one of the best examples of this cut-off-your-nose-to-spite-your-face, and only now is it beginning to rethink its policies in this regard.

In general, attitudes are changing, and the most resolute developers among Third World countries have been trying to shift from ideology to reality, offering incentives rather than discouragements to imported enterprise. This shift should make a difference, but the difference is mitigated by the facts. Chief among these is the rent-seeking character of most Third World economies: connections to power matter more than market competitiveness; office is not so much function as access to wealth; corruption is rife; and the best and brightest move where the money is.[29] So that multinational enterprises often remain isolates, linked to the rest of the economy and society more by lines of venality than by market interests.

(2) The second course of remedy, not incompatible with the first, is to find and train indigenous talent: to send students to school abroad and bring back technicians, engineers, and scientists. This is easier to contemplate than to accomplish, not so much because of cost but because these missions tend to be one-way exits. For one thing, life in the more advanced countries is often more agreeable, even for people from another culture who are exposed to the wounds of racism—and this for good reasons. Often the best of their own culture is actually more abundant and accessible in the cosmopolitan cities of the "North" than it is at home. And why not? Good musicians and cooks are also drawn by the greater monetary rewards of advanced industrial countries. By way of contrast, much of what was distinctive and satisfying in the indigenous way of life has been unfavorably altered and distorted by the pressures of colonial rule and the temptations of Western materialism. Stay away a while, and home begins to look like a very strange place. Finally, life in the industrial countries is almost invariably safer: the sheer peril of existence in much of the Third World literally consumes some of its best and brightest. (It also adds substantially to the cost of doing business.)[30]

In the meantime, the pressures of global competition have made knowledge more important than ever as a factor in commercial success. There's a paradox for you! Knowledge is largely free (unexcludable), and yet in its more recent, relatively opaque forms, it is not to be had for the asking or wanting. Even less is it to be had quickly, within competitively useful time limits. It is as though an immaterial yet real curtain had gone down between those who know and those who do not, between the advanced and the backward.

All of this is manifest in the behavior of international enterprise. For multinationals competing with one another, it is not cheap labor that makes a difference, nor machines, but rather a continuing sequence of innovation at a pace that provides a lead, however short, over the others. Time has always been crucial, but now more than ever—something the Japanese seem to have grasped ahead of their competitors, as their success in the marketing of high-tech products makes clear.[31] This is symbolized by the new Japanese approach to quality: quality, they say, is no longer simply the assurance of durability and reliability (the product works); that was the old way of thinking about it. Quality today is change, that is, ceaseless improvement, the continuing incorporation of new features that redefine the product and its uses and, so doing, make the consumer feel he wants it. Quality is the invention of needs.

In such a game, speed means market share. Whereas in the automobile industry, for example, the lead time for new models was running four years and more, the Japanese reduced it to two. This kind of entrepreneurial advantage (in the Schumpeterian sense) can be translated into durable gains, and losers find themselves on a treadmill, running hard to stay in place.

The effort to keep up with, much more catch up with, this kind of leader can and does take two forms. First, one can try to reorganize one's own mode of production so as to speed up the process that goes from conception to realization. This is not simple, because any such complex process is tied to institutional arrangements both within and without the enterprise, and these are not easy to change. At all levels, the status quo represents a kind of vested norm where technicians are only marginally quicker to change than workers in the shop.

A second and faster solution is to buy into the ways and ideas of others, to globalize and perhaps synergize innovation as well as production. To this end, an increasing number of companies have been entering into joint-venture arrangements with erstwhile competitors, at home and abroad. This process of entrepreneurial networking has gained ground very rapidly over the past decade.[32] On an international level, it has been motivated in part by the desire to get past tariff and nontariff barriers, that is, by commercial considerations. But more and more, it is the brains out there—the design, the research, the secrets—that interest the shoppers.

The search for intellectual and technological peers and partners has inevitably reinforced the interest of enterprises in advanced countries for enterprises in other advanced countries. Just as the richer nations always offered a richer market, so that international trade went far more among the rich than between rich and poor, so the new trend has focused on alliances among the strong and knowing.

It is important to note, however, that even within this small club, the relative positions of the players have been changing. In conditions of imaginative, insistent competition, no country can take its advantage for granted; the lead of today may well be the lag of tomorrow, and even among the leaders, some countries do better than others. The economist has been wont to see this as the natural manifestation of catch-up development—in other words, to put it down to convergence. Convergence in turn, as we have seen, has been explained by endogenous economic forces, in particular the tendency to a diminishing rate of return to capital and the gap between actual and potential technological practice in poorer countries.[33] To this one may add the satiety effect, that is, a diminishing appetite for gain and accumulation: one generation makes it; the next enjoys it.[34]

Such convergence, moreover, may seem to be borne out by cross-country data over a particular period.[35] Thus the postwar years have been largely the story of Japan and Europe catching up with the United States. And yet this may be an accidental result of the timing and convergence may be only a stage, a moment when new leaders overhaul the old before they pass them. It may well be that diminishing returns to capital and appetite for gain, even if general, vary from one society to another;[36] so that, like light rays passing through a lens, convergence gives way to a new divergence and to a dispersion and reordering of economies in terms of performance. Some of the rich, in other words, will continue to get richer faster than their competitors. This is what we seem to have at the moment in the continued difference in rates of growth among Japan, the richer European countries, and the United States—in descending order.[37]

The rapidly changing character of the American economy, particularly at the high-tech end of the manufacturing sector, bears witness to these trends. Between 1973 and 1987—so, less than two decades—the volume of world foreign direct investment grew fivefold, and the United States, with its huge market, large trade deficits, and hospitable attitude to foreign enterprise, has been an especially attractive destination: the American share of such investment grew from 10 to 25 per cent. Meanwhile, although American direct investment abroad has diminished relatively (48 per cent in 1973, 31.5 per cent in 1987), the American reliance on foreign affiliates has grown. In 1986 sales of high-tech products by such affiliates were twice as large as U.S. high-tech exports, and the assets of such affiliates were almost 42 per cent of the assets of the parent firms. Along with this has gone a rapid increase in the formation of international business alliances, with America taking the lead.[38] This in turn may reflect a growing failure of the United States to produce enough scientists and technicians from within its own population; hence a sharply increased American dependence on foreign talent. Just one datum: between 1975 and 1985, the proportion of young (under 36) engineering faculty of foreign birth leaped from 10 to nearly 50 per cent.[39]

> *One of Precision Sourcing's first deals was to find a company in India to make 600,000 telephones for a unit of United Telecommunications, Kansas City, Mo. United Telecommunications had bought the phones from South Korea and Taiwan until those sources became too expensive. Unit labor costs in Korea and Taiwan have been rising 20% annually, analysts say.*
>
> —*Wall Street Journal*[40]

Where does this leave the follower countries, the ones that are trying to catch up? The answer is, briefly put, they are caught between the promise and the practice. On the one hand, they presumably have the advantage of lateness: the opportunity to draw on the accumulated pool of knowledge, the prospect of a higher rate of growth with all that that entails of a self-reinforcing dynamic. On the other, it grows harder to tap into the pool; lateness creates its own incrustations, time has speeded up. To the advanced industrial nations, these would-be followers offer the advantages and temptations of cheap labor—always on condition of political security and stability. This remains the old and time-honored reason for transferring production, and today more than ever: the new communication technologies make it possible to hire skills and talent, to distribute and collect the work around the world, without movement of people. A Philippine computer programmer costs one fifth as much as a French, and he does not have to leave home, where the cost of living is low and the salary goes a long way. *Télétravail,* the French call it, and more and more it is taking place on an international level.[41]

So cheap labor helps, especially if it can learn new values and new ways, that is, if it can learn to be reliable and productive. On the other hand, there are other poor people out there, eager for work, and the pressure of competition has given rise to specialist finders whose job it is to find the lowest-cost suppliers, wherever. The very existence of such searchers is assurance that connections will not be allowed to become habit and that buyers and contractors will be ready to shift as the market dictates. Even in poor countries, the supply of satisfactory labor is not unlimited and tends to shift upward with rising demand. The wages of success is higher wages. Cheap labor, in other words, is not a durable basis for sustainable growth.[42]

Nor are raw materials a dependable, long-term asset. Aside from the fact that others have them or may turn out to have them (there's nothing like high prices to encourage prospecting), the ability of modern technology to find or create substitutes is simply not to be underestimated. Mexico thought it could dictate terms to pharmaceutical multinationals because of its monopoly of the barbasco plant, used in the manufacture of steroid drugs; but all it did was stimulate foreign companies to invent artificial steroids.[43]

What *is* a basis for sustainable growth is knowledge, because knowledge can yield a continuing, growing payoff. Intellectual autonomy if not parity is indispensable. Otherwise one is simply dependent on the interests of others. Yet knowledge and the ability to impart knowledge are exactly what the follower countries lack. As a result, they do not as yet have the cognitive resources to share in the new kinds of international business alliances, so that, even when they draw direct investment, they continue to lose ground. The foreign ventures in their midst are in effect industrial plantations comparable to the agricultural plantations of yesteryear; they have no roots in native soil. These countries may be partners, but they remain unequal partners.

The cross-sectional data on Third World economic performance confirm this ambiguity, this uncertainty of outcome. A few countries, especially in East Asia, are clearly forging ahead and catching up; others seem to move in fits and starts, looking now healthy, now crippled; others do well in some regions and languish elsewhere—a pattern that we may call mottled development; and still others have been going nowhere if not backwards.[44] The macro picture is one, then, that lends itself to more than one interpretation. For some observers, things are getting better and we can look forward to a convergence to what Simon Kuznets called Modern Economic Growth. For others—and I count myself in this number—we are witnessing a selection process. Those best prepared for development have moved or are moving in that direction. Those least prepared will likely never enter the process; that is, they may and should grow richer, but they will not achieve the kind of development that permits parity. And those in between (on the threshold) may get through if they can convert the opportunity offered by technology imports into technological creation; or, to put it differently, if they can learn to promote themselves from low-tech branches, where low wages are everything, to high-tech, knowledge-intensive production. They have in effect a window of access, an opportunity of uncertain duration to develop their own capacity for innovation and thereby absorb what would otherwise remain foreign transplants, modern enclaves in a premodern, preindustrial economy.

In the meantime, economies, like love, laugh at locksmiths: if a society cannot export merchandise, it can and will export people, or, in extreme cases, get them to sell their body parts. This too is not a basis for sustainable growth.

NOTES

1. Jonathan Raban, *Arabia: A Journey through the Labyrinth* (New York: Simon and Schuster, 1979), p. 63.
2. *Wall Street Journal,* May 16, 1991, p. 1.
3. *Wall Street Journal,* Aug. 5, 1991, p. A-4.
4. Eric Jones, *Growth Recurring: Economic Change in World History* (Oxford: Clarendon, 1988). The argument reminds one of an earlier distinction between growth and development: the first is simple increase in output per head; the second is the transformation of the techniques, organization, and composition of production in the direction of higher productivity, ordinarily with concomitant growth. The distinction has some heuristic advantages . . . so long as one keeps in mind the connections between the two processes.
5. For the experience of today's Third World countries in this regard, cf. Jan Fagerberg, "Why Growth Rates Differ," in Giovanni Dosi et al., eds., *Technical Change and Economic Theory* (London and New York: Pinter, 1988), p. 451.
6. Robert Brenner reminds me that it would be useful to say a few words here about a growth pattern that falls in between: one based on a one-time shift of factors from lower to higher productivity. Such a shift, from agriculture to industry for example, may or may not entail the introduction of new technology. The techniques may already be there, but reallocation of resources may have been impeded by institutional

(non-market) considerations. But even where the shift is triggered by innovation, it may not generate a continuing process of further innovation, whether because of persistent institutional impediments or because the technology is an alien transplant that does not take root. More of this later.

7. It is important to note the linked character of this complex of technological advances. The mechanization of cotton spinning was not the first successful example of mechanized factory manufacture. A generation earlier, Lombe built the first of a number of silk throwing mills powered by water. This technology transformed the British silk industry but it was not contagious in the sense that mechanized cotton manufacture would be—for the simple reason that silk is a luxury good and had limited potential for growth and hence derived demand effects. David S. Landes, *The Unbound Prometheus: Technological Change and Industrial Development in Western Europe from 1750 to the Present* (Cambridge: Cambridge University Press, 1969) p. 81; Donald S. L. Cardwell, "Power and Textiles in the Industrial Revolution," in *L'acquisition des techniques par les pays non-initiateurs* (Colloques Internationaux du Centre National de la Rècherche Scientifique, No. 538, Pont-à-Mousson, 28 June–5 July 1970). (Paris: Editions du C.N.R.S., 1973) 33–51, p. 38.
8. Landes, *Bankers and Pashas: International Finance and Economic Imperialism in Egypt* (London: Wm. Heinemann; Cambridge, Mass.: Harvard University Press, 1958).
9. Ironically, the economists of today have adopted the term "Dutch disease" to describe this syndrome, from the response of the economy of Holland to the discovery and exploitation of natural gas under the North Sea. As though the Dutch did not know how to make the most of these new resources.
10. Edwy Plenel, "Le conquérant oublié," *Le Monde,* September 1–2, 1991, p. 2.
11. For a rebuttal to demand-driven models, see Joel Mokyr, *Industrialization in the Low Countries, 1795–1850* (New Haven: Yale, 1977), and McCloskey in R. C. Floud and D. N. McCloskey, eds., *The Economic History of Britain since 1700,* vol. I (Cambridge: Cambridge University Press, 1981), pp. 120–23. McCloskey's argument is based on a static analysis of a closed system illustrated by parables drawn, inter alia, from Robinson Crusoe and pretends to a rare and superior common sense. "In the aggregate . . . " he writes (p. 120), "demand is not an independent factor causing income to grow. . . . Judging from the frequency with which it has eluded writers on the industrial revolution the point is an elusive one." Indeed: all those pundits misled and deceived! The exposition is laced with spoken and unspoken assumptions of a closed economy, equal returns at the margin, of full and optimum employment of inputs, and of technological autonomy, plus a few metaphors, and any connection with what really happened in 18th-century England is largely coincidental.
12. On these points, Nathan Rosenberg, *Inside the Black Box: Technology and Economics* (Cambridge: Cambridge University Press, 1982), pp. 9–11, has it right, and Patrick K. O'Brien, "Do We Have a Typology for the Study of European Industrialization in the XIXth Century?" *J. European Econ. Hist.,* 15, 2 (Fall 1986), 293, has it wrong. O'Brien confuses among other things European criticisms of the social consequences of British industrialization—what he calls "the 'British way'"—with rejection of the technology; and the responses of European travelers with those of statesmen and businessmen. As much argue that Karl Marx and his followers rejected the technology of what Marx called Modern Industry because of the abuses of capitalism.

13. David Jeremy, *Transatlantic Industrial Revolution: The Diffusion of Textile Technologies between Britain and America, 1790–1830s* (Cambridge, Mass: The MIT Press, 1981), p. 76.
14. Jeremy, pp. 36–37.
15. David S. Landes, *Revolution in Time: Clocks and the Making of the Modern World* (Cambridge, Mass.: Harvard/Belknap, 1983).
16. Brooke Hindle, "British v. French Influence on Technology in the Early United States," in Warsaw, Académie Polonaise des Sciences, *Actes du XIe Congrès international d'histoire des Sciences,* 24–31 August 1965, presided by Bogdan Suchodolski (Warsaw and Cracow: Académie Polonaise des Sciences, 1968), VI, 49–53. Hindle notes that the French, who were far more active in theoretical work, accounted for 223 of the 475 engineering titles published before 1830 and found in leading American libraries, as against only 25 for the British; and yet British influence in practical things was clearly paramount.
17. John Harris, "Michael Alcock and the Transfer of Birmingham Technology to France before the Revolution," *The Journal of European Economic History,* 15, 1 (Spring 1986): 7–57.
18. Ian Inkster, "Mental Capital: Transfers of Knowledge and Technique in Eighteenth Century Europe," *J. European Ec. Hist.,* 19, 2 (1991): 403–41, p. 403.
19. Pamela Long, "The Openness of Knowledge: An Ideal and Its Context in 16th-Century Writings on Mining and Metallurgy," *Technology and Culture,* 32, 2, 1 (April 1991): 318–55.
20. And some did it better than others. In the chemical manufacture, German dominance was directly related to the quality of scientific and technical instruction, the development of research-oriented industrial laboratories. and the close collaboration of science and industry in the development of new technology. Even though the Allied governments confiscated German patents during World War I and put them at the disposal of home manufacturers, these often proved incapable of understanding the material or detecting deliberate omissions and misinformation: and where they did understand, industry did not always possess the technical capacity to put these processes to use. One resort: hire German chemists away, along with their secrets. DuPont lured four scientists in this manner, promising salaries of $25,000 a year for five years (say, $250,000 of our money) for their services and a trunkful of secrets. The trunk was intercepted, but the scientists made it to the United States. Shades of 18th-century industrial seductions, but now it was a Continental country that was giving, albeit unwillingly, rather than receiving. F.C. Steckel, "Cartelization of the German Chemical Industry, 1918–1925," *J. European Ec. Hist.,* 19, 2 (Fall 1990): 329–52, p. 343. All of which did not prevent DuPont from concluding formal agreements with German firms when these were possible.
21. Richard R. Nelson and Edmund S. Phelps, "Investment in Humans, Technological Diffusion, and Economic Growth," *AER Proceedings,* 56, 2 (May 1966): 69–75.
22. Robert Barro, "Economic Growth in a Cross Section of Countries," *QJE,* 106, 2 (May 1991): 407–44, pp. 407–8.
23. Alexander Gerschenkron, "Economic Backwardness in Historical Perspective," in Bert Hoselitz, ed., *The Progress of Underdeveloped Countries* (Chicago: Univ. of Chicago Press, 1952). Reprinted in 1962 in Gerschenkron, ed., *Economic Backwardness in Historical Perspective* (Cambridge, Mass.: Harvard Univ. Press). This attempt at a

lapidary formulation does not quite do justice to Gerschenkron, who never, to the best of my knowledge, incorporated in his calculus the loss of product and income forgone during the period before the breakthrough to industrialization. So more exactly, late is great, but only after the spurt is under way; and even then, he emphasizes, the social and political strains of rapid development may impose great and even cruel hardship on the population. Witness tsarist and socialist Russia.

24. Robert Summers and Alan Heston, "A New Set of International Comparisons of Real Product and Price Levels: Estimates for 130 Countries, 1950–1985," *Review of Income and Wealth,* Series 34, 1 (March 1988), 1–25, and accompanying diskettes; Summers and Heston, "The Penn World Table (Mark 5): An Expanded Set of International Comparisons, 1950–1988," *QJE,* 106, 2 (May 1991), 327–88.

25. Barro, p. 409.

26. India seems to be an exception. There the Bangalore area in the otherwise poor state of Karnataka (formerly Mysore) has become an impressive center of instruction in science and engineering and of high-tech research and manufacture, to the point of producing a third of the nation's electronic goods and drawing in major foreign partners seeking not so much labor as brains. Yet firms in Bangalore are continually running up against the constraints imposed by the bureaucrats in Delhi, to the point where some foreign enterprises have found it easier to export technicians than goods—a process known locally as "body-shopping." *The Economist,* 4 May 1991: 91–92.

    This kind of brain drain also characterizes the now disintegrating Soviet Union, where the rewards and conditions of work are so poor and the frustrations so great as to dissolve the strongest bonds of cultural and personal loyalty. But of course, the present exodus would have taken place long before had the Soviet Union not forcibly prevented emigration, especially of scientists and technicians. Knowledge is important, but bad institutions can cripple knowledge and alienate its possessors. Cf. *The International Herald Tribune,* Nov. 25, 1991, p. 1.

27. D. K. Fieldhouse, *Unilever Overseas: The Anatomy of a Multinational 1895–1965* (London: Croom Helm; Stanford: The Hoover Institution, 1978) ch. 4.

28. Isaiah Frank, "MNCs and LDCs," *Harvard International Review,* 8, 5 (April 1986): 4–7, p. 5.

29. Kevin M. Murphy, Andrei Shleifer, and Robert W. Vishny, "The Allocation of Talent: Implications for Growth," *QJE,* 106, 2 (May 1991): 503–30.

30. One can make the same point by noting the contrary experience of Japan in the Meiji period. This was a country that sent some of its best young people to study abroad and got them back [Sidney D. Brown, "Okuba Toshimichi: His Political and Economic Policies in Early Meiji Japan," *Journal of Asian Studies,* 21 (1961–1962): 183–97, pp. 191–92]. Why and how? One may venture two reasons: (1) the Japanese culture these expatriates took with them was sufficiently distinctive and satisfying to make them feel less well off abroad—they couldn't wait to get home; and (2) Japanese society made good and appropriate use of them when they got back.

    China and Taiwan are other countries that have had success in bringing back their expatriate scientists and engineers. See Sheryl Wu Dunn. "McDonnell Deal: For Taiwan, a Coming of Age," *International Herald Tribune,* Dec. 3, 1991, p. 11: "One factor that remains in Taiwan's favor is a strong and growing supply of engineers and skilled workers. Two years ago the government dipped into a large pool of engineers and aerospace scientists educated and employed in the United States, recruiting a number of them to return home to help Taiwan expand its own aerospace industry."

31. Thomas I. Lee and Proctor P. Reid, eds. *National Interests in an Age of Global Technology.* For the Committee on Engineering as an International Enterprise of the National Academy of Engineering. (Washington, D. C.: National Academy Press, 1991), Figures 1.7 and 1.8.
32. Lee and Reid, Fig. 1.11.
33. Barro, p. 407 f.; Lee and Reid, pp. 14–15. On the latter, see Gerschenkron (above, n.21); Moses Abramovitz, "Rapid Growth Potential and Its Realisation: The Experience of the Capitalist Economies in the Postwar Period," in Edmond Malinvaud, ed., *Economic Growth and Resources,* vol. I (London: Macmillan, 1979), and "Catching Up, Forging Ahead, and Falling Behind," *J. Economic Hist.,* 46, 2 (June 1986): 385–406; William Baumol, "Productivity Growth, Convergence, and Welfare: What the Long-run Data Show," *American Economic Review,* 75, 4 (September 1986): 1072–85; Jeffrey G. Williamson, "Productivity and American Leadership: A Review Article," *J. Econ. Literature,* 29 (March 1991), 51–68.
34. On this last, cf. Manfred Neumann, "Zur Dynamik des internationalen Wohlstandsgefälles," *Hamburger Jahrbuch fur Wirtschaftsund Gesellschaftspolitic,* 36 (1991), 221–30.
35. Williamson, pp. 57–58. Williamson, building on William J. Baumol. Sue Anne Batey Blackman, and Edward N. Wolff, *Productivity and American Leadership: The Long View* (Cambridge and London: MIT Press, 1989), p. 103, cites as evidence of convergence data regressing annual growth rates in labor productivity (GDP per work hour) for a dozen advanced industrial countries on labor productivity in 1950. Not everyone would agree. Contrast Barro (p. 408), who regresses growth rate of GDP per capita 1960–1985 on GDP 1960 (data from Summers and Heston) for some 98 countries and finds no significant relationship. Aside from the difference in coverage, there is reason to believe that the GDP data are not always comparable (Williamson, p. 55).
36. One reason for the faith in convergence is the tacit assumption of homogeneity: economists tend to take for granted that people everywhere are alike and want to pursue the same goal of maximizing return. If they were not and did not, it would make economic theory even more difficult and unreal than it is. And yet each society has its own culture(s) (dirty word!), and these shape if not dictate all manner of institutional structures and arrangements that affect in turn the results achieved. This is not to say that these structures and arrangements are unchangeable; of course they change and are changed by circumstances and interests. But changes do not come free, the less so because of the power of vested interests and contrary responses; nor are they instantaneous, in a world where time matters more than ever.
37. Williamson, p. 65, commenting on Baumol *et al.,* discusses the possibility of a growing divergence between American and other labor productivities and exclaims that such an evolution "actually rejects the convergence hypothesis!" But of course.

    By way of comparison, here are estimates by the World Bank: *World Development Report 1991* (Washington, D.C.: World Bank, Table 1: Basic Indicators) of the rate of growth of GNP per head per year for a number of rich countries over the period 1965–89 (in per cent). The implications of extrapolation are obvious:

    Switzerland 4.6
    Japan 4.3
    Germany 2.4
    France 2.3
    Sweden 1.8
    United States 1.6

The reader will understand that such comparisons have to be assessed with caution; that rates can change markedly, for example, with changes in rates of exchange. Hence the remarkable Swiss peformance. Still, the range is such that *if such differences persist,* one may expect substantial divergence in income levels over time.

On the general question of American slowdown, see Baumol *et al.* and Williamson and the sources cited there. Baumol is an optimist and argues that the reports of American decline have been greatly exaggerated. Williamson recognizes this predilection (p. 57), but he too is basically an optimist. Among other things, he accepts the Baumol argument that slower growth in productivity relative to other countries is not harmful to economic welfare; that on the contrary, faster growth elsewhere means cheaper imports and improved material circumstances. To be sure, slow productivity gains have to be paid for in lower wages (and, I would add, loss of jobs), and to those innocents whom Williamson calls "non-economists," this would mean a decline in welfare. I agree: consolation is not compensation.

A methodological note: Baumol *et al.* spend time calculating what it would take in higher labor productivity for the United States to maintain its position vis-à-vis Germany over the next generation and conclude that it would need an increase of 1.2 per cent over the historic American rate (and an even larger increase over the current norm). Then they (and Williamson) ask what it would take to achieve that "1 percentage point increase." No need to go into the suggestions and prescriptions: suffice it to say that the assumption of these calculations is that the foreign targets will stand still. In any event, Williamson recalls here his earlier consolation, namely, that "rapid productivity advance among our competitors is a Good Thing because Americans are able to import goods cheaper" (p. 65). Even if we cannot pay for them?

In general, I have a sense here of *déjà vu:* of dozens of bright economists and so-called new economic historians reassuring the British from the late nineteenth century on that they were doing fine, while one industry after another went down the tubes; and if they were not doing fine, why, there was nothing they could do about it anyway. Ironically, this pseudo-scientific optimism is in effect a counsel of despair, a prescription for indolence, and an incentive to flee into rent-seeking. Compare Williamson's (p. 66) suggestion that it may well be "low productivity growth that encourages entrepreneurs to shift their energies into rent-seeking" (see below, n. 39).

38. Lee and Reid, 24, citing John Hagedoorn and Jos Schakenraad, *Leading Companies and the Structure of Strategic Alliances in Core Technologies* (Maastricht: Maastricht Economic Research Institute on Innovation and Technology [MERIT], 1990), and *Inter-firm Partnerships and Corporate Strategies in Core Technologies* (Maastricht: MERIT, 1990).

39. Lee and Reid, 25–26. Why this American failure to produce enough scientists and engineers is in itself an important problem. One answer, surely, lies in the failure of instruction at the elementary and secondary levels, as shown by low performance by American students on math tests that lend themselves to international comparison (cf. Lee and Reid, 61). This failure in turn is linked to the reluctance of higher institutions to set intellectual standards for admission and a general preference for subjects such as the social sciences that have no right answers (just opinions, and yours are as good as the next fellow's) over those that do (math and the natural sciences).

Another factor is the attraction, financial and other, of rent-seeking as against profit-seeking careers. Here the American predicament is summed up by the national passion for litigation (if anything untoward happens, find someone or something that may however remotely be considered responsible, and the deeper the pockets, the better) and the corresponding abundance of lawyers and legal specialists. It is not only the loss of talent from risk-taking occupations that costs; there is also the diversion of time and energy to unproductive but highly profitable disputes. On all this, see Murphy, Shleifer, and Vishny and the sources cited there.

40. *Wall Street Journal*, 8/23/1991.
41. *Libération* (Paris), 27 novembre 1991, p. 15: "Le télétravail se délocalise jusqu'en Asie."
42. Alice Amsden, "Diffusion of Development: The Late-Industrializing Model and Greater East Asia," *Amer. Econ. Rev.*, 81, 2 (May 1991): "Papers and Proceedings," 282–86, p. 284.
43. Gary Gereffi, *The Pharmaceutical Industry and Dependency in the Third World* (Princeton: Princeton University Press, 1983) ch. 2.
44. The most spectacular examples of rapid catch-up growth are those afforded by the chopstick (not the rice-bowl) countries of East Asia, in particular the so called four little dragons: Taiwan, South Korea, Hong Kong, and Singapore. Coming up behind are Thailand and Malaysia, although these have yet to show anything like the technological autonomy of the first group. This is not the place to discuss the reasons for this success, or on the other hand, to consider its political fragility. Assuming, however, the robustness of these gains and their persistence, the question of its generalizability would still remain. Some students of development would infer therefrom the promise of comparable gains by most if not all of the rest of the world. Others would emphasize the peculiar advantages, cultural more than economic, of these model developers.

6

Increasing Returns and the New World of Business

W. Brian Arthur

Our understanding of how markets and businesses operate was passed down to us more than a century ago by a handful of European economists—Alfred Marshall in England and a few of his contemporaries on the continent. It is an understanding based squarely upon the assumption of diminishing returns: products or companies that get ahead in a market eventually run into limitations, so that a predictable equilibrium of prices and market shares is reached. The theory was roughly valid for the bulk-processing, smokestack economy of Marshall's day. And it still thrives in today's economics textbooks. But steadily and continuously in this century, Western economies have undergone a transformation from bulk-material manufacturing to design and use of technology—from processing of resources to processing of information, from application of raw energy to application of ideas. As this shift has occurred, the underlying mechanisms that determine economic behavior have shifted from ones of diminishing to ones of *increasing* returns.

Increasing returns are the tendency for that which is ahead to get further ahead, for that which loses advantage to lose further advantage. They are mechanisms of positive feedback that operate—within markets, businesses, and industries—to reinforce that which gains success or aggravate that which suffers loss. Increasing returns generate not equilibrium but instability: If a product or a company or a technology—one of many competing in a market—gets ahead by chance or clever strategy, increasing returns can magnify this advantage, and the product or company or technology can go on to lock in the market. More than causing products to become standards, increasing returns cause businesses to work differently, and they stand many of our notions of how business operates on their head.

Mechanisms of increasing returns exist alongside those of diminishing returns in all industries. But roughly speaking, diminishing returns hold sway in the traditional part of the economy—the processing industries. Increasing returns reign in the newer part—the knowledge-based industries. Modern economies have therefore bifurcated into two interrelated worlds of business corresponding to the two types of returns. The two worlds have different economics. They differ in behavior, style, and culture. They call for different management techniques, strategies, and codes of government regulation.

They call for different understandings.

ALFRED MARSHALL'S WORLD

Let's go back to beginnings—to the diminishing-returns view of Alfred Marshall and his contemporaries. Marshall's world of the 1880s and 1890s was one of bulk production: of metal ores, aniline dyes, pig iron, coal, lumber, heavy chemicals, soybeans, coffee—commodities heavy on resources, light on know-how. In that world it was reasonable to suppose, for example, that if a coffee plantation expanded production it would ultimately be driven to use land less suitable for coffee. In other words, it would run into diminishing returns. So if coffee plantations competed, each one would expand until it ran into limitations in the form of rising costs or diminishing profits. The market would be shared by many plantations, and a market price would be established at a predictable level—depending on tastes for coffee and the availability of suitable farmland. Planters would produce coffee so long as doing so was profitable, but because the price would be squeezed down to the average cost of production, no one would be able to make a killing. Marshall said such a market was in perfect competition, and the economic world he envisaged fitted beautifully with the Victorian values of his time. It was at equilibrium and therefore orderly, predictable and therefore amenable to scientific analysis, stable and therefore safe, slow to change and therefore continuous. Not too rushed, not too profitable. In a word, mannerly. In a word, genteel.

With a few changes, Marshall's world lives on a century later within that part of the modern economy still devoted to bulk processing: of grains, livestock, heavy chemicals, metals and ores, foodstuffs, retail goods—the part where operations are largely repetitive day to day or week to week. Product differentiation and brand names now mean that a few companies rather than many compete in a given market. But typically, if these companies try to expand, they run into some limitation: in numbers of consumers who prefer their brand, in regional demand, in access to raw materials. So no company can corner the market. And because such products are normally substitutable for one another, something like a standard price emerges. Margins are thin and nobody makes a killing. This isn't exactly Marshall's perfect competition, but it approximates it.

THE INCREASING-RETURNS WORLD

What would happen if Marshall's diminishing returns were reversed so that there were *increasing* returns? If products that got ahead thereby got further ahead, how would markets work?

Let's look at the market for operating systems for personal computers in the early 1980s when CP/M, DOS, and Apple's Macintosh systems were competing. Operating systems show increasing returns: if one system gets ahead, it attracts further software developers and hardware manufacturers to adopt it, which helps it get further ahead. CP/M was first in the market and by 1979 was well established. The Mac arrived later, but it was wonderfully easy to use. DOS was born when Microsoft locked up a deal in 1980 to supply an operating system for the IBM PC. For a year or two, it was by no means clear which system would prevail. The new IBM PC—DOS's platform—was a kludge. But the growing base of DOS/IBM users encouraged software developers such as Lotus to write for DOS. DOS's prevalence—and the IBM PC's—bred further prevalence, and eventually the DOS/IBM combination came to dominate a considerable portion of the market. That history is now well known. But notice several things: It was not predictable in advance (before the IBM deal) which system would come to dominate. Once DOS/IBM got ahead, it locked in the market because it did not pay for users to switch. The dominant system was not the best: DOS was derided by computer professionals. And once DOS locked in the market, its sponsor, Microsoft, was able to spread its costs over a large base of users. The company enjoyed killer margins.

These properties, then, have become the hallmarks of increasing returns: market instability (the market tilts to favor a product that gets ahead), multiple potential outcomes (under different events in history, different operating systems could have won), unpredictability, the ability to lock in a market, the possible predominance of an inferior product, and fat profits for the winner. They surprised me when I first perceived them in the late 1970s. They were also repulsive to economists brought up on the order, predictability, and optimality of Marshall's world. Glimpsing some of these properties in 1939, English economist John Hicks warned that admitting increasing returns would lead to "the wreckage of the greater part of economic theory." But Hicks had it wrong: the theory of increasing returns does not destroy the standard theory—it complements it. Hicks felt repugnance not just because of unsavory properties but also because in his day no mathematical apparatus existed to analyze increasing-returns markets. That situation has now changed. Using sophisticated techniques from qualitative dynamics and probability theory, I and others have developed methods to analyze increasing-returns markets. The theory of increasing returns is new, but it already is well established. And it renders such markets amenable to economic understanding.

In the early days of my work on increasing returns, I was told they were an anomaly. Like some exotic particle in physics, they might exist in theory but would be rare in practice. And if they did exist, they would last for only a few seconds before being arbitraged away. But by the mid-1980s, I realized increasing returns were neither rare nor ephemeral. In fact, a major part of the economy was subject to increasing returns—high technology.

Why should this be so? There are several reasons:

Up-front Costs. High-tech products—pharmaceuticals, computer hardware and software, aircraft and missiles, telecommunications equipment, bio-engineered drugs, and suchlike—are by definition complicated to design and to deliver to the marketplace. They are heavy on know-how and light on resources. Hence they typically have R&D costs that are large relative to their unit production costs. The first disk of Windows to go out the door cost Microsoft $50 million; the second and subsequent disks cost $3. Unit costs fall as sales increase.

Network Effects. Many high-tech products need to be compatible with a network of users. So if much downloadable software on the Internet will soon appear as programs written in Sun Microsystems' Java language, users will need Java on their computers to run them. Java has competitors. But the more it gains prevalence, the more likely it will emerge as a standard.

Customer Groove-in. High-tech products are typically difficult to use. They require training. Once users invest in this training—say, the maintenance and piloting of Airbus passenger aircraft—they merely need to update these skills for subsequent versions of the product. As more market is captured, it becomes easier to capture future markets.

In high-tech markets, such mechanisms ensure that products that gain market advantage stand to gain further advantage, making these markets unstable and subject to lock-in. Of course, lock-in is not forever. Technology comes in waves, and a lock-in such as DOS's can last only as long as a particular wave lasts.

So we can usefully think of two economic regimes or worlds: a bulk-production world yielding products that essentially are congealed resources with a little knowledge and operating according to Marshall's principles of diminishing returns, and a knowledge-based part of the economy yielding products that essentially are congealed knowledge with a little resources and operating under increasing returns. The two worlds are not neatly split. Hewlett-Packard, for example, designs knowledge-based devices in Palo Alto, California, and manufactures them in bulk in places like Corvallis, Oregon, or Greeley, Colorado. Most high-tech companies have both knowledge-based operations and bulk-processing operations. But because the rules of the game differ for each, companies often separate them—as Hewlett-Packard does. Conversely, manufacturing companies have operations such as logistics, branding, marketing, and distribution, which belong largely to the knowledge world. And some products—like the IBM PC—start in the increasing-returns world but later in their life cycle become virtual commodities that belong to Marshall's processing world.

THE HALLS OF PRODUCTION AND THE CASINO OF TECHNOLOGY

Because the two worlds of business—processing bulk goods and crafting knowledge into products—differ in their underlying economics, it follows that they differ in their character of competition and their culture of management. It is a mistake to think that what works in one world is appropriate for the other.

There is much talk these days about a new management style that involves flat hierarchies, mission orientation, flexibility in strategy, market positioning, reinvention, restructuring, reengineering, repositioning, reorganization, and re-everything else. Are these new insights or are they fads? Are they appropriate for all organizations? Why are we seeing this new management style?

Let us look at the two cultures of competition. In bulk processing, a set of standard prices typically emerges. Production tends to be repetitive—much the same from day to day or even from year to year. Competing therefore means keeping product flowing, trying to improve quality, getting costs down. There is an art to this sort of management, one widely discussed in the literature. It favors an environment free of surprises or glitches—an environment characterized by control and planning. Such an environment requires not just people to carry out production but also people to plan and control it. So it favors a hierarchy of bosses and workers. Because bulk processing is repetitive, it allows constant improvement, constant optimization. And so, Marshall's world tends to be one that favors hierarchy, planning, and controls. Above all, it is a world of optimization.

Competition is different in knowledge-based industries because the economics are different. If knowledge-based companies are competing in winner-take-most markets, then managing becomes redefined as a series of quests for the next technological winner—the next cash cow. The goal becomes the search for the Next Big Thing. In this milieu, management becomes not production oriented but mission oriented. Hierarchies flatten not because democracy is suddenly bestowed on the workforce or because computers can cut out much of middle management. They flatten because, to be effective, the deliverers of the next-thing-for-the-company need to be organized like commando units in small teams that report directly to the CEO or to the board. Such people need free rein. The company's future survival depends upon them. So they—and the commando teams that report to them in turn—will be treated not as employees but as equals in the business of the company's success. Hierarchy dissipates and dissolves.

Does this mean that hierarchy should disappear in meatpacking, steel production, or the navy? Contrary to recent management evangelizing, a style that is called for in Silicon Valley will not necessarily be appropriate in the processing world. An aircraft's safe arrival depends on the captain, not on the flight attendants. The cabin crew can usefully be "empowered" and treated as human beings. This approach is wise and proper. But forever there will be a distinction—a hierarchy—between cockpit and cabin crews.

In fact, the style in the diminishing-returns Halls of Production is much like that of a sophisticated modern factory: the goal is to keep high-quality product flowing at low cost. There is little need to watch the market every day, and when things are going smoothly the tempo can be leisurely. By contrast, the style of competition in the increasing-returns arena is more like gambling. Not poker, where the game is static and the players vie for a succession of pots. It is casino gambling, where part of the game is to choose which games to play, as well as playing them with skill. We can imagine the top figures in high tech—the Gateses and Gerstners and Groves of their industries—as milling in a large casino. Over at this table, a game is starting called multimedia. Over at that one, a game called Web services. In the corner is electronic banking. There are many such tables. You sit at one. How much to play? you ask. Three billion, the croupier replies. Who'll be playing? We won't know until they show up. What are the rules? Those'll emerge as the game unfolds. What are my odds of winning? We can't say. Do you still want to play?

High technology, pursued at this level, is not for the timid.

In fact, the art of playing the tables in the Casino of Technology is primarily a psychological one. What counts to some degree—but only to some degree—is technical expertise, deep pockets, will, and courage. Above all, the rewards go to the players who are first to make sense of the new games looming out of the technological fog, to see their shape, to cognize them. Bill Gates is not so much a wizard of technology as a wizard of precognition, of discerning the shape of the next game.

We can now begin to see that the new style of management is not a fad. The knowledge-based part of the economy demands flat hierarchies, mission orientation, above all a sense of direction. Not five-year plans. We can also fathom the mystery of what I've alluded to as *re-everything*. Much of this "re-everything" predilection—in the bulk-processing world—is a fancy label for streamlining, computerizing, downsizing. However, in the increasing-returns world, especially in high tech, re-everything has become necessary because every time the quest changes, the company needs to change. It needs to reinvent its purpose, its goals, its way of doing things. In short, it needs to adapt. And adaptation never stops. In fact, in the increasing-returns environment I've just sketched, standard optimization makes little sense. You cannot optimize in the casino of increasing-returns games. You can be smart. You can be cunning. You can position. You can observe. But when the games themselves are not even fully defined, you cannot optimize. What you *can* do is adapt. Adaptation, in the proactive sense, means watching for the next wave that is coming, figuring out what shape it will take, and positioning the company to take advantage of it. Adaptation is what drives increasing-returns businesses, not optimization.

PLAYING THE HIGH-TECH TABLES

Suppose you are a player in the knowledge-industry casino, in this increasing-returns world. What can you do to capitalize on the increasing returns at your disposal? How can you use them to capture markets? What strategic issues do you need to think about? In the processing world, strategy typically hinges upon capitalizing on core competencies, pricing competitively, getting costs down, bringing quality up. These are important also in the knowledge-based world, but so, too, are other strategies that make use of the special economics of positive feedbacks.

Two maxims are widely accepted in knowledge-based markets: it pays to hit the market first, and it pays to have superb technology. These maxims are true but do not guarantee success. Prodigy was first into the on-line services market but was passive in building its subscriber base to take advantage of increasing returns. As a result, it has fallen from its leading position and currently lags the other services. As for technology, Steve Jobs's NeXT workstation was superb. But it was launched into a market already dominated by Sun Microsystems and Hewlett-Packard. It failed. A new product often has to be two or three times better in some dimension—price, speed, convenience—to dislodge a locked-in rival. So in knowledge-based markets, entering first with a fine product can yield advantage. But as strategy, this is still too passive. What is needed is *active* management of increasing returns.

One active strategy is to discount heavily initially to build up an installed base. Netscape handed out its Internet browser for free and won 70% of its market. Now it can profit from spin-off software and applications. Although such discounting is effective—and widely understood—it is not always implemented. Companies often err by pricing high initially to recoup expensive R&D costs. Yet even smart discounting to seed the market is ineffective unless the resulting installed base is exploited later. America Online built up a lead of more than 4.5 million subscribers by giving away free services. But because of the Internet's dominance, it is not yet clear whether it can transform this huge base into later profits.

Let's get a bit more sophisticated. Technological products do not stand alone. They depend on the existence of other products and other technologies. The Internet's World Wide Web operates within a grouping of businesses that include browsers, on-line news, E-mail, network retailing, and financial services. Pharmaceuticals exist within a network of physicians, testing labs, hospitals, and HMOs. Laser printers are part of a grouping of products that include computers, publishing software, scanners, and photo-input devices. Unlike products of the processing world, such as soybeans or rolled steel, technological products exist within local groupings of products that support and enhance them. They exist in mini-ecologies.

This interdependence has deep implications for strategy. When, in the mid-1980s, Novell introduced its network-operating system, NetWare, as a way of connecting personal computers in local networks, Novell made sure that NetWare was technically superior to its rivals. It also heavily discounted NetWare to build an installed base. But these tactics were not enough. Novell recognized that NetWare's success depended on attracting software applications to run on NetWare—which was a part of the ecology outside the company's control. So it set up incentives for software developers to write for NetWare rather than for its rivals. The software writers did just that. And by building NetWare's success, they ensured their own. Novell managed these cross-product positive feedbacks actively to lock in its market. It went on to profit hugely from upgrades, spin-offs, and applications of its own.

Another strategy that uses ecologies is linking and leveraging. This means transferring a user base built up upon one node of the ecology (one product) to neighboring nodes, or products. The strategy is very much like that in the game Go: you surround neighboring markets one by one, lever your user base onto them, and take them over—all the time enhancing your position in the industry. Microsoft levered its 60-million-person user base in DOS onto Windows, then onto Windows 95, and then onto Microsoft Network by offering inexpensive upgrades and by bundling applications. The strategy has been challenged legally. But it recognizes that positive feedbacks apply across markets as well as within markets.

In fact, if technological ecologies are now the basic units for strategy in the knowledge-based world, players compete not by locking in a product on their own but by building *webs*—loose alliances of companies organized around a mini-ecology—that amplify positive feedbacks to the base technology. Apple, in closing its Macintosh system to outsiders in the 1980s, opted not to create such a web. It believed that with its superior technology, it could hold its increasing-returns market to itself. Apple indeed dominates its Mac-based ecology. But this ecology is now only 8% of the personal computer business. IBM erred in the other direction. By passively allowing other companies to join its PC web as clones, IBM achieved a huge user base and locked in the market. But the company itself wound up with a small share of the spoils. The key in web building is active management of the cross-company mutual feedbacks. This means making a careful choice of partners to build upon. It also means that, rather than attempting to take over all products in the ecology, dominant players in a web should allow dependent players to lock in their dependent products by piggybacking on the web's success. By thus ceding some of the profits, the dominant players ensure that all participants remain committed to the alliance.

Important also to strategy in knowledge-based markets is psychological positioning. Under increasing returns, rivals will back off in a market not only if it is locked in but if they *believe* it will be locked in by someone else. Hence we see psychological jockeying in the form of preannouncements, feints, threatened alliances, technological preening, touted future partnerships, parades of vapor-ware (announced products that don't yet exist). This posturing and puffing acts much the way similar behavior does in a primate colony: it discourages competitors from taking on a potentially dominant rival. No moves need be made in this strategy of premarket facedown. It is purely a matter of psychology.

What if you hold a losing hand? Sometimes it pays to hold on for residual revenue. Sometimes a fix can be provided by updated technology, fresh alliances, or product changes. But usually under heavy lock-in, these tactics do not work. The alternatives are then slow death or graceful exit—relinquishing the field to concentrate on positioning for the next technology wave. Exit may not mean quitting the business entirely. America Online, Compuserve, Prodigy, and Microsoft

Network have all ceded dominance of the on-line computer networking market to the Internet. But instead of exiting, they are steadily becoming adjuncts of the Net, supplying content services such as financial quotations or games and entertainment. They have lost the main game. But they will likely continue in a side game with its own competition for dominance within the Net's ecology.

Above all, strategy in the knowledge world requires CEOs to recognize that a different kind of economics is at work. CEOs need to understand which positive and negative feedback mechanisms are at play in the market ecologies in which they compete. Often there are several such mechanisms—interbraided, operating over different time frames, each needing to be understood, observed, and actively managed.

WHAT ABOUT SERVICE INDUSTRIES?

So far, I've talked mainly about high tech. Where do service industries such as insurance, restaurants, and banking fit in? Which world do they belong to? The question is tricky. It would appear that such industries belong to the diminishing-returns, processing part of the economy because often there are regional limits to the demand for a given service, most services do consist of "processing" clients, and services are low-tech.

The truth is that network or user-base effects often operate in services. Certainly, retail franchises exist because of increasing returns. The more McDonald's restaurants or Motel 6 franchises are out there geographically, the better they are known. Such businesses are patronized not just for their quality but also because people want to know exactly what to expect. So the more prevalent they are, the more prevalent they can become. Similarly, the larger a bank's or insurance company's customer base, the more it can spread its fixed costs of headquarters staff, real estate, and computer operations. These industries, too, are subject to mild increasing returns.

So we can say more accurately that service industries are a hybrid. From day to day, they act like bulk-processing industries. But over the long term, increasing returns will dominate—even though their destabilizing effects are not as pronounced as in high tech. The U.S. airline business, for example, processes passengers day to day. So it seemed in 1981 that deregulation should enhance competition, as it normally does under diminishing returns. But over the long term, airlines in fact experience a positive feedback: under the hub-and-spoke system, once an airline gets into trouble, it cannot work the feeder system for its routes properly, its fleet ages, it starts a downward spiral, and it loses further routes. The result of deregulation over the long term has been a steady decline in large carriers, from 15 airlines in 1981 to approximately 6 at present. Some routes have become virtual monopolies, with resulting higher fares. None of this was intended. But it should have been predicted—given increasing returns.

In fact, the increasing-returns character of service industries is steadily strengthening. One of the marks of our time is that in services everything is going software—everything that is information based. So operations that were once handled by people—designing fancy financial instruments or automobiles or fashion goods, processing insurance claims, supplying and inventorying in retail, conducting paralegal searches for case precedents—are increasingly being handled by software. As this reengineering of services plays out, centralized software facilities come to the fore. Service providers become hitched into software networks, regional limitations weaken, and user-base network effects kick in.

This phenomenon can have two consequences. First, where the local character of service remains important, it can preserve a large number of service companies but clustered round a dominant software provider—like the large numbers of small, independent law firms tied in to the dominant computer-search network, Lexis-Nexis. Or physicians tied in to an HMO. Second, where locality is unimportant, network effects can transform competition toward the winner-take-most character we see in high tech. For example, when Internet-based retail banking arrives, regional demand limitations will vanish. Each virtual bank will gain in advantage as its network increases. Barring regulation, consumer banking will then become a contest among a few large banking networks. It will become an increasing-returns business.

Services belong to both the processing and the increasing-returns world. But their center of gravity is crossing over to the latter.

THOUGHTS FOR MANAGERS

Where does all this leave us? At the beginning of this century, industrial economies were based largely on the bulk processing of resources. At the close of the century, they are based on the processing of resources and on the processing of knowledge. Economies have bifurcated into two worlds—intertwined, overlapping, and different. These two worlds operate under different economic principles. Marshall's world is characterized by planning, control, and hierarchy. It is a world of materials, of processing, of optimization. The increasing-returns world is characterized by observation, positioning, flattened organizations, missions, teams, and cunning. It is a world of psychology, of cognition, of adaptation.

Many managers have some intuitive grasp of this new increasing-returns world. Few understand it thoroughly. Here are some questions managers need to ask themselves when they operate in knowledge-based markets:

Do I understand the feedbacks in my market? In the processing world, understanding markets means understanding consumers' needs, distribution channels, and rivals' products. In the knowledge world, success requires a thorough understanding of the self-negating and self-reinforcing feedbacks in the market—the diminishing- and increasing-returns mechanisms. These feedbacks are interwoven and operate at different levels in the market and over different time frames.

Which ecologies am I in? Technologies exist not alone but in an interlinked web, or ecology. It is important to understand the ecologies a company's products belong to. Success or failure is often decided not just by the company but also by the success or failure of the web it belongs to. Active management of such a web can be an important magnifier of increasing returns.

Do I have the resources to play? Playing one of the increasing-returns games in the Casino of Technology requires several things: excellent technology, the ability to hit the market at the right time, deep pockets, strategic pricing, and a willingness to sacrifice current profits for future advantage. All this is a matter not just of resources but also of courage, resolution, will. And part of that resolution, that courage, is also the decisiveness to leave the market when increasing returns are moving against one. Hanging on to a losing position that is being further eroded by positive feedbacks requires throwing reinforcements into a battle already lost. Better to exit with financial dignity.

What games are coming next? Technology comes in successive waves. Those who have lost out on this wave can position for the next. Conversely, those who have made a killing on this cycle should not become complacent. The ability to profit under increasing returns is only as good as the ability to see what's coming in the next cycle and to position oneself for it—technologically, psychologically, and cooperatively. In high tech, it is as if we are moving slowly on a ship, with new technologies looming, taking shape, through a fog of unknowingness. Success goes to those who have the vision to foresee, to imagine, what shapes these next games will take.

These considerations appear daunting. But increasing-returns games provide large payoffs for those brave enough to play them and win. And they are exciting. Processing, in the service or manufacturing industries, has its own risks. Precisely because processing is low-margin, operations must struggle to stay afloat. Neither world of business is for the fainthearted.

In his book *Microcosm,* technology thinker George Gilder remarked, "The central event of the twentieth century is the overthrow of matter. In technology, economics, and the politics of nations, wealth in the form of physical resources is steadily declining in value and significance. The powers of mind are everywhere ascendant over the brute force of things." As the economy shifts steadily away from the brute force of things into the powers of mind, from resource-based bulk processing into knowledge-based design and reproduction, so it is shifting from a base of diminishing returns to one of increasing returns. A new economics—one very different from that in the textbooks—now applies, and nowhere is this more true than in high technology. Success will strongly favor those who understand this new way of thinking.

7

The Knowledge-Driven Economy

Candice Stevens

The OECD economies are increasingly based on knowledge and information. Knowledge is now recognised as the driver of productivity and economic growth, leading to a new focus on the role of information, technology and learning in economic performance. It has also brought about calls for more emphasis on research and innovation, training and flexible structures of work.[1]

Knowledge, as embodied in human beings (as "human capital") and in technology, has always been central to economic development. But only over the last few years has its relative importance been recognised, just as that importance is growing. The OECD economies are more strongly dependent on the production, distribution and use of knowledge than ever before. Output and employment are expanding fastest in high-technology industries, such as computers, electronics and aerospace. In the past decade, the high-technology share of OECD manufacturing production (Table 7-1) and exports (Figure 7-1) has more than doubled, to reach 20–25%. Knowledge-intensive service sectors, such as education, communications and information, are growing even faster. Indeed, it is estimated that more than 50% of GDP in the major OECD economies is now knowledge-based.

Investment is thus being directed to high-technology goods and services, particularly information and communications technologies. Computers and related equipment are the fastest-growing component of tangible investment.[2] Equally important are more intangible investments in research and development (R&D), the training of the labour force, computer software and technical expertise. Spending on research has reached about 2.3% of GDP in the OECD area.

TABLE 7-1 Shares of High-technology Industries in Total Manufacturing, 1970–94 (%)

	Exports		*Value added*	
	1970	*1993*	*1970*	*1994*[1]
North America				
Canada	9.0	13.4	10.2	12.6
United States	25.9	37.3	18.2	24.2
Pacific Area				
Australia	2.8	10.3	8.9	12.2
Japan	20.2	36.7	16.4	22.2
New Zealand	0.7	4.6	—	5.4
Europe				
Austria	11.4	18.4	—	—
Belgium	7.2	10.9	—	—
Denmark	11.9	18.1	9.3	13.4
Finland	3.2	16.4	5.9	14.3
France	14.0	24.2	12.8	18.7
Germany	15.8	21.4	15.3	20.1
Greece	2.4	5.6	—	—
Ireland	11.7	43.6	—	—
Italy	12.7	15.3	13.3	12.9
Netherlands	16.0	22.9	15.1	16.8
Norway	4.7	10.7	6.6	9.4
Spain	6.1	14.3	—	13.7
Sweden	12.0	21.9	12.8	17.7
United Kingdom	17.1	32.6	16.4	22.2

— not available

1. Or nearest available year.

Source: OECD

Education accounts for an average 12% of OECD government expenditures, and investments in job-related training are estimated to be as high as 2.5% of GDP in countries such as Germany and Austria which have apprenticeship or dual training (combining school and work) systems. Purchases of computer software, growing at a rate of 12% per year since the mid-1980s, are outpacing sales of hardware.[3] Spending on product enhancement is driving growth in knowledge-based services such as engineering studies and advertising. And balance-of-payments figures in technology show a 20% increase between 1985 and 1993 in trade in patents and technology services.

It is skilled labour that is in highest demand in the OECD countries (Table 7-2). The average unemployment rate for people with a lower-secondary education is 10.5%, falling to 3.8% for those with university educations. Although the manufacturing sector is losing jobs across the OECD, employment is growing in high-technology, science-based sectors ranging from computers to pharmaceuti-

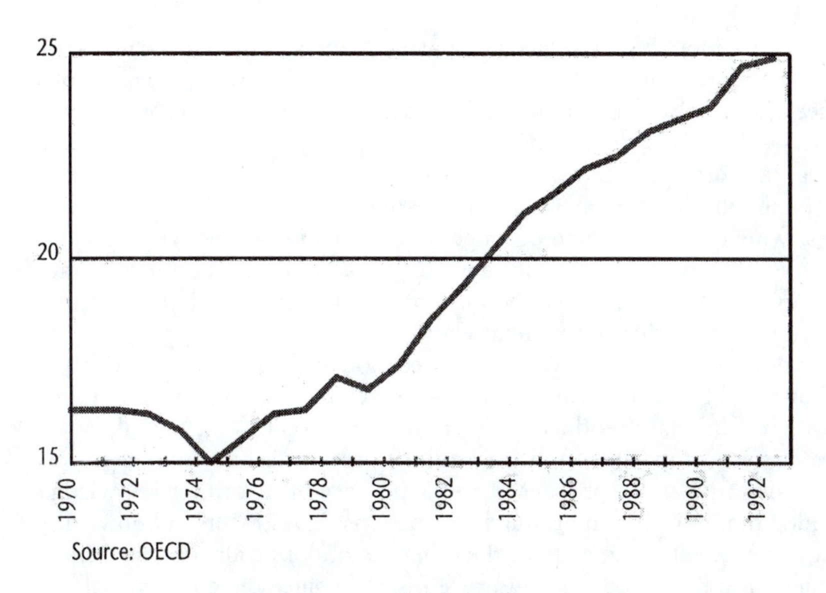

FIGURE 7-1 Total OECD High-technology Exports, 1970–93 (% of total OECD manufacturing exports)

TABLE 7-2 Employment Trends in Manufacturing, 1970–94 (%)

	Total	*Skilled*	*Unskilled*	*High-wage*	*Medium-wage*	*Low-wage*
Australia	–0.7	–0.1	–1.3	–0.6	–0.4	–1.1
Canada	0.3	0.3	0.3	1.4	0.3	0.0
Denmark	–0.8	–0.3	–1.3	0.8	–0.5	–1.5
Finland	–1.3	–0.3	–2.1	1.3	–0.6	–2.7
France	–1.2	–0.4	–1.8	–0.6	–1.1	–1.5
Germany	–0.8	–0.5	–1.1	0.4	–0.7	–1.5
Italy	–0.7	–0.4	–0.9	–1.1	–0.4	–0.8
Japan	0.2	0.9	–0.2	1.2	0.4	–0.3
Netherlands	–1.5	–1.1	–2.1	–0.8	–1.1	–2.4
Norway	–1.5	–0.8	–2.1	0.2	–1.3	–2.1
Sweden	–1.5	–0.8	–2.4	0.5	–1.5	–2.2
United Kingdom	–2.3	–1.7	–2.9	–2.0	–2.4	–2.4
United States	–0.1	0.0	–0.3	–0.1	0.1	–0.5
OECD (19)	–0.3	0.1	–0.7	0.2	–0.2	–0.7

Source: OECD

cals. These jobs are more highly skilled and pay higher wages than those in lower-technology sectors (textiles and food-processing, say). Knowledge-based jobs in service sectors are also growing strongly. Indeed, non-production or "knowledge" workers—those who do not engage in the output of physical products—are the employees in most demand in a wide range of activities, from computer technicians, through physical therapists to marketing specialists. The use of new technologies, which are the engine of longer-term gains in productivity and employment, generally improves the "skills base" of the labor force in both manufacturing and services. And it is largely because of technology that employers now pay more for knowledge than for manual work.

These trends are leading to revisions in economic theories and models, as analysis follows reality. Economists continue to search for the foundations of economic growth. Traditional "production functions" focus on labour, capital, materials and energy; knowledge and technology are external influences on production. Now analytical approaches are being developed so that knowledge can be included more directly in production functions. Investments in knowledge can increase the productive capacity of the other factors of production as well as transform them into new products and processes. And since these knowledge investments are characterised by increasing (rather than decreasing) returns, they are the key to long-term economic growth.

The most visible sign of the knowledge-based economy is the emergence of the "information society."[4] Information technology has speeded up the codification of knowledge, transforming it into a market commodity: large chunks of knowledge can be codified and transmitted over computer and communications networks. The use of personal computers has more than doubled in the last decade: almost 40% of households in the United States now have computers, and their use is expanding in other OECD countries (Table 7-3). These computers can be linked nationally and internationally: the worldwide Internet signs on around 160,000 new users every month. Through computer networks, knowledge is more accessible to a wider group of people and cheaper to acquire.

Knowledge itself is becoming a more marketable product, and its spread is transforming other goods and services and creating new markets. The spiraling number of information services available on the Internet, ranging from job searches to medical advice, is one example. The transformation of several disciplines—measurement, navigation, chemistry, music, surgery, telecommunications—by laser technology is another. And as the stock of knowledge accessible to the world economy swells, it is driving economic growth. The increase in knowledge accessibility and lower barriers to entry are also enhancing the role of the entrepreneur.

But there are some types of knowledge that are more difficult to codify and exchange in a market. There is "tacit" knowledge—skills which often cannot be reduced to mere information. Some human capabilities, such as intuition, insight, creativity and judgement, resist codification. And it is these tacit skills which are essential to selecting, using and manipulating the knowledge which can be codified. The ability to select relevant (and disregard irrelevant) information, to recog-

TABLE 7-3 Diffusion of Information Technologies, 1994 (% of households)

	United States	*Japan*	*United Kingdom*	*Germany*	*France*
User Terminals					
Personal Computer	37	12	24	28	15
Video Cassette Recorder	88	73	84	65	69
Video Game	42	—	19	8	20
Fax	—	8	2	4	3
PC modem	15	—	4	3	1
Network Infrastructure					
Digital main lines[1]	65	72	75	37	86
House with cable	65	—	4	47	9
House passed by cable	83	—	16	56	23
House with satellite	—	27	11	20	2

— not available

1. 1993

Source: OECD

nise patterns in information and to interpret and decode information is not easily bought and sold.

While codified knowledge is the material to be transformed (the "know-what"), tacit knowledge is the tool for handling it (the "know-how"). The most important tacit skill may be the ability to learn continuously and to acquire new skills.[5] The process of continuous learning is more than merely obtaining a formal education. In the knowledge-based economy, learning-by-doing is paramount. Individuals must upgrade their skills in both codified and tacit knowledge continuously so as to keep up with fast-moving technologies. On-the-job training is an ongoing process. In the major OECD countries, around 35% of the employed population is now engaged in job-related training, but this ratio should be increased.

Firms, too, have to become learning organisations, adapting their management and structures to accommodate new technologies. There is a trend in business towards downsizing, decentralisation, to forming multiple alliances with other firms, flexible working arrangements and to diffused rather than hierarchical management. As a consequence, smaller firms are becoming more important in job creation; the share of large firms (over 500 employees) in OECD employment is declining by about 1% every year. Analyses indicate that such organisational adaptations are essential to realising the productivity gains to be generated by technology. The new flexible enterprise stresses such qualities in its workers as initiative, creativity, problem-solving and openness to change, and it is willing to pay a premium for these skills. Learning, creativity and flexibility matter more in the knowledge-based economy, experience and tradition less.

BUILDING KNOWLEDGE NETWORKS

The diffusion of knowledge is as important for economic performance as the creation of new knowledge. Basic research in universities or public laboratories, for example, may be irrelevant to industry or fail to be commercialised if undertaken in total isolation from the private sector. Firms, particularly small or remote ones, may then remain ignorant of new process technologies. The success of enterprises, as of national economies, is determined by their effectiveness in gathering and using knowledge and technology. That may in turn reside in the tacit abilities of individuals and firms to link up with the right networks and use all relevant items of information. Increasingly, the ability to innovate and enhance technological performance depends on obtaining access to learning-intensive relations. The result is a society composed of networks of individuals and firms, usually linked electronically.

The rise of the knowledge networks has changed economists' ideas about the process of innovation. Traditionally, it was seen as a discovery procedure that proceeded along a fixed and linear sequence of phases. It began, so it was argued, with new scientific research, progressed through stages of product development, production and marketing, and ended with the sale of new products, processes and services. This linear model of innovation has been replaced with an interactive one. Technical advances can assume many forms, including incremental improvements of existing products and new combinations of products and services. Innovation stems largely from the feedback loops or the continuing interactions which exist between science, engineering, product development, manufacturing and marketing. It is fed by the interplay among the different institutions and individuals involved—firms, laboratories, universities and consumers. The patterns of technology-related interactions in a national economy combine to form national innovation systems which are composed of the contacts and flows between industry, government and academia in the development of science and technology. The links within this system, and its ability to diffuse knowledge and technology, influence the innovative performance both of firms and of economies as a whole. And increasingly, innovation systems extend beyond national boundaries.

Only now are systematic efforts beginning to quantify and map the paths by which knowledge and technology are diffused throughout an economy. Indicators of information technology track the use of computers, software and related networks by businesses and households. Surveys of firms are used to gauge their use of different types of technologies. Comparative data show that Japan and Sweden have the most widespread use of advanced manufacturing technologies and robotics in industry, while the United States has a wider diffusion of computer-based engineering applications. In Canada, 48% of manufacturing firms use the latest technologies, mostly for inspection and communications.

It is more difficult to trace the diffusion of ideas and know-how in an economy. Analysis of how often patents and scholarly articles are cited is one tool for mapping the flow of ideas. Analysis of patent data in the United States, for instance, shows that 75% of some industrial innovations flow to users outside the originating industry—for example, medical genetics by the food industry and aerospace materials by the automobile sector. Similar techniques are used to measure the cross-fertilisation of ideas from universities to industry, from public laboratories to academia and also through international transactions. Another approach counts the movements of highly skilled personnel, who carry with them their codified and tacit knowledge, from one sector to another.

Innovation surveys of firms, which ask questions about the sources of information and equipment and the extent of technology cooperation with outside bodies, are now yielding the most complete portraits of national innovation systems. They show, for example, that most industry research is directed to product rather than process innovation, that technical analysis of competitors' products is an important source of information, that researcher mobility is considered an asset, that joint ventures are crucial to high-technology firms and that domestic public research is used more than foreign sources.

KNOWLEDGE INDICATORS

Knowledge is not a traditional economic input, like steel or labour, and presents enormous difficulties of measurement. As a result, the understanding of what is happening in OECD economies is circumscribed by the indicators available. Intangibles such as knowledge stocks and flows, knowledge distribution and the relationship between the creation of knowledge (in the form of research and development, for example), and economic growth are still virtually unmapped.[6] In many respects, the knowledge-based economy remains more of a concept than a measurable entity.

The first task is to improve indicators of inputs, such as R&D, training and other intangible investments, by enhancing coverage of both small and large firms and services. Development of indicators of the flows of knowledge and of the acquisition and use of technology will yield more accurate measurement of the knowledge-intensity of industries and economies. And in view of the importance of tacit as well as codified knowledge, indicators are required to track the flow of ideas. Surveys of innovation in individual firms and similar techniques can help characterise strategic alliances and inter-active innovation processes. With these objectives in mind, the OECD is continually updating its manuals on collection and interpretation of science and technology statistics.

Although current data indicate that investments in knowledge are the key to growth, as shown by the outstanding performance of high-technology sectors, the extent and soundness of this conclusion must be tested on a broader basis. Further indicators are thus required to show the private and social rates of return to R&D and other knowledge inputs. This step involves gauging the benefits v. the costs of investment to individuals, firms and entire sectors, measured in employment, output, productivity and competitiveness. Both enterprises and governments want concrete measures of the results of their investments in science and technology. Firms are calling for information on where investment would be most profitable—in long-term research, improvements to product quality, or in advertising? Countries want to know where to target expenditures to improve their competitiveness—to tax incentives to R&D, training the labour force or encouraging computer networks? Until better indicators are developed, the effects of technology on the economy and employment will not be completely understood.

In knowledge-based economies government policies have to put more emphasis on upgrading human capital through providing access to general education and incentives to continuous work-related training.[7] Education is at the center of the knowledge-based economy, and learning is the tool of individual and organisational advancement.

Science and technology policies are looking for a new emphasis. Support to innovation should be broadened from "mission-oriented" projects aimed at specific research outcomes, such as a new combat aircraft, to "diffusion-oriented" programmes, such as educating small firms about new products and processes. The links and networks between public, private and academic sectors are also a prime factor in innovation, and the dissemination of technology to a range of sectors and firms a vital element of productivity growth. Governments are responsible for providing the framework conditions for innovative collaborations, technology dissemination and development of information infrastructures—all crucial to performance in knowledge-based economies.

NOTES

1. *Science, Technology and Industry Outlook*. OECD Publications, Paris, 1996.
2. Jeremy Beale. "The Information Explosion." *The OECD Observer,* No. 196, October/November 1995.
3. Vivian Bayar and Pierre Montagnier. "The Information Technology Industry." *The OECD Observer,* No. 198, February/March 1995.
4. *Information Technology Outlook*. OECD Publications. Paris, 1995.
5. Jean-Claude Pave. "Making Life-long Learning a Reality for All." *The OECD Observer,* No. 193, April/May 1995.
6. Graham Vickory and Gregory Winzburg. "Intangible Investment. Missing Pieces in the Productivity Puzzle." *The OECD Observer.* No. 178, October/November 1992.
7. Abrar Hasam and Albert Tuijnman. "Linking Education and Work" *The OECD Observer,* No. 199, April/May 1996.

Part Three

Measuring and Managing the Intangibles of Knowledge

8

On Some Problems in Measuring Knowledge-Based Growth

Peter Howitt

INTRODUCTION

The title of this conference [The Implications of Knowledge-Based Growth for Micro-Economic Policies] seems to imply that there is something new about growth being based on knowledge, as does the oft-heard remark that we are now in a knowledge era, in which knowledge is somehow more important than it was in the past. This idea is misleading. It has long been the consensus among economists who have studied the problem that long-term growth is always based on the growth of technical and organizational capabilities. Likewise, every era of rapid sustained growth has been one in which new knowledge transformed people's lives. The information revolution we are now living through is dramatically raising the premium on particular kinds of knowledge and skills, while rendering others obsolete. But the same was true of the explosion in technological knowledge in textiles in the late 18th and early 19th centuries, and of technological progress in agriculture in the first half of the 20th century, to pick just two examples.

What is new about knowledge from the economist's point of view is that we are now beginning to incorporate it into our framework of analysis, not as an extraneous outside influence but as one of the main unknowns whose evolution we seek to explain as the outcome of economic forces. Although many of the ideas of endogenous growth theory go back to such writers as Schumpeter, and even as far back as John Rae (1834), and although economic historians and specialists on technology had been analyzing the sources of knowledge and productivity growth for many years before the rise of endogenous growth theory, it was only with the work of Romer (1986), Lucas (1988) and their followers that economists were able to incorporate these ideas into simple dynamic, stochastic, general equilibrium models.

In the simplest aggregate growth models, knowledge is treated much as if it were just another good, capable of being accumulated like capital and aggregated with the same precision (or lack of precision) as capital. Output equals AK, where A measures knowledge and K measures capital, and where there are separate but similar technologies for making A and K grow, each using the existing A and K as an input to the growth process. However, most growth theorists, even within the neoclassical tradition, take seriously the idea that knowledge is not a commodity and cannot be modeled as one. The biggest theoretical accomplishment of endogenous growth theory has been to discover how to modify standard neoclassical general equilibrium models, which were originally designed to deal with the production, exchange and use of commodities, to analyze the production, exchange and use of knowledge, while recognizing some of the essential differences between knowledge and commodities.

Although there has been progress in modeling knowledge at the theoretical level, less progress has been made at the empirical level. If knowledge is indeed different from other goods, then it must be measured differently from other goods, and its relationship to the price system must be different from that of other goods. But, the theoretical foundation on which national income accounting is based is one in which knowledge is fixed and common, where only prices and quantities of commodities need to be measured. Likewise, we have no generally accepted empirical measures of such key theoretical concepts as the stock of technological knowledge, human capital, the resource cost of knowledge acquisition, the rate of innovation or the rate of obsolescence of old knowledge.

To some extent, the situation is one of theory before measurement, to paraphrase one of the apostles of real business cycle theory (Prescott, 1986). But to lay the blame on empirical economists or on data-gathering agencies would be disingenuous. It would be more accurate to say that formal theory is ahead of conceptual clarity. As the Cambridge, United Kingdom side of the Cambridge capital controversy used to insist, the real question is one of meaning, not measurement. Only when theory produces clear conceptual categories will it be possible to measure them accurately.

This paper discusses some of these conceptual issues, suggests ways in which they might be clarified and points out problems they raise for the understanding of technical change and economic growth. It develops the main point that because of our inability to measure properly the inputs and outputs to the creation and use of knowledge, standard measures of Gross National Product (GNP) and productivity give a misleading picture. In particular, our failure to include a separate investment account for knowledge the way we do for physical capital means that much of an economy's annual output is simply missed.

These measurement problems have important implications for measuring growth even in a steady state. But they particularly distort standard measures of growth during a period of transition such as we are going through now when the information revolution has greatly enhanced the opportunities for knowledge creation. In particular, they imply that GNP and productivity may appear to be slowing down when in fact they are surging. The discussion that follows is aimed at clarifying the nature of this measurement problem during such a period of transition as well as during periods of steady-state growth.

KNOWLEDGE AS A CAPITAL GOOD?

I define knowledge in terms of potentially observable behaviour, as the ability of an individual or group of individuals to undertake, or to instruct or otherwise induce others to undertake, procedures resulting in predictable transformations of material objects.[1] The knowledge can be codified, as when it is transmitted by mathematical theorems or computer programs that can be reproduced through known procedures; or it can be tacit, as when it exists only in the minds of particular individuals or in the established routines of organizations, and is not capable of routine transmission or reproduction.

This definition restricts knowledge to the capabilities of individuals and organizations. It could alternatively be defined as imbedded in goods, as when a computer program is encoded in a file on a diskette. I prefer to think of such a diskette as a unique commodity which can be used in consumption or production, the creation of which required knowledge in the possession of some individual or group of individuals. But there is probably nothing fundamental at stake here. One might just as well think of a properly inscribed diskette in the same terms as a properly indoctrinated graduate student. All that really matters at this stage is to be as clear as possible.

The above definition also rules out knowledge in the abstract. Books, blueprints and computer programs are instruments that different people use to create similar knowledge, not instruments for them merely to use previously existing knowledge. This interpretation alters the usual distinction between the production and diffusion of knowledge, for it implies that the reader creates knowledge much as the writer did. What is different in the two cases is the process by which the knowledge is created, and the degree to which the knowledge being created substitutes for pre-existing knowledge. The writer probably took more time and effort, and the knowledge created during the writing of the book had a greater scarcity value at the time of writing than did the knowledge created by the millionth reader. One reason for defining knowledge this way is that much of what is commonly thought of as costless imitation is, in fact, a costly process that resembles, in many ways, the process of innovation. Any time an individual sets out to learn something, some of it will come from observing what others have done, and some of it will be novel.

A piece of knowledge thus defined is like a capital good. It can be produced, exchanged and used in the production of other goods, or in the production of itself. It can also be stored, although subject to depreciation, as when people forget or let their skills deteriorate, and subject also to obsolescence, as when new knowledge comes along to supersede it. In each case, however, there are important differences between knowledge and capital goods.

PRODUCTION

The production of knowledge is, to some extent, a by-product of activities with other purposes, as when people learn from the experience of producing or consuming some good, or when they learn of others' experiences by word of mouth. More generally, it takes place for the same reason as the production of any capital good. Firms spend resources, in the form of research and development (R&D), training, market research, sending people to conferences, etc., with the intended objective of creating knowledge. Households also undergo sacrifices to create knowledge by acquiring an education. Even the activities of learning by doing and learning by using are not as serendipitous as theory often portrays them, as firms can and do go out of their way to experiment, to solicit information from clients and from workers, and to reflect on the lessons of experience.

One big difference between the production of capital goods and the production of knowledge is that the latter typically entails a deeper element of uncertainty. Uncertainty has not yet played a big role in endogenous growth theory, although those working in the evolutionary tradition have rightly focused on it as one of the chief salient characteristics of knowledge. The idea, typical in endogenous growth models, that people have rational expectations about the consequences of innovative activity, is almost a contradiction in terms, since to innovate is to do what no one had thought of before. Of course, when new knowledge consists of the capability of producing new capital goods, then investment in those new capital goods will be subject to the same sort of uncertainty. But to the extent that much physical investment consists of replicating existing capital structures in familiar situations, uncertainty affects it less than it does the creation of new knowledge.

Another difference between the production of capital goods and the production of knowledge is the form of the output. Most types of physical capital take the form of physical implements whose value can be readily appropriated by a single controlling agent, although there are, of course, public capital goods, such as roads and monuments, that entail sizeable transaction costs when appropriated for use. Knowledge, on the other hand, is embodied in people and organizations. In the first case, it takes the form of human capital—a notoriously difficult concept to measure accurately. In the latter case, it takes a form that so far has eluded endogenous growth theory—that of organizational routines.

A digression on organizational routines is in order here, given the difficulty of incorporating them into neoclassical economics. When a large business firm learns to implement new production methods or to reorganize its divisional structure to take better advantage of individual initiative, much of the knowledge is dispersed among the different members of the organization. As in Hayek's (1945) famous vision of the decentralized economy, the organizational routines may allow the knowledge of individual participants to be aggregated efficiently even though no individual has a detailed understanding of the entire operation. In that sense, the organization "possesses" knowledge which may not exist at the individual level. Indeed if, as Hayek can be interpreted as saying, much of the individual knowledge used by the organization is tacit, it may not even be possible for one individual to acquire the knowledge embodied in a large corporation.[2]

Perhaps the most important difference between the production of capital goods and the production of knowledge arises from the fact that many of the methods of producing knowledge use the knowledge of other people or other firms as an input. That is, one can observe nature or one can observe others, or what others have done. Given the practical difficulty of monitoring what others are observing, this implies a social aspect not necessarily present in other forms of production. This social aspect makes it difficult, and in many cases impossible, to appropriate the full social benefits accruing to the creation of knowledge. Even with patents that fully protect a monopoly of certain types of knowledge that can be codified, there will be a spillover. For example, the ease with which others can reproduce the knowledge I create, once they hear about it, or once they do some reverse engineering, will allow them to generate further knowledge, as one new insight sparks another.

The positive externality from knowledge-generating activities that this implies is a central aspect of almost all endogenous growth theories. It is also present in the production of physical capital (as the original studies of ship and aircraft production indicated) but only to the extent that production of knowledge and capital is a joint activity. It is often just the knowledge emerging from this activity that is hard to appropriate. For instance, an aircraft can be sold, and its benefits appropriated, much as would be the case for any other good, but the producer will not be compensated for all the resulting increases in knowledge of how to improve aircraft production.

The main implication of all these considerations is that most knowledge-creating activities are imperfectly measured. We do have survey-based measures of R&D activities of business firms and government agencies (see Dosi, 1988 for an international comparison of aggregate measures) and, of course, we have measures of input in the educational sector. It is commonly acknowledged, however, that there are lots of informal training, learning, observing, experimenting and other activities taking place within firms and households that go completely unmeasured. More specifically, although wages and other incomes earned by the factors involved may be recorded as part of national income, they are treated as payments for inputs into the creation of goods and services, whereas in truth they are payments for inputs into the creation of knowledge.

EXCHANGE

Strictly speaking, the above definition of knowledge implies that it cannot be exchanged between two individuals in the sense usually envisioned by neoclassical price theory. That is, I can share ideas with someone in a conversation or correspondence, and each of us can thereby acquire some of the other's knowledge. One of us might even pay the other for the exchange, as in a consulting relationship. But this "exchange" does not require either of us to give up any of the knowledge being transacted. One way to look at this is to say, as Romer (1990) has emphasized, that knowledge is a "non-rival good," like many public goods, which can be shared by many people without diminishing the amount available to any one of them. But to remain consistent with our definition of knowledge as capability rather than as a disembodied idea, we must instead view any such procedure for "exchanging" information as involving the production of new knowledge. Pure exchange per se is not possible.

While this view of exchange, as necessarily involving an act of creation much like that of the usual notion of production, may strike many economists as odd, it ought to be more common in economics. The standard parable of a pure exchange economy, in which people somehow exchange goods on a large scale without the costly intermediation of business firms that create, operate and maintain markets, and continually strive to improve them, is far removed from anyone's daily life in a modern economy. It is hard to think of any significant transaction activities that people undertake that do not involve establishments that exist mainly to facilitate such transactions—usually business firms but often government or other non-profit agencies. According to the estimates of Wallis and North (1986), the facilitation of transactions absorbs more resources in the U.S. economy than does the pure transformation of inanimate nature. As Clower and Howitt (1995) have argued, the typical act of exchange is one in which two parties—one of which is a specialist business enterprise—lay out resources in order that one of them ends up with money and the other with command over some object or objects. When the object being exchanged is knowledge, the resource cost incurred by the seller need not include a sacrifice of his or her own command over the object.

There is another major difference, however, between the exchange of information and the exchange of capital goods, and that has to do with asymmetric information. A central theme of modern economic theory is that someone wanting to buy something from someone who knows more about it is likely to suffer from problems of moral hazard and adverse selection, and the anticipation of these problems may prevent the transaction from occurring. The problems are unavoidable when knowledge is being traded, in which case, the asymmetry of information that can create market failure is a necessary precondition for there to be a gain from the exchange in the first place. The problems are particularly intractable when tacit knowledge is being sold. Since it cannot be codified, but must instead be taught in a more personal manner, such knowledge is, in the terminology of modern contract theory, non-contractible. Failure of the seller to deliver what was agreed on cannot be remedied easily through the courts—a point which Stigler's (1973) satire on "truth in teaching" illustrates.

Because of these asymmetries of information, together with the difficulty of observing others' use of information, most industrial R&D is done in house

(Dosi, 1988) rather than licensed or contracted out. A firm cannot resolve all the agency problems which these asymmetries imply[3] but can presumably internalize them more effectively than can impersonal markets. Although a considerable part of R&D is "sold" to government agencies, private purchases of R&D are relatively scarce.[4] In short, there are few markets in which newly created industrial knowledge is traded, and hence few market prices (as opposed to notoriously unreliable internal transfer prices) to use as a measure of even the private value of R&D. And of course, the problem of appropriability implies that even those prices that do exist do not accurately reflect social values.

USE, DEPRECIATION, AND OBSOLESCENCE

Knowledge can be used for many of the same general purposes as can commodities. People can use it as a consumption good, as when they read or do research out of pure intellectual curiosity. They can also use it to produce other goods, to create new market opportunities or to generate still more knowledge. Economists have little to say about the purely private activity of consumption that would distinguish knowledge from other commodities. But certain features of knowledge that make its use, as a producer's good, somewhat different from the use of capital goods can be identified.

The first such feature lies at the heart of endogenous growth theory, namely that the use of knowledge necessarily entails increasing returns to scale. As an example, consider a firm attempting to produce a new line of products. If it succeeds, the cost of the R&D which allowed the firm to create the new line will appear as a sunk cost to the firm's subsequent operations. Each time it produces a batch of the new goods, the firm will have to spend more on capital and labour, but it will not have to pay for more knowledge by redoing the R&D.

The problem of increasing returns is that it is incompatible with the standard framework of general equilibrium under perfect competition. Under conditions of competitive equilibrium, firms must be too small to have market power and must earn normal profits. But this would not be an equilibrium situation, if a firm that increased its scale to the point where it had some market power could operate more efficiently and thereby reap supernormal profits. This means that if general equilibrium is modelled in such an economy, there either must be imperfect competition, or the economies of scale must be external to the firms. In the latter case, no individual firm would see itself as being in a position to gain from economies of scale by expanding its operations, since the economies depend on the scale of the entire industry or economy, not of its own operations.

The second feature of knowledge that makes its use in production essentially different from the use of capital goods is that it automatically creates obsolescence of other knowledge, as well as of other capital goods. In the early 19th century, the knowledge of how to build power looms created devastating losses for handloom weavers, whose human capital was highly valued. They were quickly rendered obsolete by the new power looms. Knowledge of how to produce and use personal computers and word processors is similarly rendering obsolete typewriters, plants for producing typewriters and the specialized knowledge of how to produce and use typewriters. In short, the creation of new knowledge almost always involves what Schumpeter called creative destruction.

At one level, creative destruction means that the activity of producing knowledge entails negative externalities. As Aghion and Howitt (1992) showed, in the context of a Schumpeterian growth model, there is a rent-seeking aspect to the creation of knowledge which means that, under laissez faire, society may spend more than the optimal amount of resources in the generation of new knowledge. But there is a deeper implication, according to which one of the major uses of knowledge is enabling firms to compete with each other. For, as Schumpeter stressed, the essence of the competitive struggle in a free economy has little to do with whether or not firms take prices as parametric, as in textbook price theory. Instead, it involves the very innovative process that gives rise to creative destruction. The firms that survive this struggle do not respond to adversity by reallocating resources and manipulating prices within known technological parameters. They respond by innovating, by finding previously undiscovered ways to trim costs and open up new markets, and by creating new products that can be sold even in hard times.

The final aspect of knowledge that makes its use different from that of capital is that, to a large extent, it is used not just to produce more goods at a lower cost (as in the case of a pure process innovation) but to produce goods that didn't exist before. Equivalently, knowledge can also be used to raise the quality of previous goods to a level never before experienced. Of course, quality improvements are notoriously hard to measure, and the difficulty of doing so is something that has long plagued the construction of reliable price indexes and measures of real output, at both the aggregate and sectoral levels.

MEASURING OUTPUT, PRODUCTIVITY, AND KNOWLEDGE

The main implications of the above discussion for endogenous growth theory can be summarized by saying that the very features which make knowledge distinct from capital goods create four major measurement problems. The first is the "knowledge-input problem." That is, the amount of resources devoted to the creation of knowledge is certainly underestimated by standard measures of R&D activity, by resources used in the educational sector (which exclude a lot of informal activities routinely undertaken by firms and individuals) and by the private cost of education borne by individuals. Many workers, who are counted as engaged in production, management or other non-research activities, spend a considerable amount of their time and energy looking for better ways to produce and sell the output of the enterprise they are employed by and, hence, their compensation should be counted, at least in part, as contributing to the cost of creating knowledge.

The second major measurement problem is the "knowledge-investment problem." That is, the output of knowledge resulting from formal and informal R&D activities is typically not measured at all, because it does not result in an immediate commodity with a market price. From the Haig-Simons point of view, the creation of knowledge ought to be treated like the creation of capital goods since, in either case, there is an expenditure of resources that could alternatively have been used to produce current consumption but which has instead been devoted to the enhancement of future consumption opportunities. Yet the national accounts include no category of final expenditure that would capture a significant amount of the annual increment to society's stock of knowledge the way it captures the annual increment to society's stock of capital—except for the output of the educational sector and for R&D undertaken by or sold to the government sector. None of the new knowledge generated by R&D undertaken by business firms on their own account (which includes most of industrial R&D) results in a direct positive contribution to current GNP or to the current value added of that sector of the economy, as it would if the resources had instead been devoted to the creation of new capital goods.

To make this point more explicitly, consider the case of a firm that hires additional R&D workers at a cost of $1 million during the current year. The only result of the additional expenditure is a new patent discovered at the very end of the year, which will enable the firm to earn additional profits in future years, with an expected discounted value of $2 million. Since firms are not permitted to capitalize such R&D expenditures, this sequence of events will not result in any increase in current output from that sector as far as the national income accounts are concerned. Likewise, from the income side of the accounts, although there has been an additional $1 million in wages and salaries (assuming that the workers were hired from out of the labor force), there has been an offsetting decrease in profits, since the expenditure by the firm resulted in no increased current revenue. If instead of the patent, the workers had produced a machine worth $2 million, GNP would have been higher by $2 million.[5]

Of course, to the extent that R&D results in more or better goods being produced, it does eventually affect measured GNP. But new knowledge should also be counted as output when it is created, just as physical investment is counted when it is created even though it eventually has a further effect on GNP by increasing the potential to produce other goods. Furthermore, to the extent that R&D results in better goods, many of its future effects on GNP will not be measured, because of the third major measurement problem, the "quality-improvement problem." As many writers have observed, to the extent that knowledge creation within business firms results in improved goods and services, the practical difficulties of dealing with new goods and quality improvements in constructing price indexes imply that much of the resulting benefit goes unmeasured.

The fourth problem is the "obsolescence problem." If standard measures of GNP ought to include a separate investment account for the production of knowledge then, by the same token, Net National Product (NNP) and national income ought to include a deduction corresponding to the depreciation of the stock of knowledge that takes place as it is superseded, or otherwise reduced in value, by new discoveries and innovations. Furthermore, the creation of new knowledge is also a factor accounting for the depreciation of existing physical capital. Depreciation is a notoriously difficult problem to account for in any case. The timing and extent of replacement investment are endogenous variables that the national income accountant can only capture in rough measure by applying simple mechanical formulas. But the problem becomes even more acute when a wave of innovations accelerates the rate of obsolescence of old knowledge and capital.

In a steady-state economy, the most serious of these measurement problems would be that of quality improvement. Much of the growth of productivity and output, in the long run, is the result of product innovations that generate new and improved goods whose contributions to output are only partially measured. Gordon (1990) for example, has estimated that correcting properly for quality improvements in capital goods alone would at least double the growth rate of aggregate real investment in the United States over the period from 1947 to 1983. Many of the gains from better capital goods are eventually reflected in GNP growth when the improved capital goods boost output in other sectors. But even then, the problem will distort measured productivity growth in different sectors, as when the airline industry is credited with productivity growth that actually occurred in the airframe and engine industries. Furthermore, to the extent that the improved capital goods allow other sectors to create new and improved products, the productivity gains may not even be measured in those sectors, as when more powerful computers allow banks to produce a better quality of service.[6]

By contrast, neither the knowledge-input problem nor the knowledge-investment problem would necessarily create distorted measures of growth in a steady state. Since productivity growth in all sectors would be the same and knowledge inputs would be growing at the same rate as production inputs, the failure to include the knowledge sector when measuring output would not distort growth rates. The effect on the level of output, however, would be potentially quite large. A country that devoted 2.5 percent of its inputs to R&D investment and 20 percent to physical investment would have to add 12.5 percent to the investment component of GNP to correct for this aspect of the knowledge-investment problem, if the two kinds of investment activities yielded the same rate of return. If, as many have argued, R&D investment has a social productivity that is much higher than the social productivity of physical investment, and if the level of knowledge input broadly conceived were much higher than 2.5 percent of total resources, then the unmeasured investment output would be correspondingly higher than 12.5 percent of measured investment.

By the same token, the obsolescence problem by itself would not cause any great distortions in a steady state, where the essential problem for the national income accountant would be to apply the right average rate of depreciation to each class of investment goods. This is, of course, not a trivial problem, but it would exist even in the absence of new knowledge.

During a period of adjustment to a cluster of fundamental innovations, such as we are now experiencing, the combined effect of the four problems probably produces a downward bias in conventional measures of GNP growth and productivity growth. Consider first the quality-improvement problem. Just as it causes part of economic growth to go unmeasured in a steady state, it also causes much of the surge of economic growth resulting from better computers and related goods to go unmeasured. Part of this problem has been dealt with by the adoption, in the United States and Canada, of hedonic measures of quality improvement in the computer industry. But similar measures have not been undertaken in other industries, e.g., the electronic equipment industry that manufactures chips.

Baily and Gordon (1988) have argued that the quality-improvement problem cannot account for much of the slowdown in productivity that took place in the late 1960s and early 1970s, mainly because the failure to measure quality improvements properly has been too steady over time. Moreover, the use of Paasche price indexes in the national income accounts, rather than Divisia indexes, creates a measurement bias in the other direction, especially now that the output of the computer sector has been adjusted to reflect quality improvements more accurately. That is, the output of goods whose quality improvements have been measured will contribute excessively to measured economic growth, since it will be weighted by base period prices that do not reflect the falling real price resulting from technical progress.

Griliches (1994) claims, however, that the fruits of the information revolution have been used disproportionately in sectors where quality improvements are next to impossible to measure. He estimates that over three quarters of the output of the computer industry is used in what he calls the unmeasurable sectors. Furthermore, the information revolution is contributing to an increase in the relative size of the unmeasurable sectors, which Griliches estimates now account for 70 percent of GNP in the United States.

Consider next the knowledge-input problem. When computers first started to change the way work was done throughout the economy, a long period of learning had to take place.[7] At first, people looked for ways in which the new tool could simply replace old ones without a radical change in operating techniques. Although some gains were obtainable in that direction, the added cost of information service departments was often larger than the benefits. Gradually, through a process of trial and error, people are now beginning to exploit the enormous potential of computers, but for many years there were no visible productivity gains associated with the adoption of sophisticated information technologies.

Part of the problem is that the time people spend learning to use computers efficiently, and all the associated costs of training and experimentation, are unmeasured knowledge input. When the opportunities for such knowledge-creating activities are enhanced by the arrival of new fundamental technologies, workers spend less time producing output and more time creating new knowledge. The fact that output does not seem to be rising as fast as before reflects this reduction in real production input. But, since there is no corresponding reduction in measured production input, it appears as if productivity growth has slowed down. Indeed, from a broader perspective, one might see the costly restructuring of firms and the sectoral reallocations involved in learning to exploit fundamental technologies better as an unmeasured knowledge input with similar effects on measured productivity growth.

Next, consider the knowledge-investment problem. Part of the effect of this problem during such a transitional period is the converse of the knowledge-input problem. The learning and restructuring that goes on, as people adjust to a new general-purpose technology, have an unmeasured output, in the form of knowledge accumulation. Even costly mistakes create knowledge of what not to do. If that output were properly measured, it would compensate for the fall in measured output that takes place when firms and workers start devoting more time to learning how to use their new tools.

Even beyond this, however, more workers go into knowledge-creating activities when new opportunities open up because the return to these activities has risen by more than the return to production activities. Thus, it seems likely that the knowledge investment that goes unmeasured is even greater than the fall in output that is measured. So, even if knowledge inputs were measured correctly, the knowledge-investment problem would imply that measured output and productivity growth would fail to reflect what has been, in fact, an increase in overall growth. Neither the inputs nor the outputs of a sector whose productivity and output are growing faster than average would be counted.

Finally, consider the obsolescence problem. To some extent, it moderates the distortions created by the knowledge-investment problem, because the net increase in society's stocks of capital and knowledge resulting from the information revolution would be overstated, if the accelerated obsolescence of pre-existing capital and knowledge were not considered. Thus, if we were to solve the knowledge-investment problem without dealing with the obsolescence problem, we would certainly overstate the gain in NNP and national income taking place during a technological transition, even though measures of GNP and gross productivity would not be affected by the omission.

Aside from this effect, the obsolescence problem generates a separate distortion which reinforces the understatement of productivity gains caused by the other problems during a wave of fundamental innovations. To the extent that unmeasured obsolescence reduces the effective stock of capital, standard measures of total factor productivity (TFP) will overstate the capital services component of inputs to the production process, and will thereby understate the productivity of those inputs.

A FORMAL MODEL

To make these ideas more concrete, this section presents a simple abstract model to highlight the four measurement problems identified above. The model abstracts from all aspects of human capital, and focuses only on the question of the creation of new knowledge by the business sector. It assumes, for simplicity, that there are only two sectors of the economy: one producing capital goods (sector K) and one producing consumption goods (sector C).

Aggregate output from sector C is governed by the technological relationship:

$$C = Q_c\,(A_c)\,F_c\,(A_c, L_c^p, K) \tag{1}$$

where A_c represents the average stock of knowledge among firms in the C sector; F_c is the measurable number of units of some standardized consumption good being produced; Q_c is the average quality of these goods; L_c^p is the input of production labor in C; and K is the stock of capital. The stock of knowledge embodies both process and product innovations. The former are captured in the F_c function and the latter in the Q_c function.

The flow of aggregate gross output from sector K is governed by the technological relationship:

$$I = Q_k\,(A_k)\,F_k\,(A_k, L_k^p) \tag{2}$$

where the terminology is defined analogously to that of the first equation. For simplicity, and in order to highlight the use of computer capital in other sectors, I suppose that capital is used only in sector C.

The gross flow of new knowledge in the two sectors is governed by the relationships:

$$IA_k = (\lambda\, A_k\, G_k\,(L_k^r) \tag{3}$$

$$IA_c = H\,(A_c, A_k)\,G_c\,(L_c^r) \tag{4}$$

where G functions represent the technology of knowledge creation; L^r represents labour input into knowledge creation in the two sectors; and λ is a parameter affecting the productivity of knowledge-creating activities in sector K. A wave of fundamental innovations, such as those involved in the ongoing information revolution, would be represented by an exogenous increase in λ. I suppose that the growth of knowledge in the two sectors is affected not only by current labor inputs but also by the accumulation of past knowledge. Knowledge in sector K is assumed to affect the growth of knowledge in sector C, because more sophisticated capital goods open up opportunities for more sophisticated applications in sector C, as when computers allow banks to invent new kinds of deposits.

The rate of obsolescence of old capital is assumed to be an increasing function of the rate of gross investment (because it takes new investment to render old capital obsolete) and of the rate of creation of new knowledge in sector K. Hence:

$$\dot{K} = \kappa(I, IA_k, K,) \equiv I - \delta(I, IA_k)K \tag{5}$$

where the net-investment function κ is increasing in gross investment I and decreasing in the other two arguments. The depreciation function δ includes the effects of obsolescence as well as physical wear and tear, and is increasing in both arguments.

The rate of obsolescence of old knowledge of either type is also assumed to be an increasing function of the rate of creation of that kind of knowledge. Hence:

$$\dot{A}_i = \alpha_i (IA_i, A_i) \equiv IA_i - \delta_i^a (IA_i) A_i \quad ; \quad i = c, k \tag{6}$$

The final aggregate relationship is the market clearing condition for labor:

$$L_c^p + L_k^p + L_k^r + L_c^r = L \tag{7}$$

where L is the aggregate supply of labor.

To make the measurement problems discussed above operational, I define growth in terms of GNP.[8] Ideally, GNP should include investment in all three categories (physical capital and the two kinds of knowledge):

$$Y \equiv C + \mu I + \mu_c IA_c + \mu_k IA_k \tag{8}$$

where μ refer to shadow prices representing the value to society of incremental units of the respective stocks, in terms of the consumption good. In the standard theory of growth without technological change, there would be just the one μ representing the shadow price of capital, which would be Tobin's q. The rate of growth is therefore:

$$g = (\dot{C}/C)(C/Y) + (\dot{I}/I + \dot{\mu}/\mu)(\mu I/Y) + g_A \tag{9}$$

where g_A represents the direct contribution of growth in investment in knowledge:

$$g_A \equiv \frac{I}{Y} \frac{d}{dt} (\mu_c IA_c + \mu_k IA_k) \tag{10}$$

Total factor productivity growth is g minus the contribution of increased inputs of capital and labor. The latter contributions are measured at market factor prices. The rental price of capital is taken to be the price of capital μ multiplied by the sum $r+\delta$, where r is the long-run average rate of interest and δ the long-run average rate of depreciation of capital:

$$\tau = g - \frac{\mu\,(r+\delta)\dot{K} + w(\dot{L}_c^p + \dot{L}_k^p)}{Y} \tag{11}$$

TFP growth in producing consumption goods is:

$$\tau_c = \frac{\dot{C}}{C} - \frac{\mu(r+\delta)\dot{K} + w\dot{L}_c^p}{C} \tag{12}$$

The knowledge-input problem can be captured simply by supposing[9] that the measured labor input into production in each sector includes a fraction ε_r of workers who are actually engaged in research:

$$Lm_i^p = L_i^p + \varepsilon_r L_i^r\,; \quad i = c,k \quad 0<\varepsilon_r<1 \tag{13}$$

The quality-improvement problem can be captured by supposing that the measured growth rate of quality improvement for each period in each sector is only the fraction $1-\varepsilon_q$ of the actual growth rate $dln(Q)/dt$. Assume there is some base year in which both actual and measured quality are defined to equal unity. Then measured consumption will differ from real consumption according to:

$$Cm = Q_c\,(A_c)^{1-\varepsilon_q}\,F_c^p\,(A_c,L_c^p,K) = Q_c\,(A_c)^{-\varepsilon_q}\,C \tag{14}$$

Likewise, under the same normalization assumption for the quality of capital goods:

$$Im = Q_k\,(A_k)^{1-\varepsilon_q}\,F_k^p\,(A_k,L_c^p,K) = Q_k\,(A_k)^{-\varepsilon_q}\,I \tag{15}$$

Because the quality of capital and consumption goods is mismeasured, so are their total quantities and their relative price μ. Assume, however, that the total dollar values of consumption and investment can be measured every year. Then, by dividing these two nominal quantities we get a measure of the relative values of the annual output from the two sectors: $\mu I/C$. The measured relative price will be consistent with this magnitude. Hence:

$$\mu m = \mu\,(I/Im)\,/\,(C/Cm) = (Q_k\,(A_k)/Q_c\,(A_c)^{\varepsilon_q}\,\mu \tag{16}$$

Equation (16) implies that, as Gordon (1990) has stressed, if quality improvements are larger in capital goods than in consumption goods, then the relative price of capital goods will be overstated.

Under these assumptions, measured output will equal:

$$Ym = Cm + \mu m_0 Im \tag{17}$$

which differs from its real counterpart Y in (8) by:

- not including anything representing current investment in knowledge;
- having measured instead of real consumption and investment; and
- having a fixed, measured relative price of capital instead of the current true relative price.

Note that, aside from the knowledge-investment and the Laspeyres quantity-index problems, the only quality-measurement problem that would distort the measure of GNP is the problem of measuring the quality of consumption goods.

Any understatement of physical investment would be offset by an overstatement of the relative price of capital. That is, if the measured base price μm_0 was replaced in (17) by the measured current price μm as defined by (16), measured GNP would equal $Q_c(A_c)^{-\varepsilon_q}(C+\mu I)$, which differs from Y only by the non-inclusion of knowledge investment and the mismeasurement of the quality of consumption goods.

Corresponding to (17), the measured growth rate of GNP is:

$$gm = (c\frac{\dot{C}m}{Cm} + (1-c)\frac{\dot{I}m}{Im}) = (c\frac{\dot{C}}{C} + (1-c)\frac{\dot{I}}{I}) - \varepsilon_q (c\frac{\dot{Q}_c}{Q_c} + (1-c)\frac{\dot{Q}_k}{Q_k}) \tag{18}$$

where c is the measured share of consumption in GNP. The measured rate gm differs from the actual growth rate g defined in (9) in four ways. First, c might not equal the actual share of consumption. Second, gm excludes the g_A term measuring the contribution of knowledge investment. Third, gm makes no allowance for the changing relative price of investment. None of these would matter in a steady state with balanced growth. Fourth, the quality-improvement problem tends to make $gm < g$, since $\varepsilon_q > 0$. As discussed above, this last problem would exist even in a steady state with balanced growth.

To discuss the issue of productivity measurement, I first examine the special case in which the economy is in a steady state, where the rate of depreciation δ is constant and known. Then the measured capital stock will be:

$$Km(t) = \int_0^t e^{-\delta(t-\tau)}\, Im(\tau)d\tau + e^{-\delta t}\, Km(0) \tag{19}$$

As time passes and the effect of the initial guess $Km(0)$ wears off, the fact that investment is underestimated will imply that the capital stock is also underestimated. Hence, the effects of mismeasurement that tend to underestimate the growth of output will be offset to some extent by underestimation of the growth of capital.

To be more precise, in a steady state with investment growing at the constant proportional rate g, and with the quality of capital goods Q_k growing at the proportional rate ηg $(0<\eta<1)$, the capital stock will be underestimated by proportionately less than investment. That is, in such a steady state:

$$\frac{Km(t)}{K(t)} = \frac{\int_0^\infty e^{-\delta s}\, I(t-s)Q_k(t-s)^{-\varepsilon q}\, ds}{\int_0^\infty e^{-\delta s}\, I(t-s)\, ds} = \frac{Im(t)}{I(t)} \frac{\int_0^\infty e^{-[\delta+g(1-\eta\varepsilon q)]s}\, ds}{\int_0^\infty e^{-(\delta+g)s}\, ds} > \frac{Im(t)}{I(t)} \tag{20}$$

The reason behind this result is that the proportional measurement error in investment grows over time, and the capital stock, which is just a weighted sum of past investments, has a proportional measurement error which is a weighted sum of past proportional measurement errors.

Since the proportional measurement error on depreciation is the same as on the capital stock, it follows that the proportional measurement error on net investment in a steady state will exceed that on gross investment, because depreciation will not be understated by as much as will gross investment:

$$\frac{\dot{K}m(t)}{\dot{K}(t)} < \frac{Im(t)}{I(t)} \tag{21}$$

Measured TFP growth will be:

$$\tau m = gm - \frac{\mu m(r+\delta)\dot{K}m}{Ym} - \frac{w(1-\varepsilon_r)(\dot{L}_c^p + \dot{L}_k^p)}{Ym} \tag{22}$$

In a steady state, the deduction for the growth in capital input in (22) will be understated. According to (16), the proportional measurement error for this deduction would have been the same as for consumption if gross investment had been used but, since net investment is used, the error will be larger than this.

This error in the numerator is offset, however, by the fact that the denominator is also undermeasured. Since the use of a Paasche index does not create any distortion in a steady state with the relative price of capital constant, the analysis following (17) implies that the proportional measurement error of the denominator is also greater than that of consumption. Then in a steady state, where the last term in (22) vanishes, TFP growth will be underestimated by approximately the same amount as GNP growth, and both changes will be attributable to the quality-improvement problem. In transitional periods, however, as mentioned above, all four problems will interact to distort measured TFP growth.

Measured TFP growth in sector C will be:

$$\tau m_c = \frac{\dot{C}m}{Cm} - \frac{\mu m(r+\delta)\dot{K}m}{Cm} - \frac{w(\dot{L}_c^p + \varepsilon_r \dot{L}_c^r)}{Cm} \tag{23}$$

A comparison of (12) and (23) shows that, contrary to the case of aggregate TFP growth, the steady-state mismeasurement of TFP growth in sector C is likely to be less than that of GNP growth. For in this case, the underestimate of the numerator in the deduction for growth in capital input is not fully offset by any underestimate in the denominator. That is, according to (16) and (21), the value of net investment will be underestimated relative to consumption.

During transitional periods, the distortion of productivity growth in sector C will be more complicated. In particular, the information revolution is likely at first to create a bigger quality improvement problem for net investment than consumption, thus tending to create an overestimate of TFP growth in the consumption sector. But this will also be offset by the obsolescence problem, which will cause standard accounting procedures to miss the accelerated depreciation of capital. Unmeasured knowledge-input growth in sector C induced by the radical change in capital inputs will also cause TFP growth in sector C to be understated.

CONCLUSION

If the critical component of this paper has been larger than the constructive component, this is mainly attributable to the fact that the issue at hand is not likely to be fixed by minor tinkering with national income accounting practices. The underlying problem is that the very conceptual foundations on which national income accounting is based assume away the mainspring of long-term economic growth, by taking knowledge as unchanging and freely available. In such a world, market prices and quantities are all one needs to measure economic activity. In a world where growth is based on the creation, acquisition and use of knowledge, however, we need to look at other magnitudes, and a better conceptual foundation is needed before we know just what magnitudes to look at and how.

The paper suggests some general directions in which to look for better measures. First, to deal with the knowledge-input problem it would be helpful to ask business firms for more detailed information concerning their training, market research, brainstorming, exploration and other activities, both formal and informal. At least some attempt could then be made to construct a more comprehensive measure of knowledge input, which could be used to get better measures of productivity in knowledge creation, and could be subtracted from other inputs to get better measures of productivity in narrower production activities. Of course, Canada's experience with the scientific research tax credit scheme in the 1980s shows that there is also a danger of going too far, that it might be possible to construe almost any activity as constituting R&D. But just because a problem is difficult, does not mean that nothing should be done about it.

Better measures of knowledge input would also help in dealing with the knowledge-investment problem. One way of dealing, at least imperfectly, with this issue is to impute, to the resources used in R&D, an investment value equal to the value of the resources used. The characteristic uncertainty and externalities of knowledge investment make this hazardous, since the value of knowledge will have a large random component, and even its expected social value will differ from the expected private value reflected in the value of R&D resources used.

In dealing with the knowledge-investment problem, one can seek better measures of output as well as input. Thus, data on patents and the rate of introduction of new goods,[10] new firms and new jobs all give clues to the extent of knowledge creation. These various quantitative measures have well-known problems,[11] most notably that knowing how many goods, patents, etc., have been created does not indicate what their social or even private value is. But it should be possible to use the sort of hedonic methods to attribute values to these characteristics of new knowledge that have been used since Griliches (1961) to assess the characteristics of new goods in dealing with the quality-adjustment problem. Moreover, a large part of the knowledge-investment problem will be solved if the new satellite accounts being set up by Statistics Canada, as recommended by the 1993 *System of National Accounts,* eventually result in the capitalization of R&D expenditures for national income accounting purposes.

The quality-improvement problem is perhaps the most susceptible to economic analysis, as it has been recognized and dealt with for many years within the economics discipline. What is needed is a more systematic use of hedonic regressions among statistical agencies, as has been done in the case of computers, to deal with quality improvements in other industries. But the use of hedonic measures is itself subject to well-known problems, most notably that measures are crucially dependent on judgments as to how the prices of new goods affect those of old goods in imperfect competition, how the introduction of new goods hastens quality improvements in old goods[12] and, most important in our context, how the sort of deep structural change the world is now undergoing affects the relationships between particular characteristics and social value.[13]

Finally, the obsolescence problem would be mitigated by studies such as Caballero and Jaffe (1993), which has provided at least a preliminary estimate of the rate of obsolescence of patentable ideas. More frequently revised estimates of the rate at which old capital is scrapped would also be helpful, and should be fairly straightforward to obtain. The fact that a large fraction of current investment in recent years has been in new computers, whose rate of obsolescence continues to be much higher than that of the average piece of business equipment, creates an overstatement of net investment that could and should be corrected by surveying business enterprises on the frequency of replacement.

NOTES

1. This definition is broad enough to include knowledge used in service industries, where the material objects can include such items as hair (in the case of haircutting services) or even electrons (in the case of many information services). When all that is received is advice, as in many business service industries, for example, the output of that industry is itself knowledge.
2. Arrow (1994) makes a similar point about Hayek's conception of the use of knowledge.
3. Aghion and Tirole (1994) analyze how these problems might affect the organization of R&D.
4. This is not to deny the existence of joint research ventures and contracted R&D. Rose (1995) presents evidence from a survey of 3566 large R&D-performing firms indicating that 328 of the firms surveyed received funds from another company for conducting research.
5. The working group which produced the international *System of National Accounts* (OECD, Paris, 1993) considered recommending the capitalization of R&D expenditures for just these reasons. In the end, they decided to drop the recommendation, in view of the problems of measuring and evaluating such an intangible investment, although they did recommend the setting up of satellite R&D capital accounts on an experimental basis.
6. This point is made forcefully by Griliches (1994) in a paper summarizing a lifetime of research on the question of measuring the productivity gains from R&D and attributing them to the right sector.

7. David (1991) presents a provocative discussion of this problem.
8. See Usher (1980) for a comprehensive treatment of alternative measures of economic growth, including a discussion of the implications of different measures for the knowledge-investment problem.
9. Of course, statistical agencies cannot make any such supposition. They do the best they can, which we suppose, for simplicity, leaves a constant fraction of research workers misrepresented as being engaged in production.
10. See Klenow (1994), for example.
11. See Griliches (1979), for example.
12. This is the famous "sailing-ship" phenomenon that many economic historians have commented on.
13. See Jorgensen and Landau (1989) and Gordon (1990) for recent discussions of these problems.

REFERENCES

Aghion, Philippe and Peter Howitt. "A Model of Growth through Creative Destruction." *Econometrica.* 60, (March 1992): 323–251.

Aghion, Philippe and Jean Tirole. "On the Management of Innovation." *Quarterly Journal of Economics.* 109, (November 1994): 1185–1209.

Arrow, Kenneth J. "Methodological Individualism and Social Knowledge." *American Economic Review.* 84, (May 1994): 1–9.

Baily, Martin Neil and Robert J. Gordon. "The Productivity Slowdown, Measurement Issues, and the Explosion of Computer Power." *Brooking Papers on Economic Activity.* 2, (1988): 347–420.

Caballero, Ricardo J. and Adam B. Jaffe. "How High are the Giants' Shoulders: An Empirical Assessment of Knowledge Spillovers and Creative Destruction in a Model of Economic Growth." In *NBER Macroeconomics Annual, 1993.* Cambridge, MA: MIT Press, 1993, pp. 15–74.

Clower, Robert W. and Peter Howitt. "Money, Markets and Coase." In *Is Economics Becoming a Hard Science?* Edited by Antoine d'Autume and Jean Cartelier. Proceedings of conference in Paris, October 1992.

David, Paul. "Computer and Dynamo: The Modern Productivity Paradox in a Not-Too-Distant Mirror." In *Technology and Productivity.* Paris: Organization for Economic Cooperation and Development, 1991, pp. 315–348.

Dosi, Giovanni. "Sources, Procedures, and Microeconomic Effects of Innovation." *Journal of Economic Literature.* 26, (September 1988): 1120–1171.

Gordon, Robert J. *The Measurement of Durable Goods Prices.* Chicago: University of Chicago Press, 1990.

Griliches, Zvi. "Hedonic Price Indexes for Automobiles: An Econometric Analysis of Quality Change." In *The Price Statistics of the Federal Government.* Washington, DC: National Bureau of Economic Research, 1961, pp. 173–196.

———. "Issues in Assessing the Contribution of Research and Development in Productivity Growth." *Bell Journal of Economics.* 10, (1979): 92–116.

———. "Productivity, R&D, and the Data Constraint." *American Economic Review.* 84, (March 1994): 1–23.

Hayek, F. A. "The Use of Knowledge in Society." *American Economic Review.* 35, (September 1945): 519–530.

Jorgensen, Dale W. and Ralph Landau, eds. *Technology and Capital Formation.* Cambridge, Mass: MIT Press, 1989.

Klenow, Peter J. "New Product Innovations." Unpublished, University of Chicago, January 1994.

Lucas, Robert E. Jr. "On the Mechanics of Economic Development." *Journal of Monetary Economics.* 22, (January 1988): 3–42.

Prescott, Edward C. "Theory Ahead of Business Cycle Measurement." In *Carnegie Rochester Conference Series on Public Policy.* Vol. 25, 1986, pp. 11–66.

Rae, J. *Statement of Some New Principles on the Subject of Political Economy.* Boston: Hilliard, Gray and Co., 1834.

Romer, Paul M. "Increasing Returns and Long-Run Growth." *Journal of Political Economy.* 94, (October 1986): 1002–1037.

———. "Endogenous Technological Change." *Journal of Political Economy.* 98, (October 1990): S71–S012.

Rose, Antoine. "Strategic R&D Alliances." *Service Indicators—4th Quarter 1994.* Ottawa: Statistics Canada, Cat. No. 63-016, Vol. 1, No. 3, 1995.

Stigler, George. "A Sketch of the History of Truth in Teaching." *Journal of Political Economy.* 81, (March–April 1973): 491–495.

Usher, Dan. *The Measurement of Economic Growth.* New York: Columbia University Press, 1980.

Wallis, John J. and Douglass C. North. "Measuring the Transaction Sector in the American Economy, 1870–1970." In *Long-Term Factors in American Economic Growth.* Edited by Stanley Engerman and Robert Gallman. Chicago: University of Chicago Press, 1986.

9

The Management of Intellectual Assets: A New Corporate Perspective

Richard Hall

With the recent growth of the service sector in the West (in 1985 only 26 per cent of UK employment was in manufacturing; HMSO Regional Trends 1986), and the rapid development of the information technology industry, the role of intellectual assets has become of significant importance. The strategic management of intellectual assets is becoming a major policy area for any modern corporation.

There is an emerging literature in professional journals on the valuation of intellectual property, in particular brandnames,[1,2] and also on the subject of intellectual assets and corporate strategy.[3,4] In addition there is an established literature covering intellectual property rights.[5,6,7] No serious attempt has yet been made to bring these subjects together in one framework which can encompass the broad area of the management of intellectual assets.

The purpose of this paper is to argue the case for a new perspective in the management of corporate affairs. The importance of reputation, know-how etc., like the value of motherhood, is readily acknowledged; but until recently there has been little attempt to identify, and give structure to, the nature and role of intellectual assets in the strategic management of a business. This is largely due to the fact that intellectual assets rarely have an exchange value, either because property rights have not been, or cannot be, established; and/or because the intellectual assets have not been, or cannot be, the subject of a transaction. In consequence they often lie outside the province of the commodity based models of economics and accountancy.

Assets can be viewed as inputs to, and outputs from, a commercial or industrial transformation process (the operations strategy perspective), or as financial factors which can be used to match liabilities (the accountancy perspective). This

Reprinted by permission of The Braybrooke Press Ltd. From *Journal of General Management* 15, no. 1 (Autumn 1989): 53–68.

paper will identify the different types of intellectual asset, the relevance of the operations and accountancy perspectives, and the application of these ideas to business policy.

An asset is "property available to meet debts; any possession; a person, or thing having any useful quality" (Concise Oxford Dictionary). Two key attributes can be identified as a result of this definition. They are ownership and value.

Ownership may be established in law, as for example the ownership of land which is established by means of title deeds, or the ownership of a trademark which is established by a state grant of a monopoly of use; or it may not have a place in any legal context, for example the ownership of good customer relations.

The valuation of assets in financial terms lies in the province of the accounting profession where the key concept is that of exchange value. The exchange value is the answer to the question "What sum of money has been exchanged for ownership?" This is the basis of nearly all financial valuations. Some valuations however have only a very tenuous link with an exchange; examples are the revaluation of a building by a surveyor, or the valuation of a brand name which has been developed in-house, as opposed to one which was bought in.

The term "intellectual assets" is used in this paper to identify those assets whose essence is an idea or knowledge, and whose nature can be defined and recorded in some way. Intellectual assets may reside in the minds of customers, e.g., skills and experience; they may reside in the minds of employees, e.g., reputation and confidence; or they may reside in the corporate mind, e.g., databases and the know-how of the group. They may also be independent and separable from any individual or organisation as is the case with a patent which can be treated as a commodity.

Intellectual assets may be further categorised into the two groups of (a) those which have property rights—intellectual property, and (b) those which do not have property rights—here defined as "knowledge."

The intellectual property asset includes patents, trademarks, copyright and registered designs; whilst the knowledge asset includes reputation, goodwill, organisational and personal networks, databases, and the knowledge and experience of skilled employees.

THE NATURE OF ASSETS—THE ACCOUNTANCY PERSPECTIVE

The accountancy profession identifies different categories of asset. The definitions used in the sections which follow apply to the UK.[8] The purpose of reviewing the accountancy categorisation is so that these concepts may be applied, where appropriate, to the treatment of intellectual assets which will be put forward in this paper.

Fixed and Current Assets

Assets which are used to generate revenue, and which are not held primarily for resale are classed as fixed. These assets are usually depreciated according to one or other of the accounting conventions. Fixed assets typically include plant and buildings.

Assets which are held with the intention of conversion into cash are classed as current. Current assets include stocks, debtors, and bank deposits. Stocks are valued at the lower of cost or market value; whilst debtors retain their face value.

An alternative test is to identify the length of time an asset is to be retained by an organisation; thus assets which are to be held for a relatively long period are classed as fixed; whilst those which are to be held for a short period are classed as current.

Usually the same classification is arrived at irrespective of the test used; the key to meaningful classification is to identify the nature of the company's business; for example if the company is a motor trader the cars which it owns are current assets as they are held for a short term, and with a view to turning them into cash; if on the other hand the firm is a pharmaceutical wholesaler the cars which it owns are held as fixed assets as they are held for a long term and are used to generate revenue.

Intangible Assets

Intangible assets result from expenditure incurred, i.e., an exchange, in return for which nothing tangible or physical is received, but from which a benefit may accrue beyond the accounting period in question.

There are three main types of intangible asset: research and development; goodwill; and intellectual property (patents, trademarks, and copyright).

Goodwill is the difference between the net asset value of the company as defined by the accounts, and the value assigned to the total organisation as a result of an exchange. Whilst conceptually goodwill represents such things as the quality of relations with customers, the value assigned to it is the balancing figure between the net asset value, and the total sum paid. In the interests of caution the accounting profession prefers to amortise (depreciate) goodwill over a short period, usually the current year.

Research and development is an asset which comes about usually as a result of expenditure incurred internally; i.e., it is rarely the result of an arm's length transaction between independent parties. In addition it may or may not represent an asset which enjoys property rights, and it is unlikely to have a value if separated from the organisation. In the light of these characteristics the professional accounting bodies prefer that expenditure on pure and applied research is written off in the year in which it is incurred. Development expenditure can be written off over a longer period (i.e., capitalised and then amortised) but only if certain conditions apply.

Intellectual property, by definition, enjoys property rights; i.e., title can be established in law, trespassers can be prosecuted, and it can be bought and sold. Accountancy convention allows the valuation of patents and trademarks but until recently only where ownership had resulted from an exchange which enabled an historical cost to be established. Because patents have a finite life it is clear that an amortisation policy applied. Trademarks however enjoy an indefinite life (if renewed as required), and under these circumstances the need for an amortisation policy is less clear; indeed some would argue that most brand names increase in value with age.

In the UK there is considerable controversy regarding the financial valuation of registered brandnames. Recent takeovers involving very large sums of money classed as goodwill have prompted the identification of the amount of goodwill which can be ascribed to trademarks, so that a less onerous amortisation policy may be applied to the trademarks than to the goodwill element; i.e., the amortisation of the trademarks can be spread over a number of years as opposed to the amortisation of goodwill in the current financial year. This practice is viewed with less concern than the practice of valuing brandnames which have been developed in-house and which have not been the subject of an exchange. This latter practice inevitably involves a degree of subjective assessment with which most professional accountants are uncomfortable as it is a fundamental departure from the commodity based paradigm of the discipline.

In summary therefore the accountancy profession recognises a variety of asset types, and valuation methodologies. The treatment of intellectual property, both in terms of recognition as an asset, and its valuation, is in a state of flux.

THE NATURE OF ASSETS—THE OPERATIONS PERSPECTIVE

An operating system is a configuration of resources combined for the provision of goods or services by means of the functions of manufacturing, transport, trading and service; and operations management is concerned with the design and the operation of systems for these four functions.[9]

This may be conceptualised as the classic "Input; Transformation Process; Output" sequence; where the input is resources (materials, machines, labour, intellectual assets etc.); the transformation process is one or more of manufacturing, transport, trading or service; and the output is goods or services that customers wish to buy. The assets which are inputs, and outputs, to the system are current assets; whilst the assets which are required to operate the transformation process are fixed assets. Operating systems can be described in terms of storage, flow, process, and queues. The three concepts of storage, flow and process can be adapted for use in information/knowledge systems, and can be more conveniently described as identification, retrieval, processing, transmission and storage.

The purpose of all transformation processes is to add value to the input. Modern manufacturing philosophy concentrates on the objective of constantly adding value to the work in progress, so that resources are standing idle for as little time as possible. This results in a departure from a preoccupation with the utilisation of fixed assets (machinery), to a preoccupation with the utilisation of current resources (work in progress). Information technology is concerned with adding value to the data input to produce enriched data, i.e., knowledge.

In processes other than those concerned solely with the transformation of data into knowledge, there is always the opportunity to enrich the intellectual asset base; be it in terms of extra skill and experience, extra data, better relations with customers, etc. Itami puts forward the view that every turn of the business cycle should be adding value to the organisation's intellectual asset base in the relevant core know-how areas (alternatively known as the areas of key competencies[10]). Whilst the concept of core competencies is understood by most major companies, the concept of constantly adding value to the intellectual asset base is less widely accepted.

INTELLECTUAL ASSETS—THEIR NATURE AND CHARACTERISTICS

Intellectual property rights such as patents, trade marks, registered designs and copyright afford legal protection to the owners of certain classes of intellectual assets. To qualify for such protection the intellectual asset must be recordable and definable in certain ways, and in addition it must be possible to demonstrate exclusive authorship. When legally enforceable title has been established, usually by means of the state granting a monopoly which is enforceable in law, it becomes possible to value, to buy, to sell, to let, to mortgage, and to count as an asset the intellectual property in question.

Trade Marks

Of the four main categories of intellectual property, the trademark is the oldest. The earliest evidence of a maker's mark is on pottery made 7,000 years ago. Property rights for trademarks were incorporated in Roman law, where the emphasis was on protecting the customers from being cheated with fraudulent goods, rather than protecting the intellectual property of the manufacturer. Nowadays trade and service marks afford protection in the use of devices, names, signatures, etc., used to describe a product or service. In an age when the brand name can represent the essence of the ideas and feelings associated with a product, the protection afforded by a trade mark can be crucial to the well-being of a company in order to avoid unfair competition and the use of its reputation by rivals. To have a mark registered in the UK the requirements are that it has to be: distinctive, not descriptive of the product, and different from other trade marks. Generally speaking a trade mark cannot be a surname or a geographical name. Examples of world class brandnames which are registered as brandnames, and which have been valued very highly, are "Bisto," "Bell's Scotch Whisky," and "Hovis" bread.

Unlike patents and copyright which have finite duration, trade marks can be renewed indefinitely.

Patents

The formal recognition of an inventor's right of ownership to his invention was first conceived in Venice in 1421 when the state granted a monopoly to Phillipo Brunillesci in respect of his invention of a floating architectural crane. This was followed in England in 1449 when Henry VI granted a monopoly to one John of Utyman who was installing the stained glass windows in Eton college chapel. In 1474 the first patent law was enacted in Venice.

When a patent is granted a contract is made between the state and the inventor whereby the inventor is granted a monopoly in his invention for a limited period of time in the state's territory, in return for the inventor disclosing his invention and it being made available to the world at large; the very word "patent" derives from the Latin *literae patentes* meaning open letter. It can be seen therefore that the basis of patent protection is the concept of the ownership of a new idea (the invention); and consequent upon the demonstration of that ownership, the establishment of a contract between the state and the inventor. The information contained in patents is clearly intended for the benefit of the public, and in fact the patent databases constitute one of the richest information crops which it is possible to harvest.

Copyright

The need for copyright did not arise until the invention of the printing press in the 16th century, when the copying of documents became easy. In England a monopoly was granted to the Stationers' Company. Members of this company were the only people who could print documents, and in exchange for this monopoly they undertook to censor, on political and religious grounds, everything which was printed. This is another example of a contract between the state and the owner of the intellectual property. Nowadays no such contract applies as in the UK copyright is automatic, and there is no need to register a document in a central registry.

Whereas patents are meant to protect an inventive idea, copyright is meant to protect an embodiment of that idea. For example the plots of "The Taming of the Shrew" and "Romeo and Juliet" are Shakespeare's original ideas, and "Kiss Me Kate" and "West Side Story" are embodiments, fashioned by others, of those ideas. These embodiments have their own protection in copyright. Copyright protects original literary, dramatic, musical, and artistic works, sound recordings, films and broadcasts by giving legal rights to the originators so that they may control the copying, adaptation, publishing, performing and broadcasting of the material. Additionally in the UK it is often possible to protect the design of an industrial product by means of the copyright which resides in the original drawings on which the product is based. Copyright is a collection of separate legal rights each of which is specific to the type of material in question.

Registered Designs

A registered design enables the eye appeal of a commercial article to be protected. Design registration is concerned only with the appearance, e.g., of a soft drinks bottle. Designs may be two dimensional, e.g., a fabric print; or three dimensional, e.g., a tea pot. Designs which are purely functional, and which lack eye appeal, will not be registrable; however it may be possible to obtain copyright protection for those designs, as mentioned above. For a design to be registrable it must not have been published or offered for sale.

KNOWLEDGE

The knowledge asset includes reputation, organisational and personal networks, databases, and the knowledge and experience of skilled employees. The common feature of these assets is that they are all conceived in the mind, and in one manner or another they reside in the mind.

Itami identifies three types of knowledge as shown in Table 9-1.

TABLE 9-1

		Flows	
Type	*Example of Knowledge*	*From*	*To*
Environmental Knowledge	Market Intelligence Technology Political Factors Supplier Relations Customer Relations	Environment	Organisation
Corporate Knowledge	Reputation Company/Brand Image Advertising & Promotion	Organisation	Environment
Internal Knowledge	Corporate Culture Morale Databases Employee Know-How Corporate Know-How	Starts and Finishes in the Organisation	

The environmental source is concerned with the flow of information from the environment to the organisation. The organisation needs to gather constantly all the available information from the environment which is pertinent to its affairs. It is too easy to leave this crucial activity to chance. As well as identifying the regular sources of environmental information, e.g., technical journals, trade journals, patent and trademark journals etc., attention should be given to the nurturing of personal networks.

The corporate source is concerned with the flow of information from the organisation to the relevant outsiders. It is therefore concerned with such issues as public relations, advertising and promotion, reputation gained by word of mouth, etc. In consumer products the asset of supreme importance is the stable of brandnames. The efficacy of branding lies in its ability to coalesce the constellation of ideas and concepts surrounding a product or service and thereby facilitate the communication process.[11] Relevant outsiders can include many groups other than customers; examples of other groups are: suppliers, licensors, shareholders, bankers, stockbrokers, environmental groups, legislators, employees and others.

The internal source is concerned with knowledge which accumulates in the minds of employees, and the corporate mind, as a result of training, but also as a result of the operation of the business. It was suggested earlier that all organisations have two transformation processes working in parallel, the explicit one concerned with producing the output for sale, but also the implicit one which has the capability to add value to the intellectual asset base of the organisation. The key point is to recognise the opportunities which the existence of the second process affords, and having recognised them to concentrate on the benefits which they can make available.

Recent theories of human intelligence suggest that far from comprising one global faculty, intelligence consists of a series of relatively interdependent modules, each preadapted to serve particular forms of experience. This theory helps to explain prodigious abilities in art or mathematics in persons who may be of average intelligence in other respects.[12] The corporate mind seems to behave, for whatever reason, in a similar way, and in addition it seems to have a synergistic characteristic whereby the corporate know-how is greater than the sum of the know-how of the individuals.

THE MANAGEMENT OF INTELLECTUAL ASSETS

Intellectual assets have the following characteristics: they are difficult to acquire and accumulate; they are capable of simultaneous multiple uses; they can, like money, be both inputs to, and outputs from, the business process.

Intangibles, such as esteem and trust, take time to acquire: unlike conventional assets they cannot be bought. Conversely they can be lost almost instantaneously. When Sir Clive Sinclair launched his Sinclair C5 battery-operated vehicle apparently without adequate research and testing, he not only lost a great deal of money when it failed to sell, but arguably he also lost, almost overnight, some of his reputation as a businessman. It is obvious that the stewardship of resources as fragile as reputation should rank very highly as a management responsibility.

A good brand name can be used simultaneously on a multiplicity of compatible products. For example the Honda (TM) brandname was first used on motorcycles and scooters: by sensible diversification it is now applied, with advantage, to both cars and mowing machines.

The operation of the business process should be not only cash positive but also information positive. Each turn of the business cycle should result in the organisation having more skill, experience, information database, and reputation. Itami suggests that this is a key criterion for judging alternative strategies.

The business cycle can easily be information negative, if for example a brand name is used on an incomptabile product; not only is the new product unlikely to succeed, but the quality of the brand name will be degraded. If Coca Cola launched a range of toilet preparations under the Coca Cola name, the chances are that the new range would not do well, and that the existing soft drinks range would suffer.

One acquires physical assets in a coherent, not a haphazard, manner; this policy should also apply to intellectual assets. An organisation should systematically build up its core intellectual assets: manufacturing/service know-how, complementary brand names, etc. This will not only result in an increasing competitive advantage, but will also constitute an effective entry barrier to potential competitors.

The life cycle curve of an intellectual asset may take a variety of interesting shapes. There is the steadily increasing curve of the established world famous brand name whose value increases every time a product is sold, say Coca-Cola, illustrated in Figure 9-1(a). There is the classic life cycle of growth, maturity and decline which applies to the value of the copyright in a popular song, illustrated in Figure 9-1(b). And there is the paradox of the ultra successful brand name such as Hoover or Walkman where the world passes into general use and by virtue of that passage ceases to have any value to the original owner, illustrated in Figure 9-1(c).

A NEW STRATEGIC PERSPECTIVE

This section will draw together the concepts introduced in the preceding sections, and develop a new perspective. Intellectual assets do not fit readily into the accountancy disciplines. A trademark which is licensed, as for example in a franchise agreement, can be classed as both a current and a fixed asset of the licensee's business. It is exchanged for cash in the everyday course of business, the current asset classification; and it is also the asset, above all others, which the licensee expects to retain in the long term to generate revenue, the fixed asset test.

The same trademark, or more precisely the intellectual property which resides in the mark, can be said to constitute an infinite resource for the licensor, and one which he can sell at zero variable cost. This view can be taken because when a royalty payment becomes due from the licensee to the licensor, due to the licen-

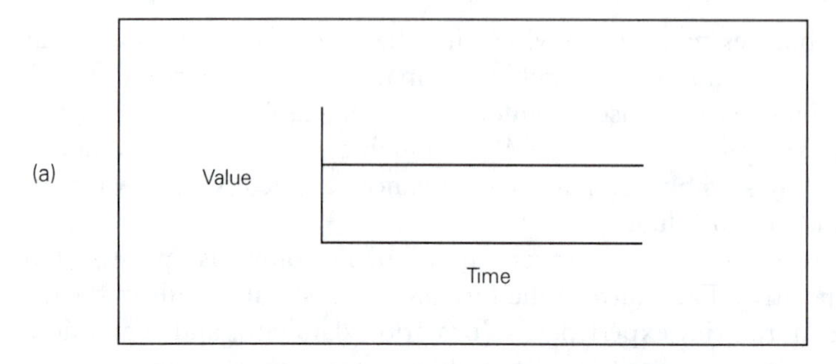

THE LIFE CYCLE OF A WORLD FAMOUS BRAND NAME

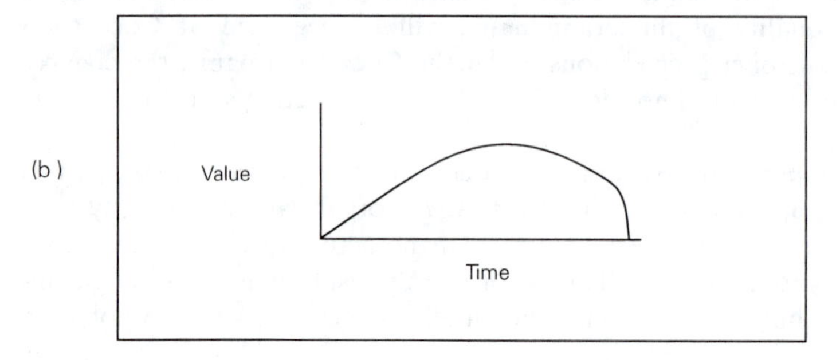

THE LIFE CYCLE OF A POPULAR SONG'S COPYRIGHT

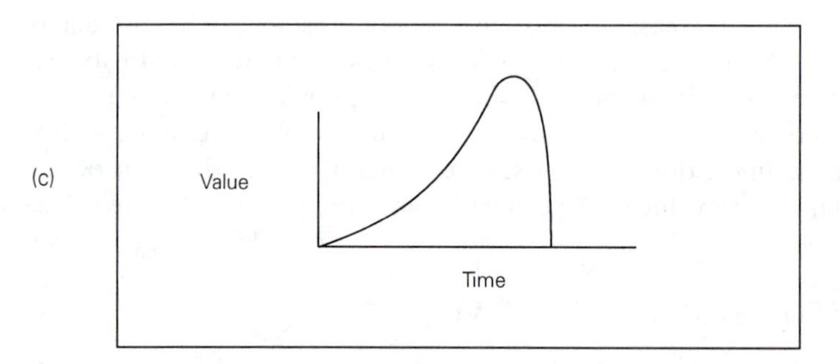

THE LIFE CYCLE OF A BRAND NAME WHICH BECOMES GENERIC

FIGURE 9-1

see making a sale to a third party, the licensor has incurred no variable cost when his intellectual property was "sold." It can also be argued that his "stock" of intellectual property has increased as a result of the sale to the third party, due to the marginal increase in fame and esteem which has resulted from the increased exposure his intellectual property has received. This was illustrated above in Figure 9-1(a).

The fact that the intellectual assets which have been accumulated by a company usually do not result from an exchange, but are more often developed in-house, is not a good reason for them to be excluded from the accounts. The assets in question must, of course, enjoy property rights as it is not possible to count as an asset something whose ownership cannot be demonstrated and protected. The task facing the accounting profession is to conceive a valuation methodology which gives consistent results when used by different practitioners. If the auditors are reluctant to countenance a balance sheet valuation of intellectual assets the directors of a company should still address the issue of the value of these assets, and if considerations of security allow, include their conclusions in notes to the accounts.

Those companies which have valued brandnames have demonstrated that the value of these marks can constitute the major portion of shareholders' funds. In the case of the Ranks Hovis McDougal valuation carried out in 1988 the valuation of brand names resulted in shareholders' funds increasing from £250 million to £920 million: an increase of 268 per cent. When the assets in question are as valuable as this it is clear that they should be managed with the utmost care and attention. In particular the practice of appointing a brand manager for a set term of, say, three years has been questioned as this can often result in, at best, defensive management, and at worst inconsistent practice.

Major companies operating in the consumer goods field are increasingly pro-active in the way they manage brandnames. They use intellectual property rights as a sword as well as a shield, for example by simultaneous exploitation of brandnames, licensing agreements, etc. This does not seem to be the case with small/medium sized enterprises (SME's). This may be due to ignorance, or it may be due to a cynical attitude towards the value of intellectual property rights when one has not available substantial funds to prosecute trespassers. Organisations with slender resources should at least avail themselves of the considerable information which is available from the Patent and Trademark Journals.

As stated earlier the commercial operations management concepts of storage, flow and process can be adapted for use in information/knowledge systems, and can be more conveniently described as identification, retrieval, processing, transmission and storage.

Using this terminology, and Itami's three types of knowledge: environmental, corporate and internal, it is possible to construct a framework to formalise the administration of intellectual assets, as shown in Table 9-2.

It is quite likely that most organisations are well organised with respect to the identification, retrieval, processing, transmission and storage of the necessary environmental and corporate information. It is much less likely that attention has been given to the identification of the core know-how areas, and the identification of the operation's focus which will result in the best accumulation of knowledge in these core areas. For example a crucial decision for most manufacturing companies is to identify the centre of gravity in the make/buy spectrum. The apparent tendency in the west is to move the centre of gravity towards the "buy-in" end of the spectrum; whilst the apparent tendency in the east is to move it towards the

TABLE 9-2 Example of Part of an Intellectual Asset Audit System

1. Environment Knowledge	
1.10 Competitive Activity—Patents	
(a) Identify Source	Patent Database
(b) Retrieve Information	Weekly review of all patents published by competitors
(c) Process Information	Analyse to determine if, for example, a portfolio is being established
(d) Transmit Information	Circulate to relevant R&D who will produce monthly summary
(e) Store Information	File by product category, and by competitor
1.11 Competitive Activity—Field Intelligence	
(a) Identify Source	Customers
(b) Retrieve Information	Sales Force
(c) Process Information	Sales Manager to summarise field reports by competitor
(d) Transmit Information	Summary circulated to board
(e) Store Information etc.	Filed by competitor

"make" end of the spectrum. It is possible that an imbalance towards the "buy-in" end will eventually result in a weakening of a manufacturing company's intellectual asset base and a less defensible strategic position.

The latter point is illustrated by the allegorical tale of an engineering company, operating in a high technology area, which over the years manufactured less and less and bought in more and more. Eventually the company's main component supplier destroyed the company by offering ten of the company's senior executives an equity stake in a new company making the same product.

The author believes that whilst the condition of being information positive is the essence of service organisations, it is also of fundamental importance to organisations in all other sectors where a, usually unrecognised, data transformation process is taking place in parallel with the main process. At the worst it is possible that the information transformation process is negative and destructive rather than constructive and positive. For example every contact with a customer is an opportunity to improve the relationship, and to learn more about the market; it can also be an occasion for degrading the relationship, and for deducing the wrong things about the market. Perhaps the common criterion of successful organisations is that they recognise the fact that they should always be in a learning mode.

The accumulation of intellectual assets can represent the strategy which provides the best defensible position. Intellectual assets take time to accumulate and often cannot be bought. In consequence they can constitute a "wall" which it is very difficult to penetrate from outside the organisation. Conversely it must be recognized that intellectual assets are fragile to erosion from within, and can be destroyed quickly by careless and inefficient management. Whilst a company's reputation can be attacked from within by disinformation etc., it can be eroded more quickly by disaffection on the part of employees.

CONCLUSION

This paper has sought to identify the nature of intellectual assets; to show how the nature and characteristics of intellectual assets fit, or do not fit, with the disciplines of accountancy and operations management; and to suggest that the accumulation of intellectual assets in core know-how areas is an under-utilised criterion for evaluating alternative corporate strategies.

The significance of intellectual property rights seems to be poorly recognised. The emerging literature on brandname valuation devotes little attention to the question of the quality of title, for example, class of mark, product categories covered, territories covered, etc.

Whilst some large organisations are pro-active in the field of intellectual property rights, there seems to be a widespread disinterest in SME's in the protection which can be obtained. As has been postulated above this may be due to ignorance, or it may be due to cynicism about the quality of the protection which the law affords if one does not possess large financial resources with which to prosecute trespassers.

The accountancy profession seems to be uneasy with the issue of intangible assets in general, and intellectual property rights in particular. Whatever the difficulties of measuring such assets as brandnames, it is clear that a method must be devised when it has been demonstrated by acquisition activity that the bulk of the worth of many companies lies in these intellectual assets.

The fundamental valuation issue however is the degree to which the measurement of conventional assets is a relevant criterion of the worth of a business at all. The traditional measure based on conventional assets will continue to be relevant for manufacturing and trading, but is increasingly irrelevant for services, i.e. for those organisations whose output is an intangible benefit, and whose resources are essentially information based. The worth of a university is only trivially related to the value of the land and buildings which it owns; the resources which are of strategic significance are reputation, research momentum, skill and experience of academic staff, etc. The same is true of advertising agencies, consultancies, computer bureaux, etc. For many service companies the value of the business is better measured by the degree to which it is not only cash positive, the short term measure, but information positive, the medium term measure.

The author believes that a characteristic of all successful organisations is the recognition, explicitly or implicitly, of the learning process which runs in parallel to all operations. Recognition of the fact that every commercial activity is shadowed by opportunities to enhance the intellectual asset base, or to degrade it, leads to a concentration on the accumulation of intellectual assets in the core competency areas.

Whilst the importance of intellectual assets is implicitly accepted, like the value of motherhood, the fact that there is little research and education in the subject suggests that a more formal recognition is overdue. In particular the role of intellectual asset management in business policy needs to be more clearly understood.

NOTES

1. Holgate, P., *The Accounting Rules on Intangibles and Goodwill.* Working paper, Deloitte Haskins & Sells, London, 1988.
2. Mullen, M., *How the Professional Advisor Values Brands Trademarks and other Intangible Assets,* Working Paper, Coopers and Lybrand, London, 1988.
3. Itami, H. and Roehl, T.W., *Mobilizing Invisible Assets,* Harvard University Press, Cambridge, Massachusetts, 1987.
4. Lloyd, I. and Sveiby, K.E., *Managing Know-How,* Bloomsbury, London, 1987.
5. Hodkinson, K., *Protecting and Exploiting New Technology and Designs,* E. and F.N. Spon. London, 1987.
6. Eisenschitz, F.S., *Patents Trademarks and Designs in Information Works,* Croom Helm, London, 1987.
7. Johnston, D., *Design Protection,* Design Council, London, 1986.
8. Arnold, J., Hope, I. and Southworth, A., *Financial Accounting,* Prentice-Hall, London, 1985.
9. Wild, R., *Essentials of Production and Operations Management,* Holt, Rinehart and Winston, London, 1984.
10. Itami, H. and Roehl, T.W., op. cit.
11. Wills, G.S.C., *The Penguin Management Handbook,* Penguin, London, 1987.
12. Bullock, A., Stallybrass, O. and Trombley, S., *Dictionary of Modern Thought,* Fontana, London, 1988.

10

Measuring and Managing Technological Knowledge

Roger E. Bohn

Knowledge is power.

—Francis Bacon

As we move from the industrial age into the information age, knowledge is becoming an ever more central force behind the competitive success of firms and even nations. Nonaka has commented, "In an economy where the only certainty is uncertainty, the one sure source of lasting competitive advantage is knowledge."[1] Philosophers have analyzed the nature of knowledge for millennia; in the past half-century, cognitive and computer scientists have pursued it with increased vigor. But it has turned out that *information* is much easier to store, describe, and manipulate than is *knowledge*. One consequence is that, although an organization's knowledge base may be its single most important asset, its very intangibility makes it difficult to manage systematically.[2]

The goal of this paper is to present a framework for measuring and understanding one particular type of knowledge: technological knowledge, i.e., knowledge about how to produce goods and services. We can use this framework to more precisely map, evaluate, and compare levels of knowledge. The level of knowledge that a process has reached determines how a process should be controlled, whether and how it can be automated, the key tasks of the workforce, and other major aspects of its management. Better knowledge of key variables leads to better performance without incremental physical investment.

Two examples illustrate the importance of technological knowledge in the form of detailed process understanding. Chaparral Steel, a minimill, was able to double output from its original electric furnace and caster. Semiconductor companies routinely increase yields on their chip fabrication lines from below 40 percent to above 80 percent during a period of several years. In these cases, the incre-

Reprinted from *Sloan Management Review*, Fall 1994, pp. 61–73, by permission of publisher.

mental capital investments are minimal. The improvements are instead due to multiple changes in the manufacturing process, including different procedures, adjustments of controls, changes in raw material recipes, etc. Why weren't these changes implemented at startup? The reason is that the knowledge about the process and how to run it is incomplete and develops gradually through various kinds of learning.

Many authors have noted that there is a difference between data and information. A few have also noted that there is a difference between information and knowledge.[3] Although not always clear-cut, the distinction among the three in production processes is very important. *Data* are what come directly from sensors, reporting on the measured level of some variable. *Information* is "data that have been organized or given structure—that is, placed in context—and thus endowed with meaning."[4] Information tells the current or past status of some part of the production system. *Knowledge* goes further; it allows the making of predictions, causal associations, or prescriptive decisions about what to do.

For example, consider a stream of measurements of the critical dimension of a series of supposedly identical manufactured parts—raw *data*. If the data are plotted on a control chart, they provide *information* about the status of the production process for those parts. The measurements may have a trend, may be beyond the process control limit, may be out of the allowed tolerance, or may even show no discernible pattern. All of these are *information,* but not knowledge. *Knowledge* about the process might include, "When the control chart looks like that, it usually means machine A needs to be recalibrated" (causal association and prescriptive decision), or "When the control chart is in control for the first hour of a new batch, it usually remains that way for the rest of the shift" (prediction). This paper is about technological knowledge, not data or information.

To explain why some types of knowledge are more complete and useful than others, a colleague and I developed an ordinal scale for describing how much is known about a process. Originally we studied ramp-up of new production in high-tech industries (VLSI fabrication, hard disk drives). Subsequently, we found that the same concepts worked well in traditional industries such as firearms, pulp and paper, and steel cord.[5]

In the next section, I give a detailed scheme for measuring the extent of technological knowledge and several brief examples, ranging from semiconductors to consulting. The third section examines the implications of the level of knowledge for how to manage production processes. The fourth section looks at learning, i.e., the evolution of knowledge over time. In the penultimate section, I use a familiar technology, baking, as an extended illustration. In conclusion, I look at some of the implications for managing technological knowledge itself.

A SCALE FOR MEASURING KNOWLEDGE ABOUT A PROCESS

A company's knowledge about its processes may range from total ignorance about how they work to very formal and accurate mathematical models.[6] For our purposes, a process is defined as *any repetitive system for producing a product or service, including the people, machines, procedures, and software, in that system.* A process has inputs, outputs, and state variables that characterize what is happening inside it. The inputs are often further broken down into raw materials, control variables, and environmental variables (see Figure 10-1). For example, environmental variables include temperature, humidity, air pressure, dust, seismic vibration, electrical power, etc.

Here I define technological knowledge as *understanding the effects of the input variables on the output.* Mathematically, the process output, Y, is an unknown function f of the inputs, x: Y = f(x); x is always a vector (of indeterminate dimension). Then technological knowledge is knowledge about the arguments and behavior of the function f(x).[7] The manager's or process engineer's goal is to manipulate the raw materials, controls, and environment to get output that is as good as possible. It is customary to treat the environmental variables as exogenous and uncontrollable. However, with enough knowledge, the environmental variables can be turned into control variables and, therefore, are not exogenous.

I start by looking at well-defined manufacturing processes such as building a car door or cooking in a fastfood restaurant. Later I will show how knowledge about less tangible processes, such as marketing and legal services, can be described by the same scale. Whatever the process, better technological knowledge gives the operators better ability to manage the process effectively.

I have identified eight stages of technological knowledge, ranging from complete ignorance to complete understanding. Each stage describes the knowledge about a particular input variable x's effect on the process output, Y. Why so many stages? We are used to the idea of a spectrum of knowledge "from art to science," but intuition suggests that only three or four stages should be sufficient to describe the spectrum. Most analyses of production processes, however, look only at things

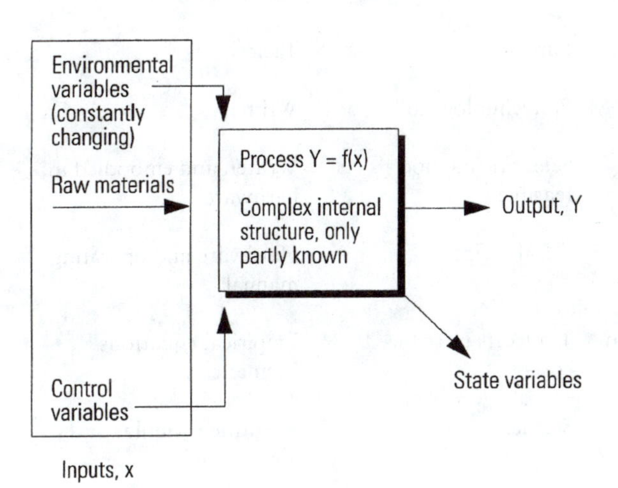

FIGURE 10-1 Diagram of a Process

that are already reasonably well understood. Variables in the first three stages are usually considered exogenous, in that it is impossible to control them. Nonetheless, it is important to recognize their existence since important variables may be at one of those stages, and management of the process needs to take that into account. The stages are summarized in Table 10-1.

In contrast to most approaches for measuring knowledge, the nature of the knowledge changes qualitatively with each stage in this framework. The process of learning from one stage to the next also changes. Each stage is described as follows:

Stage One—Complete ignorance. You do not know that a phenomenon exists, or if you are aware of its existence, you have no inkling that it may be relevant to your process. The history of technology is full of phenomena that were initially not recognized, yet had potentially major effects on a production process (e.g., quantum mechanics, germs in the treatment of wounds, contamination in a number of processes). At stage one, there is nothing you can do with the variable, and its effects on the process appear as random disturbances.

Stage Two—Awareness. You know that the phenomenon exists and that it might be relevant to your process. There is still no way to use the variable in your process, but you can begin to investigate it in order to get to the next stage. Learning from stage one to stage two often occurs by serendipity, by making analogies to seemingly unrelated processes, or by bringing knowledge from outside the organization.

TABLE 10-1 Stages of Knowledge

Stage	*Name*	*Comment*	*Typical Form of Knowledge*
1	Complete ignorance		Nowhere
2	Awareness	Pure art	Tacit
3	Measure	Pretechnological	Written
4	Control of the mean	Scientific method feasible	Written and embodied in hardware
5	Process capability	Local recipe	Hardware and operating manual
6	Process characterization	Tradeoffs to reduce costs	Empirical equations (numerical)
7	Know why	Science	Scientific formulas and algorithms
8	Complete knowledge	Nirvana	

Stage Three—Measure. You can measure the variables accurately, perhaps with some effort. This requires development and installation of specific instrumentation. Stage three variables cannot be controlled. However, if the variable is important enough, you can alter the process in response to the variable in order to exploit or ameliorate its effects. An example of a stage three variable is weather; many outdoor processes are halted or done differently during bad weather.

There are two kinds of learning at stage three. One kind consists of passive, natural experiments to determine the relationship between this variable and the output. A second learning process studies ways of controlling the variable to reach stage four, control. Knowledge about how to control the variable is, in effect, a subprocess with its own inputs and output (the level of the input variable for the main process). For certain variables, knowing how to measure it (stage three) leads almost automatically to knowing how to control it (stage four). These are primarily variables where feedback-based control is feasible, such as furnace temperatures.

Stage Four—Control of the mean. You know how to control the variables accurately across a range of levels, although the control is not necessarily precise. That is, you can control the mean level, but there is some variance around that level. Stage four provides a quantum leap in process control, since, at a minimum, you can now stabilize the process with respect to the mean of that variable. Variables that were previously viewed as exogenous disturbances to the process can now be treated as control variables. Reaching stage four also makes further learning easier, because you can now perform controlled experiments on the variable to quantify its impact on the process.

Stage Five—Process capability (control of the variance). You can control the variables with precision across a range of values. When all of the important variables reach stage five, your process can manufacture products by following a "cookbook," i.e., a consistent recipe. The product still may not meet quality standards, however, so final inspection will be needed.

Learning from stage four to stage five is a matter of learning to control the various disturbances that affect the input variable. This is a nested subproblem that passes through the stages of knowledge on the way to good control of the input variable. That is, producing the correct level of an input, x, is a process in its own right and must be learned. Fortunately, accumulated technological knowledge gives cookbook methods for controlling many variables. The process engineer can look it up in a catalog or handbook. This means that you do not have to "reinvent the wheel" each time; you just have to learn enough to control the variable using known "wheels."

Stage Six—Process characterization (know how). You know how the variable affects the result, when small changes are made in the variable.[8] Now you can begin to fine-tune the process to reduce costs and to change product characteristics. You can also institute some feedback control on the output using any stage six variable that is both easy to change and has a major impact. This increases the quality of the output by reducing its variability. To reach stage six, you run controlled experiments with different levels of the variable to determine its effects.

Stage Seven—Know why. You have a scientific model of the process and how it operates over a broad region, including nonlinear and interaction effects of this variable with other variables. At this stage, you can actually optimize the process with respect to the stage seven variables. Feedback and some feed-forward control are broadly effective. Control can be turned over to microprocessors, which will be able to handle most contingencies. You can even use your knowledge to simulate the process to study settings you have never tried empirically, such as ways of making new products using the same process. Learning from stage six to stage seven involves tapping scientific models, running broad experiments across multiple variables to estimate the models, and finding interactions among input variables.

Stage Eight—Complete knowledge. You know the complete functional form and parameter values that determine the result, Y, as a function of all the inputs. Process and environment are so well understood that you can head off any problems in advance by feed-forward control. Stage eight is never reached in practice because it requires knowing all the interactions among variables. However, it can be approached asymptotically by studying the process in more and more detail.

The stages of knowledge can be applied to diverse tasks and industries:

- High-tech manufacturing requires rapid learning about multiple variables in new products and processes. We can frame a definition in terms of the stage of knowledge: *high-tech processes are those in which many of the important variables are at stage four or below.* This makes the process difficult to control and work with, so a lot of effort goes into raising the knowledge level as quickly as possible. Because of customer and competitive pressures, no sooner is knowledge raised for one product than higher performance products are demanded, which brings in new low-stage variables. Thus managing in high-tech industries requires both rapid learning and the ability to manufacture with "immature" (low stage of knowledge) technologies.
- VLSI semiconductor design and fabrication processes are driven by the ability to reproduce very small features with high reliability at high volume. The process is very complex, with multiple layers and hundreds of variables potentially affecting each layer. As feature sizes get smaller with each new generation, new equipment is needed and new variables become important. These new variables start at low stages of knowledge. For example, as feature sizes go below one micron, heat dissipation problems begin to push designers to engineer chips for three volts instead of five volts. This has a number of advantages but requires many changes in both chip design and fabrication. As these changes are made, the vari-

ables that were at stage six or seven for the old process "regress" to stage five; engineers know how to control them, but don't know their effects on the new process.

- Consumer marketing has made many strides toward higher stages of knowledge in the past thirty years. Many of the breakthroughs have been based on developing effective ways to measure variables (stage three). For example, bar-code scanners at supermarket checkouts have provided masses of disaggregated data about who is buying what, whether they use coupons, etc. Some stores are now using customer ID cards to match this data with information about individual households, their demographics, what TV commercials they received, and other environmental variables to allow development of stage six and seven models of the marketing mix's effects on consumer behavior.[9]
- Professional services such as legal services run the range of knowledge stages. For example, preparing a will has reached stage six or even seven for many people, so that it can be done by a $30 software program. At the other extreme, high-profile criminal trials used to be at stage three or below. Recently, a number of law firms have attempted to move jury selection to stage six, using methods such as customized polling of population groups from which a particular jury will be drawn. Other aspects of trial strategy, presumably, remain at stage three or four; they can be measured but not controlled well. For example, an important type of "input" to litigation is judicial rulings on motions. Lawyers can use the judge's ruling to measure whether the judge agrees with them on a motion, but they have only limited control over that decision (stage four). Pretrial aspects of litigation, on the other hand, are generally better understood.
- In strategic consulting, the Boston Consulting Group's four-quadrant matrix (cash cows, dogs, stars, and question marks) was an attempt to reduce acquisition and divestiture decisions to two quantitative variables—market share and growth rate.[10] It is possible to write equations that describe the effects of market share and growth rate on business unit profit, so these two variables are at stage six. But there are many other important variables that also influence the outcome and that are at much lower stages of knowledge. Many consulting firms claim knowledge about these other variables, but they perform strategic analysis using a heavy mix of expertise, implying an awareness that some of their knowledge is at a low stage.

DYNAMIC EVOLUTION OF KNOWLEDGE AND PERFORMANCE

Important variables are those that, in fact, have great economic implications for the process. Ideally, a company would like to have a high stage of knowledge about all the important variables and a low stage about all the variables that have negligible effects. But, instead, the organization is likely to know very little about some important variables, especially for immature processes. Conversely, it may have stage six knowledge about unimportant variables, such as the color of paint on the machine and the type of clothing workers wear. Of course, in certain processes, these variables may be important, but there may be little way to know this until you learn enough to bring them to a high stage. For example, paint inside a machine may affect process chemistry, paint outside a machine may affect worker morale, and worker clothing can affect contamination-sensitive processes.

One way to visualize overall technological knowledge is as a tree (see Figure 10-2). The trunk of the tree is Y, the process output that we want to control. The branches from the trunk are variables that directly affect Y, (x_1, x_2, ...). Branching off from each of these are subvariables ($x_{1.1}$, $x_{1.2}$, ...) that collectively determine x_1, and so on, to any level of detail. The shading of each branch represents the organization's stage of knowledge, with white (invisible) representing stage one, while black is stage seven. The thickness of the branch represents its importance. Every knowledge tree trails off into a haze of dimly seen but potentially important variables and eventually becomes invisible, because there are always some variables at a still finer level of detail whose existence is unrecognized.

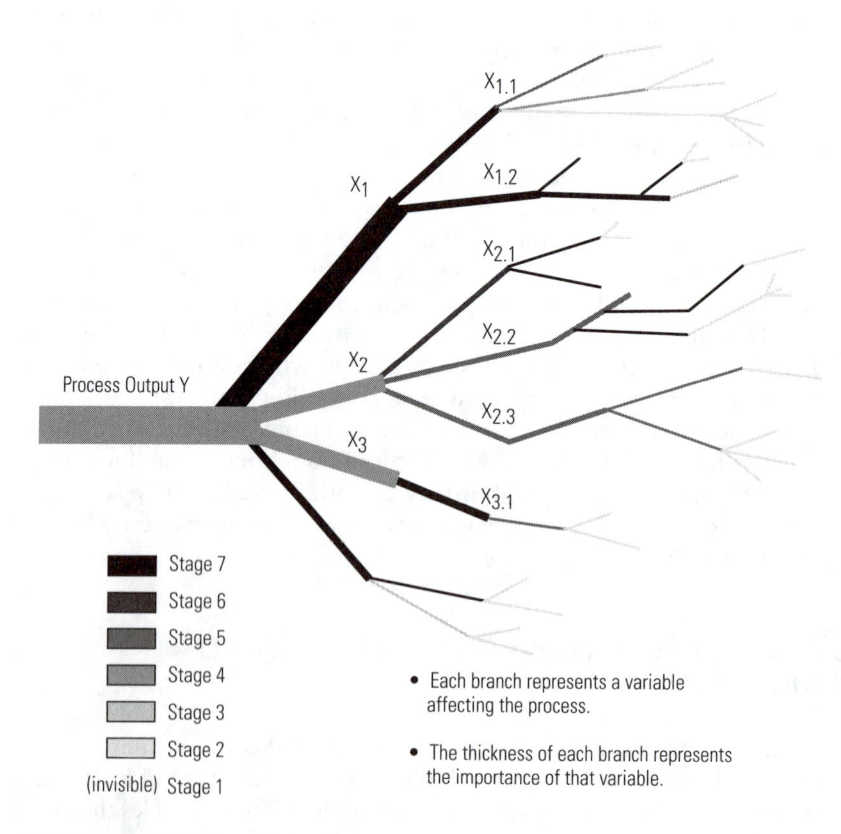

FIGURE 10-2 A Knowledge Tree

As the tree illustrates, a single process has many variables that are inevitably at different stages of knowledge. As more is learned about part of the process, old variables are brought to higher stages, but new variables also emerge from the mists of ignorance. The process as a whole can do no better than the knowledge about its most important drivers. If even a few key variables are at low stages of knowledge, the process can be considered at a low stage of knowledge overall.

RELATIONSHIP TO THEORIES OF ORGANIZATIONAL LEARNING

Experience in conducting a task generally leads to improvement, a concept formalized in the literature on learning curves.[11] Most learning curve models skip the intermediate stages of causality and statistically link cumulative production directly to costs (see Figure 10-3, part A). But it is clear that how the production and learning processes are managed has a big impact on whether and how fast learning occurs.[12] Indeed, the large amount of literature on quality improvement concerns systematic learning methods to achieve more improvement in a shorter period of time. Thus learning can be a directed activity, not just a by-product of normal production. Part B in Figure 10-3 shows a more complete model of technological learning, with explicit recognition of knowledge.[13]

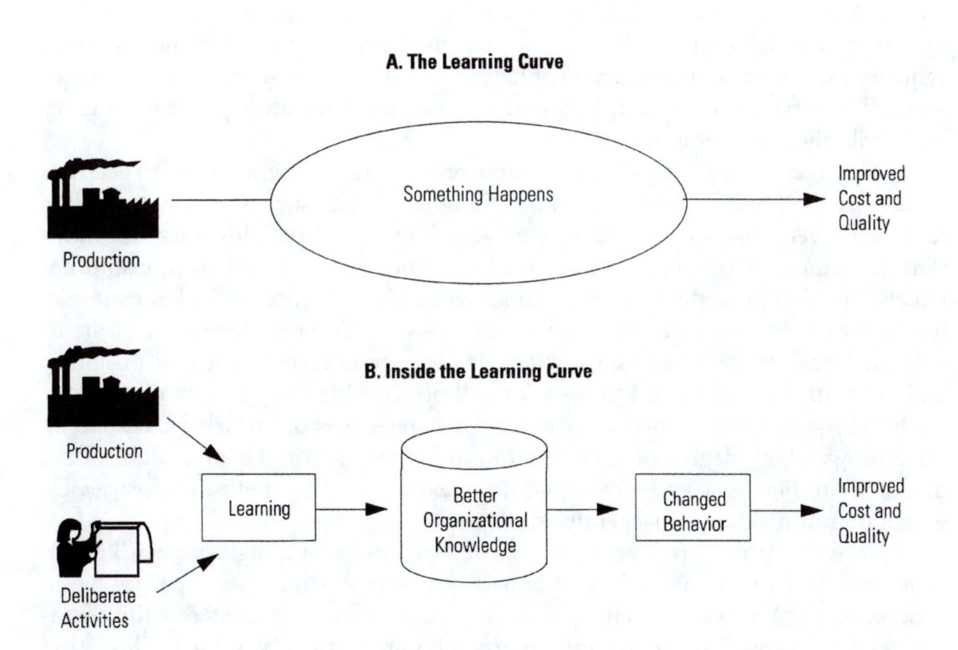

FIGURE 10-3 Learning Curve and Knowledge-Based Views of Organizational Improvement

It is no coincidence that the knowledge tree of Figure 10-2 resembles causal trees like those used in quality improvement efforts.[14] These trees, also called fishbone or Ishikawa diagrams, are often used as a way of listing potential causes of problems. A process engineer may have fifty variables (or corresponding problems) at stages two through four that are potentially important. Various methods can be used to guess which ones will turn out to be the most important.[15] The stages of knowledge provide a way of mapping current knowledge and estimating how hard it will be to go further on particular variables. That is, they provide a detailed scorecard for process improvement efforts.

HOW TO MANAGE AT EACH STAGE OF KNOWLEDGE

The knowledge stage of different process variables is important because it determines how to manage both the knowledge and the production process. The higher the stage of knowledge, the closer the process is to "science," and the more formally it can be managed. Conversely, low-stage processes, such as creative endeavors, do not do well under formal management methods, and should be treated more as "art."

One of the most basic system-design decisions is the degree of procedure. There are different ways of performing a given task, requiring different kinds of people, training, and tools. At one extreme is pure procedure, i.e., a completely specified set of rules about what to do under every possible set of circumstances. At the other extreme is something we can call pure expertise or pure art—a style of action in which every situation is dealt with as if it were new and unique. This requires experienced and skilled people who use their own judgment at each moment. These people have tacit knowledge, meaning that although they can carry on a task, they are not able to explain it.

Managers can attempt to operate a process anywhere along the spectrum from pure expertise to pure procedure. The microprocessor has made it possible to execute very complex procedures at very low cost.[16] But this does not mean that procedural approaches are always best. There is a natural relationship between degree of procedure and stage of knowledge (see Figure 10-4). For example, in order to automate a process, all key variables should be understood at least to stage six, and preferably to stage seven. If they are not, unanticipated problems will crop up frequently, and the system will not be able to deal with them effectively. Those portions of processes that are at low stages of knowledge should be done using a high degree of expertise and little automation. Locations above the diagonal in Figure 10-4 correspond to inexpensive but ineffective processes, which do not produce consistently good output.

Conversely, if a process or portion of a process is at a high stage of knowledge, it is inefficient to use lots of expertise to carry it out. An expertise-based process may still work (although people lose attentiveness in purely repetitive situations), but you will pay extra for experts who are not really needed. This is the area below the diagonal in Figure 10-4.

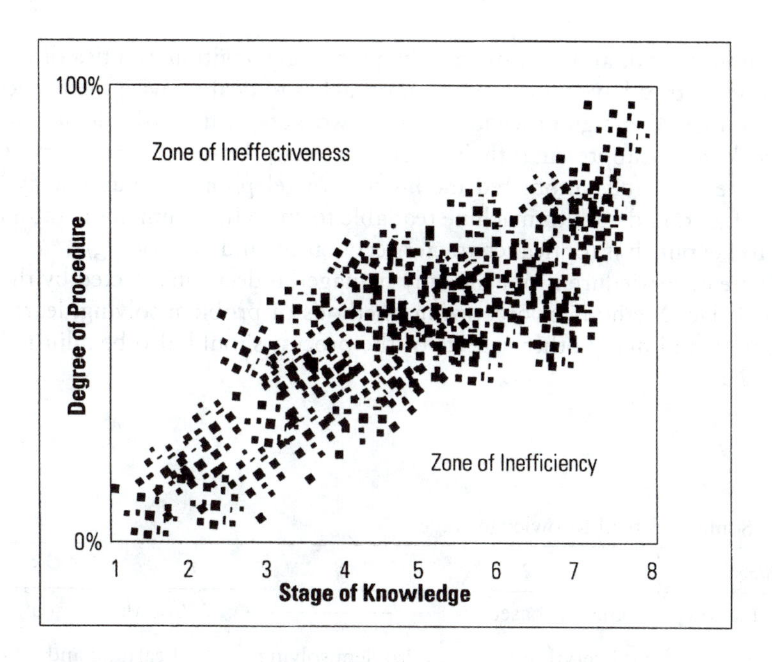

Source: R.E. Bohn and R. Jaikumar, "The Development of Intelligent Systems for Industrial Use: An Empirical Investigation," in *Research on Technological Innovation, Management and Policy*, ed. R. Rosenbloom (London and Greenwich, Connecticut: JAI Press, 1986), pp. 213-262.

FIGURE 10-4 Ideal Operating Method and the Stage of Knowledge

Why do companies find themselves off the diagonal of Figure 10-4? A common reason during the early 1980s was hubris: overoptimism about the firm's knowledge of production processes and its associated ability to build, debug, and operate new factories. This led to numerous attempts to solve manufacturing competitiveness problems by automation, as exemplified by the slogan "automate, emigrate, or evaporate." When automation was undertaken without a solid base of process knowledge, the results were counterproductive: "The automation of a large, complex, poorly understood, conventional manufacturing process leads to a large, complex, poorly understood, unreliable, expensive, and automated manufacturing process."[17] Perhaps one of the most conspicuous and expensive examples of this syndrome was General Motors, which, in the early 1980s, invested approximately $40 billion to build a number of automated auto assembly plants, many of which never worked properly.

At the other, perhaps less common extreme are companies that use expensive labor to perform repetitive tasks, leading to inefficiency. Examples include information-based services such as manual letter sorting (e.g., the U.S. Postal Service) and routine telephone services (directory assistance). Although human judgment is very useful in these processes for handling exceptions, the bulk of the work is routine, well understood, and uses mainly the pattern recognition abilities of the human brain. Industries have taken several approaches to dealing with the resulting inefficiency, including high proceduralizing of workers, which risks dehumanizing the work and suppressing their expertise (e.g., United Parcel Service industrial engineering and automated monitoring of telephone operators), and finding ways of getting data into machine readable form so that human operators do not have to keypunch it (optical character recognition and bar coding).

The degree of procedure is not the only managerial decision affected by the stage of knowledge. Methods of organizing, methods of problem solving, learning, and training, and many other aspects of the process should also be adjusted (see Table 10-2).

TABLE 10-2 Some Effects of Knowledge Stages

Knowledge at Stage . . .	*1 2*	*3 4 5*	*6 7 8*
Nature of production	Expertise based	———————	Procedure based
Role of workers	Everything	Problem solving	Learning and improving
Location of knowledge	Workers' heads	Written and oral	In databases or in software
Nature of learning	Artistic	Natural experiments	Controlled experiments, simulations
Nature of problem solving	Trial and error	Scientific method	Table look-up
Method of training new workers	Apprenticeship, coaching	———————	Classroom
Natural type of organization	Organic	Mechanistic	Learning oriented
Suitability for automation	None	———————	High
Ease of transfer to another site	Low	———————	High
Feasible product variety	High	Low	High*
Quality control approach	Sorting	Statistical process control	Feed forward

*R. Jaikumar,, "From Filing and Fitting to Flexible Manufacturing: A Study in the Evolution of Process Control" (Boston: Harvard Business School, working paper, 1988).

Yet, as shown in Figure 10-2, most processes have important variables at widely differing stages of knowledge. The ideal management style for the process as a whole is an uncomfortable hybrid. The traditional approach to this issue was to segregate work into different functional departments, which are then managed according to their own needs. A common example of this in traditional manufacturing companies is R&D (low stages) versus manufacturing functions (high stages, or so it was believed). This Taylorist approach has broken down in modern manufacturing, especially for technologies that are evolving rapidly, because the less mature portions of the process are inevitably at low stages of knowledge.[18]

There are at least two other approaches to this paradox. One is to use microprocessors (or other automation) to execute procedures, but with human oversight to select the appropriate program and to recognize unprogrammed contingencies and take control. Examples include accounting, continuous manufacturing processes such as paper mills, and commercial aviation. A final approach is to use low-skilled workers to execute the better understood tasks, with experts monitoring and directing them. The low-skilled workers may be apprentices to the experts or on a separate career track. For example, law offices use both junior associates (apprentices) and paralegals.

All three approaches have weaknesses. For example, it is difficult for pilots to monitor autopilots reliably during long flights without taking an active role themselves, yet respond quickly and appropriately in emergencies.[19] If lower skilled workers perform the better understood and therefore more procedural tasks, this can lead to excessive division of labor, poor coordination, and lost opportunities for learning. In addition, cultural conflict is a common result when an organization is split into sections operating at different stages of knowledge. Thus there is no ideal solution to the problem of working at multiple stages of knowledge, or if there is one, we don't yet know it. Nonetheless, this situation is increasingly common.

A SIMPLE EXAMPLE OF KNOWLEDGE PROGRESSION OVER TIME

Knowledge increases through learning. Much learning is simply increasing the precision and accuracy of parameter estimates within a single stage, but sometimes learning shifts the knowledge to the next stage. To illustrate, using familiar technology, suppose you are baking cookies for the first time. You hope to make chocolate chip cookies, but have only a vague idea of a good recipe (raw materials) and procedure (control variables). You have a standard oven, which you were told to set at 350 degrees.[20]

The first step is to define your output measure, Y. It consists of a combination of taste, texture (hard or soft), and appearance.

Stage One—Complete Ignorance. You don't even know what influences cookie characteristics, so when the results change, you consider it "random."

Stage Two—Awareness. You rack your memory, observe others in the kitchen, and begin to build a list of possibly relevant input variables, including the list of ingredients, baking time, outdoor weather (rainy, cloudy, clear), time of day, amount and brand name of each ingredient, and a vaguely defined "mixing procedure."

Stage Three—Learning to *measure* key variables. You use your watch to measure cooking time, measuring cups to measure raw materials, an outdoor thermometer and hygrometer for the weather, and a clock for the time of day. You have no detailed metric for mixing procedure, so you throw everything into one bowl and count strokes of the mixing spoon.

Stage Four—Control of the mean. You get a count-down timer and develop a procedure to take the cookies out of the oven after a set amount of time. You can control outdoor weather only crudely, by baking on days when the weather is of a particular type. You decide not to bother controlling for time of day since it does not seem to make any difference. Control of the ingredients is straightforward, using a standard measuring cup; that is, for the raw materials, stage three leads immediately to stage four.

Stage Five—Process capability and a recipe. You practice measuring ingredients until you can do it with 95 percent repeatability. You write down a set of instructions (recipe) that seems to produce "adequate" cookies. Your cookies now have a reasonably consistent taste, but texture and appearance are still variable and some cookies are burned.

Stage Six—Process characterization. You run a series of experiments on many variables, including baking time, baking temperature, mixing time, and the exact amounts of flour, sugar, and liquid ingredients. You discover the effects of a 10 percent change in each of these variables on the cookie characteristics. If a friend asks for a better baked cookie, you can now achieve it by varying either the time or the temperature. You discover that some variables, including weather and time of day, have no detectable effect on the output.

Stage Seven—Know why, including interactions among input variables. You go to the local university library and take out textbooks on baking, which give mathematical formulas for outcome variables such as sweetness and surface texture. You calibrate those models using data from your own baking process. You can now produce a "near perfect" chocolate chip cookie. If someone asks for a healthier cookie (less sugar), you can produce it, and you know how much to adjust the baking temperature. Similarly, if you are in a hurry, you know how to increase the temperature and decrease the baking time without burning the cookies.

Repeat for secondary variables. Although you now have stage five control (a recipe) for about ten variables and a stage seven understanding (know why) of five of them, there will always be a host of secondary variables in your knowledge tree that have smaller effects. And there is no guarantee that you will learn about the most important variables first. For example, you may not realize that cookie size is important (stage two) until you are well into stage five for other variables. You can subject these additional variables to the same progression through the stages of knowledge. Variables include the brand and characteristics of raw materials (butter versus margarine versus inexpensive margarine, types of flour), the importance of sifting dry ingredients together before mixing, type of baking tray (aluminum versus glass versus iron), and use of a scale instead of measuring cups for more accurate measurement of raw materials. For casual baking, you would never bother to learn about some of these variables, but if you wanted to reduce costs or improve consistency, you would have to delve much deeper into these secondary variables.

Stage Eight—Complete knowledge. Since there is an infinitude of potential secondary variables, you can never have complete knowledge of the cookie-making process.[21] But for practical purposes, you can say that you have reached stage eight when you have a model that will predict output (cookie) characteristics to an accuracy of one-tenth of the tolerance band, for changes in inputs across a 2:1 range, and including all interactions.

Amateurs may stop when they have stage five knowledge about the primary variables that affect taste. They can then bake decent cookies and throw away batches ruined by low knowledge about secondary variables. But professional bakeries must track down additional secondary variables, especially those that influence costs. Here is a description of the situation at one famous baking company:

> *Since early this decade, Nabisco has been worried about its bakery technology, which, according to a 1981 study, had fallen far behind that of even some tiny rivals. . . . The biscuit company, to this day, uses a lot of equipment made decades ago at Nabisco's former Evanston, Illinois, machine shop.*
>
> *And to this day, baking at Nabisco remains something of an art. Oreos have uneven swaths of cream filling. The exact number of Ritz crackers in a box is anybody's guess. Some 5 percent to 7 percent of Nabisco's cookies and crackers emerge from its ovens broken.*
>
> *Similarly, the company still has poor inspection methods for the tons of commodities it purchases, such as flour and cocoa, according to a former executive of the baking unit. The bakers must repeatedly test-bake batches of cookies and crackers to adjust ovens and other gear to slight variations in commodity composition.* [In our terms, they had stage four knowledge of raw materials and were attempting to compensate for it by using stage six knowledge about how to adjust the ovens.] *Such trial-and-error methods make quality control, among other things, difficult.*
>
> *So, sixteen months ago, . . . the company planned to spend some $1.6 billion on complete retrofitting of four existing bakeries and close five other plants.*

> *The plan called for a microchip revolution in Nabisco's bakeries. At least one-third of the project's cost was to be for the purchase of computerized weighing, mixing, packaging, and process-control equipment, says a senior Nabisco manufacturing engineer who recently resigned.*
>
> *Such high-tech gear would eventually halve the company's 8 percent "give-away" rate—the overweight amount in an average package of Nabisco biscuits—and sharply reduce its 5 percent to 7 percent breakage.*[22]

Nabisco's automation will be most effective with stage seven knowledge (know why) about all of the key variables. It is possible that Nabisco's equipment vendors sell machines that already embody that knowledge, but it is likely that some of it (including the specific variables uniquely affecting Nabisco's cookies) would have to be developed as part of the automation program.

APPLYING THE STAGES OF KNOWLEDGE

Now that we have a framework for measuring and understanding technological knowledge, we can look at some principles for managing knowledge to improve production processes.

Understand How Much You Know and Don't Know

In order to understand how much you already know about a process, you need to ask a number of questions:

- What are the important variables for the process?
- At what stages are these variables? Which variables in the process would give the most leverage if you could get them to a higher stage?
- How can you manage the process well at these stages of knowledge? What limits and opportunities does the process impose? Are your management methods consistent with knowledge levels (Figure 10-4 and Table 10-2)? How should you handle the inevitable variables that you know less about yet are still important?
- How can you learn to reach higher stages of knowledge?

You also need to beware of what you think you know about a process that you really don't. One of the most painful forms of ignorance is false knowledge. If your company believes that it has stage six or higher knowledge about a variable, but in fact that knowledge is based on past experience and is incorrect for the present process, you will operate the process in an inferior way. A common version of this is the belief that "variable x does not matter." It may not have mattered ten years ago because of a small contribution to process variance. But what was considered small ten years ago may be quite important today. A newer competitor, unburdened with this false knowledge, can control or change the level of x to get superior quality or lower cost.

The countermeasure for this problem is to realize that as your company's process changes, its effective knowledge regresses to earlier stages. In particular, stage six knowledge, which is generally derived by empirical observation, often regresses to stage five for a new process. You still know how to measure and control the variable, but you no longer know its true impact.

Understand and Manage the Locations of Knowledge

Knowing where knowledge resides for the process you are managing is important for effectively managing and using that knowledge. It has implications for accessibility, transmission to new locations, and ability to extend the knowledge, among other things. Technological knowledge may be located in people's heads, word of mouth, or other informal mechanisms; in formal procedure sheets for operators, handbooks, other written documentation; or embodied in machinery, firmware, and software. How well is it documented? How easy is it to change? How much do users know about how to use its features?

As I have discussed, the feasible and desirable locations of knowledge depend on its stage. There are also broader issues surrounding more general forms of organizational memory.[23]

Be Wary of Deskilling the Workforce and Freezing Processes

The Taylorist model of manufacturing, as it is commonly applied, moves technological knowledge about the process away from line workers and puts it in the heads of staff engineers. These engineers will be less available when problems come up, or they may leave the company. If workers do not understand the process, they cannot handle unanticipated situations, nor can they do much to improve the process, even if they are motivated. Therefore, one of the revolutionary effects of the total quality management movement has been to return knowledge to the workers and make them capable of doing process improvement in small groups, without relying on the traditional staff experts.

Even if you fully understand a process today, the world will change in a few years. Some of your current knowledge will be obsolete, and it will be important to reevaluate it. Once a firm assumes, for whatever reason, that it has nothing more to learn about a production process, it tends to "lock in" the present production methods by specifying rigid procedures that can deskill the workforce and cut back on product and process engineering. A firm may use time and motion studies to find the "one best way" to produce and lose interest in root cause analysis.[24] While this may work well in the short run, five years from now the company may find competitors making superior products at two-thirds its cost.

For example, Jaikumar compared the development and use of flexible manufacturing systems (FMS) in the United States and in Japan.[25] He found that the U.S. systems had been developed with overly ambitious goals for flexibility, up-time, labor use, etc. These goals were not achieved by the initial designs; the knowledge base was not adequate to make them possible. Yet the projects were often declared complete, and workers with much lower skills were brought in to run the FMS. The result was that the users were afraid to experiment and learn about the systems, and the systems were in fact used in a very inflexible way. In contrast, in the successful Japanese systems, the original developers stayed with the system for the first year or more of operation, and continued to improve it during that time. The result was systems that were very flexible and robust enough to run unattended.

Learn Carefully and Systematically

As we have seen, different stages of knowledge require very different methods of learning. For example, Chew and others recommend sequential use of four different methods of learning about problems that occur during the installation of new technology:

- Vicarious learning—learning from other organizations with similar situations.
- Simulation—building a model of your process and experimenting with the model.
- Prototyping—taking a subset of your process and using it for testing and refining.
- On-line learning—experimenting systematically on the full process.[26]

Many organizations become proficient at only one or a few methods of learning, which makes it difficult for them to deal with variables that are at different stages of knowledge.[27] For example, many plants avoid the use of pilot lines and simulators to pretest process changes.

CONCLUSION

Lord Kelvin, in the 1890s, commented on the value of knowledge:

> *When you can measure what you are speaking about, and express it in numbers, you know something about it; but when you cannot measure it, when you cannot express it in numbers, your knowledge is of a meager and unsatisfactory kind: it may be the beginning of knowledge, but you have scarcely, in your thoughts, advanced to the stage of science.*

In terms of my framework, Kelvin was advocating the value of stage three knowledge (measure) over stage two knowledge (awareness). As I have shown, being able to measure is only the beginning; the stages of knowledge beyond stage three (control, capability, characterization, and know why) give additional power and economic value to a company's processes. The stages-of-knowledge framework provides powerful leverage to efforts to improve processes and conveys information about how to manage. A company can make explicit decisions about which portions of the knowledge tree to pursue most vigorously.

For example, a high-volume, forty-year-old, continuous process was controlled using incremental extensions of the original sensors. These operated on a time scale from seconds to hours. A consultant recognized that the company did not have knowledge of the variables at time scales below a second. Once it learned how to measure events in the millisecond range, a large new subtree of variables became visible. By learning about these variables and their implications for the process, the process engineers were able to reduce quality problems by a factor of three within a few months. Development and exploitation of the new variables continues today.

NOTES

1. I. Nonaka, "The Knowledge-Creating Company," *Harvard Business Review,* November-December 1991, pp. 96–104.
2. Peter Drucker has commented, "In fact, knowledge is the only meaningful resource today. The traditional 'factors of production' have not disappeared, but they have become secondary." See P.F. Drucker, *Post-Capitalist Society* (New York: Harper Business, 1993), p. 42.
3. Harlan Cleveland distinguishes data, information, knowledge, and wisdom. However, he then intermixes the four concepts. See: H. Cleveland, "The Knowledge Dynamic," *The Knowledge Executive* (New York: Human Valley Books, 1985).
4. R. Glazer, "Marketing in an Information-Intensive Environment: Strategic Implications of Knowledge as an Asset," *Journal of Marketing* 55 (1991): 1–19.
5. R. Jaikumar, "From Filing and Fitting to Flexible Manufacturing: A Study in the Evolution of Process Control" (Boston: Harvard Business School, working paper, 1988); and A.S. Mukherjee, "The Effective Management of Organizational Learning and Process Control" (Boston: Harvard Business School, doctoral dissertation, 1992).
6. R.E. Bohn and R. Jaikumar, "The Structure of Technological Knowledge in Manufacturing" (Boston: Harvard Business School, working paper 93–035, 1992); and R.E. Bohn and R. Jaikumar, "The Development of Intelligent Systems for Industrial Use: An Empirical Investigation," in *Research on Technological Innovation, Management and Policy,* ed. R.S. Rosenbloom (London and Greenwich, Connecticut: JAI Press, 1986), pp. 213–262.
7. This formalism is pursued in Bohn and Jaikumar (1992).
8. $\partial f/\partial x_i$ in a local region.

9. Glazer (1991); and N.R. Kleinfield, "Targeting the Grocery Shopper," *New York Times,* 26 May 1991.
10. J.A. Seeger, "Reversing the Images of BCG's Growth/Share Matrix," *Strategic Management Journal* 5 (1984): 93–97.
11. J. Dutton and A. Thomas, "Treating Progress Functions as a Managerial Opportunity," *Academy of Management Review* 9 (1984): 235–247.
12. P.S. Adler and K.B. Clark, "Behind the Learning Curve: A Sketch of the Learning Process," *Management Science* 37 (1991): 267–281.
13. R. Jaikumar and R.E. Bohn, "A Dynamic Approach to Operations Management: An Alternative to Static Optimization," *International Journal of Production Economics* 27 (1992): 265–282.
14. J.M. Juran and F.M. Gryna, eds., *Juran's Quality Control Handbook* (New York: McGraw-Hill, 1988), Chapter 22.
15. These methods include Pareto charts, use of analogies to similar but better understood processes, screening experiments, and other methods discussed in the quality control literature. Notice that screening experiments are possible only if the variable is already at stage four or higher.
16. G.V. Shirley and R. Jaikumar, "Turing Machines and Gutenberg Technologies: The Post-Industrial Marriage," *ASME Manufacturing Review* 1 (1988): 36–43.
17. J. Flanagan, "GM Saga a Lesson four America," *Los Angeles Times,* 27 October 1992, p. A1.
18. Bohn and Jaikumar (1992).
19. K.E. Weick, "Organizational Culture as a Source of High Reliability," *California Management Review,* Winter 1987, pp. 112–127.
20. Experienced bakers will realize that the following account is highly simplified. A case simulation of some of the following issues is provided in: R.E. Bohn, "Kristen's Cookie Company (B)" (Boston: Harvard Business School, Case 9-686-015, 1986).
21. For example, eggs, flour, and chocolate are relatively complex agricultural products, of imperfect consistency over time.
22. P. Waldman, "Change of Pace: New RJR Chief Faces a Daunting Challenge at Debt-Heavy Firm," *Wall Street Journal,* 14 March 1989.
23. J.P. Walsh and G.R. Ungson, "Organizational Memory," *Academy of Management Review* 16 (1991): 57–91.
24. Bohn and Jaikumar (1992).
25. R. Jaikumar, "Postindustrial Manufacturing," *Harvard Business Review,* November-December 1986, pp. 69–76.
26. W.B. Chew, D. Leonard-Barton, and R.E. Bohn, "Beating Murphy's Law," *Sloan Management Review,* Spring 1991, pp. 5–16.
27. Learning is obviously of central importance in knowledge-based competition, but detailed analysis is beyond the scope of this paper. A very interesting study of how machine developers become aware of new variables (stage two) through field use is provided by: E. von Hippel and M. Tyre, "How Learning by Doing Is Done: Problem Identification in Novel Process Equipment," *Research Policy.* forthcoming.

   For a description of how one company manages learning as an integral part of the manufacturing process, see:

D. Leonard-Barton, "The Factory as a Learning Laboratory," *Sloan Management Review,* Fall 1992, pp. 23–38.
For a discussion of the characteristics of organizations that learn successfully, see:
D.A. Garvin, "Building a Learning Organization," *Harvard Business Review,* July–August 1993, pp. 78–91.
For a general typology of methods of technological learning, see:
R.E. Bohn, "Learning by Experimentation in Manufacturing" (Boston: Harvard Business School, working paper 88-001, 1987).

Part Four

Learning Organizations in the Global Knowledge-Based Economy

11

The Coming of Knowledge-Based Business

Stan Davis and Jim Botkin

The next wave of economic growth is going to come from knowledge-based businesses. What will those businesses and their products look like?

A tire that notifies the driver of its air pressure and a garment that heats or cools in response to temperature changes are early versions of knowledge-based, or "smart," products already on the market. Diapers that change color when wet and tennis rackets that glow where they strike the ball would be smart versions of other common products.

These products are smart because they filter and interpret information to enable the user to act more effectively. Smart products, created by knowledge-based businesses, can be identified by a variety of characteristics: they are interactive, they become smarter the more you use them, and they can be customized. We will discuss these and other characteristics, but we are sure that many more will become apparent as the knowledge era generates more such products.

Consumers become learners when they use smart products, which both oblige and help them to learn. Businesses will move toward making their offerings smarter because they will profit from doing so. When their customers use those products, they will be engaging in an educational process.

Seeing customers as learners requires a major change in thinking. But over the next two decades, businesses will come to think of their customers as learners and of themselves as educators. They will promote the learning experience for profit, and their customers will profit from that experience.

In the years ahead, people's use of knowledge-based products both as consumers and on the job will be critical to their economic success. The value of a business will be similarly determined: businesses that are based on providing information to customers will do better than those that are not, and businesses that know how to convert information into knowledge will be the most successful.

FROM DATA TO INFORMATION TO KNOWLEDGE

Changing technology is driving the next wave of economic growth. To take advantage of that growth, we will have to apply not only new technology but also new thinking. First and foremost will be our ability to understand the shift in the economy from data to information to knowledge.

Data are the basic building blocks of the information economy and of a knowledge-based business. Or, as Robert Lucky, a former director of AT&T Bell Laboratories, says, they are the "unorganized sludge" of the information age. In the early years of this economy, we focused on data that came to us in four particular forms: numbers, words, sounds, and images. What we did with those data—how we processed, stored, or otherwise manipulated them—determined their value.

Information is data that have been arranged into meaningful patterns. Numbers are data; a random number table is information. Similarly, sounds (converted into notes) are data that can be arranged in an infinite number of systems to produce the information we call music. Whether a piece of music becomes the stuff of *knowledge*—whether, that is, it enables those who hear it to learn—depends not only on the composition but also on the skill and purpose of the performer. For a beginning pianist, a halting rendition of a waltz can be a learning experience. The same waltz performed by a virtuoso can be a source of knowledge for his or her audience.

The importance of data as an economic factor first became apparent in the 1950s and 1960s, when room-sized computers made it possible to collect, sort, and store vast amounts of data, which then had to be programmed by users to produce information. With the advent of electronic computers, including the microprocessor and standard software, that process became more sophisticated and more useful, to the point where the information a business produced often became more valuable than the business itself. Computer-generated airline guides and reservation systems such as American Airlines' SABRE are well-known examples of information that often is more profitable than the businesses it was created to serve.

Yield management is another example of how information can enhance or even transform a business. In the airline industry, yield management allows carriers to maximize revenue on a fixed asset by varying prices—which is why there can be 20 different prices for the coach seats on a single flight. In agriculture, yield management can provide benefits for the farmer—and it created a new business for tractor manufacturer Massey Ferguson.

Farmers used to guesstimate the average yield of an entire field, but with Massey Ferguson's yield mapping system they can practice small-scale farming on a large scale and maximize the yield of each square yard in every field. The system links the farmer's tractor to a satellite-based Global Positioning System, which records the latitude, longitude, and yield of every square yard. The traditional harvesting operation does not have to change in any way. The data are automatically sent to the farmer's desktop computer, which generates yield maps showing where variations are above or below target. Armed with this specific information, the farmer can investigate selected areas and pinpoint the reasons for the variations (soil compaction or nutrient imbalance, for example), quantify them in financial terms, and find out if it is economical to implement remedies. Soil sampling, for example, can be much more selective than it is using traditional random methods. Today this knowledge-based system is being used to provide a competitive edge. In the future, it may be worth more than Massey Ferguson's primary business.

As these examples suggest, businesses that generate information often begin as adjuncts to the "real" work of the company, and the information seems nothing more than a by-product of the core business. Over time, however, the importance of the information increases, until the value added by its content outweighs the value of the original business itself.

Now the process of change is about to take place again. As an economy, we are on the cusp of the transition from information to knowledge, with *knowledge* meaning the application and productive use of information.

An intuitive way to appreciate the difference between information and knowledge is to substitute the word data every time you see or hear the word *information.* Chances are it won't feel right. A chief information officer, for example, has a very different role and set of responsibilities than a data processor has. Data today are commodities, neither as powerful nor as valuable as the information derived from them. Within a decade, we will feel the same kind of resistance if we try to substitute *information* for *knowledge,* because knowledge will have superseded information just as information has now superseded data.

The shift from a data to an information economy involved two sequential developments, one technological and the other behavioral. AMR Corporation (the holding company of American Airlines) used its technological expertise to diversify into myriad information activities ranging from handling medical and insurance claims for the Travelers Corporation and Blue Cross Blue Shield to managing the Warsaw airport for the Polish government. Only after technology had led the company into new lines of business did the people involved realize that those businesses would call for different ways of managing and organizing.

The shift from information to knowledge, however, is giving rise to a different phenomenon: awareness of the value of knowledge is exceeding the ability of many businesses to extract it from the goods and services in which it is embedded. How can businesses, for example, extract the knowledge value from a pair of socks, a home mortgage, an electric bill, or a foreign exchange credit? Those that can figure it out will derive as much power and profit as data and information brought in their turn. But to do so, they will have to understand the basic elements of knowledge-based business.

SIX ELEMENTS OF KNOWLEDGE-BASED BUSINESS

We have identified six characteristics of knowledge-based business. Although they are interrelated, not all of them are necessarily present in any one smart product or service. Nevertheless, they provide guidelines on how a mature business can become a knowledge-based business by upgrading its offerings in a way that puts information to productive use.

1. The more you use knowledge-based offerings, the smarter they get. The Ritz-Carlton hotel chain is installing a knowledge-based system that tracks customers' preferences and needs and automatically transmits the information worldwide. If a customer in Boston asks for six hypoallergenic pillows, for example, she will find them in her room the next time she checks in to a Ritz-Carlton, whether it is in Boston or Hawaii or Hong Kong. Thus the system has learned more about the customer and can put the new information to productive use. Similarly, credit-card transactions are sources of data, and each customer's monthly bills are information; but when Citibank Aadvantage calls up to inquire about unusual activity on your account, it's putting what it has learned about you to work for both you and the card provider. The system has gotten so smart that it can recognize buying patterns that are out of character for a particular cardholder and may be a sign of fraud.

2. The more you use knowledge-based offerings, the smarter *you* get. Some knowledge-based goods and services not only get smarter themselves but also enable their users to learn. Consider CAMS, General Motors' Computer Aided Maintenance System. Designed as a tutor to help novice mechanics diagnose and repair cars, it has evolved into an even more sophisticated system that allows expert mechanics to refine their skills. Now every mechanic can benefit from the combined expertise of all the mechanics on the system.

As recently as 1965, a mechanic who had absorbed 500 pages of repair manuals could fix just about any car on the road. Today that same mechanic would need to have read nearly 500,000 pages of manuals, equivalent to some 300 Manhattan telephone books. Access to CAMS makes mechanics smarter without manuals. While one could claim that the increased knowledge resides in the system and not in any particular person, the fact is that many mechanics are smarter because they now have the experience of all the other mechanics. The system itself continually improves because it is always learning new techniques from the best mechanics. The result, of course, is better service for the customer.

3. Knowledge-based products and services adjust to changing circumstances. A fixed offering is simply not as valuable as one that assesses new situations and modifies itself accordingly. We have long been accustomed to refrigerators that "know" when to defrost. The simple home thermostat that senses a room's temperature and then calls for heating or cooling is another pre-computer-age smart product. When knowledge is built into a tangible product, it might even be built in at the atomic or molecular level, as in chemicals that are engineered to biodegrade when they reach a noxious or dangerous stage. Phase-change materials, or micro-PCMs, are more recent developments that are also independent of computers yet have the ability to adjust. When the cloth of a micro-PCM ski jacket senses cold, it turns warm. The same micro-PCMs can be embedded in car seats, curtains, insulation materials, and wallpaper.

Another new material that adjusts to changing conditions is designed to be applied to glass windows. Cloud Gel, developed by Suntek in Albuquerque, New Mexico, can reflect—or transmit—90% of the sun's rays depending on the temperature or the intensity of the sun. When it's 68 degrees Fahrenheit, for example, a treated window or skylight will let in more warmth, but when it's 71 it will start to bounce radiant heat back into the atmosphere. Each year, some 6 billion square feet of new glass are installed worldwide. If all that glass were coated with this substance, Suntek claims, energy consumption would drop by 17% and more than 1 billion tons of air pollution would be eliminated.

Today, computer chips are routinely built into products, such as the chip in an oven that buzzes when the turkey is done and turns off the heat if the cook doesn't. Other smart products and services tell you how to act. For example, automobile tires tend to lose air, reducing performance and gobbling gas. Goodyear has developed a "smart tire," which contains a microchip that collects and analyzes data about air pressure. Eventually it may be able to flash a message to the dashboard that says, "Low Tire Pressure—Time for a Pit Stop." The first part of the message conveys information; the second, the knowledge component, will tell you what to do. It will be up to you to make the wise move.

4. Knowledge-based businesses can customize their offerings. Knowledge-based products and services can determine customers' changing patterns, idiosyncrasies, and specific needs. For example, the telephone companies are working intensively to produce phones with knowledge-based features. Your telephone credit card will soon know which language you want to use when you call a long-distance operator. It will also allow you to create your own distinctive ring so that your best friend knows it's you calling. This new smart service can also recognize your most frequently called numbers not just by number but also by name, so when you pick up the phone and say, "Call my travel agent," the system will know who that is. Voiceprint recognition will soon be a major step in customizing many products and services such as telephone credit cards and may even replace the card itself.

5. Knowledge-based products and services have relatively short life cycles. Patent protections on intellectual property are still not nearly as developed as they are on "hard" technologies, so the half-life of proprietary information is short. Consider the foreign exchange advisory services offered by commercial and investment banks. This knowledge is highly specialized, and the products are often customized for corporate clients. Because those products depend on the existence of certain market conditions, their viability is short-lived. Yet because information about the markets is widely disseminated, proprietary products can be copied quickly by competitors. Therefore, to maintain their profits—and their proprietary edge—the banks must constantly upgrade their products. The managerial challenge for those running foreign exchange advisory services is getting their professionals in New York, London, and Tokyo to cooperate so that they can develop the next generation of offerings faster than their competitors can.

6. Knowledge-based businesses enable customers to act in real time. Information becomes more valuable when it can be acted on instantly. AAA Triptiks and TourBooks have long given drivers information about highways, hotels, and hot spots. Automakers are preparing to deliver such information into vehicles electronically, in real time. Not only will drivers be provided with routing services, but the information will also be continually updated with traffic reports displayed on a dashboard screen. It will be up to the driver, of course, to apply the information wisely by taking a suggested detour, waiting out a traffic jam, or stopping at the "best" place for dinner. If the service can be made interactive so that it responds to a motorist's questions, its value will be even greater.

Knowledge-based products can also act in real time. This is what happens when the Otis service agent shows up to fix elevator 8 in a skyscraper and the building manager says nothing is wrong with it: "Yes, but there's going to be," says the service agent, who has just received a call from the elevator, "and I'm here to prevent that." Xerox also provides preventive maintenance for some of its large machines with a built-in modem and a telephone that automatically calls for field service.

KNOWLEDGEBURGERS AND OTHER SMART PRODUCTS

Any product or service has the potential to become knowledge based. How, for example, could you turn a hamburger business into a knowledge-based business? Start with some basic hamburger data, including its ingredients and its benefits, such as nutrition, convenience, low price, and tastiness. When the company puts those data into a meaningful pattern, it knows both the menu and the target market. In short, it knows what business it is in.

If this business is truly to become a knowledge-based business, however, in addition to serving tasty, inexpensive food, it must give customers a way to use the nutritional information. Perhaps the calorie and fat content could be calculated and printed out alongside the items on the bill—or even presented before the order is placed—so that customers could make more informed judgments about their meals. One result might be market pressure for more nutritious offerings—in other words, the beginning of a business transformation.

Selecting television programs, to use another example, will likely become a knowledge-based experience, incorporating several of the characteristics we described above. With more than 100 channels to choose from, and 500 to 1,500 on the way, viewers will have to be able to filter and select more effectively than present systems allow. Flipping channels is simply selecting among data. When these choices are organized into lists, whether in a printed version like *TV Guide* or in electronic form on a special channel, they become an information-based product.

If an electronic program guide were interactive, however, with the viewer and the guide getting smarter about each other with use, it would have the potential to become a smart product. But nothing ensures that it will be used as such. If viewers do nothing more than control the speed at which the choices scroll past, then they will be using the guide only to get information. But if they ask the guide for all the comedies televised that week, or all the programs on pollution or cooking fish, they will be elevating the information to knowledge.

The Federal Communications Commission's 1992 decision to allow telephone companies to transmit television programming is making electronic program selection a reality. The fiber optic or wireless digital networks on which this programming will run will not be in place until the end of the century. But when they are, schools and businesses, students and consumers will be able to browse through electronic libraries that offer everything from soap operas and movies to scientific texts and medical files. Using that information wisely will be up to the viewer. The FCC decision will ultimately mean interactive multimedia programming on demand—spawning knowledge-based businesses that we cannot yet imagine.

Billing summaries for credit cards, telephone calls, and the like provide another instance of the opportunities a knowledge-based mind-set can open up. American Express was the first to distinguish itself from its competitors by sorting a year's worth of transactions into categories that are useful for tax and business purposes. The individual charges are the data, and the monthly bill is the information; but the billing summary becomes a knowledge tool when it helps the user control travel expenses and prepare tax forms.

Some credit-card companies now provide this summary at year-end for a nominal fee. But why not extend the service with monthly and year-to-date displays as well? Why not offer a menu of alternate variables for displaying the data or, for a onetime fee, organize charges by category instead of by date? New knowledge-based businesses can be built around fee-based services that give customers choices about how they can put information to the most productive use.

BUSINESS AS EDUCATOR

The development of knowledge-based business is a reflection of an even larger transformation occurring in our society. The market for learning is being redefined dramatically to encompass not just formal students but also lifelong learners. A new meaning of education and learning is bursting on the scene.

Learning in agricultural economies is often church led, focuses on children between 7 and 14 years of age, and is sufficient to last all the years of a working life. In industrial economies, learning has been government led, and the age range of students is between 5 and 22. In knowledge economies, the rapid pace of technological change means that learning must be constant and that education must be updated throughout one's working life. People have to increase their learning power to sustain their earning power.

Knowledge is doubling about every seven years, and in technical fields in particular, half of what students learn in their first year of college is obsolete by the time they graduate. In the labor force, the need to keep pace with technological change is felt even more acutely. For companies to remain competitive, and for workers to stay employable, they must continue to learn. This shadow education market is underestimated.

Consumers as a learning segment are also underestimated: they will be the newest and largest learning segment in the twenty-first-century marketplace. As information technologies become so much friendlier and smarter, and as they become intrinsic to more and more products and services, learning will become a by-product (and by-service) of the customers' world. Never before have customers considered themselves learners, and businesses considered themselves educators.

Business, more than government, is instituting the changes in education that are required for the emerging knowledge-based economy. School systems, public and private, are lagging behind the transformation in learning that is evolving outside them, in the private sector at both work and play, with people of all ages. Over the next few decades, the private sector will eclipse the public sector as our predominant educational institution.

12

Organisational Foundations of the Knowledge-Based Economy

John Mathews

INTRODUCTION

Flexibility, adaptability, responsiveness and a capacity to innovate rapidly—these are coming to be seen as the elements of "best practice" organisational architecture in the knowledge-based economy. These are the attributes of successful firms which can bring new products to market swiftly, which can draw on the skills and knowledge of their workforce in effecting continuous process improvement, and which can implement joint learning with suppliers and customers to keep abreast of and in front of competitors.

Conventional organisational theory, and management science, has been concerned with structure and strategy in a more stable world. Organisations consist of structures created to get tasks done in an accountable and orderly fashion. The strength of organisations has lain in their cohesion, which is established and reinforced through hierarchical structures of command and control. This structure is linked tightly to a business strategy aiming for the orderly production of mass goods and services designed to extend and create new markets: the standardisation of goods and services called for the standardisation of labour, of organisation and, ultimately, of management processes themselves.

The world described by this closed model has, of course, changed. In the new environment of rapidly shifting markets and changes in technology, the very rigidity that was a source of strength now becomes a major liability. Hence over the past decade an enormous effort of scholarship has been devoted to understanding how firms adapt to changing circumstances, and utilise their experience in doing so.[1]

The concept of *organisational* learning has been advanced to capture this sense of continuous adaptation to a changing commercial environment, drawing on a repertoire of skills and routines ("organisational knowledge") that can be brought to bear on any particular circumstance. The concept depends for its effect on a sense of cognitive dissonance: learning is an attribute of human beings, so how can it be said that organisations "learn"? To ask the question is to initiate an inquiry into the means and purposes of adaptation to changing circumstances at the organisational level.

How then do firms learn and unlearn, and how does their learning contribute to national prosperity? These are questions that have entered the mainstream of economic and industry debate in all OECD countries, as the advantages of flexibility and adaptation in the face of market and technological turbulence have become apparent.[2]

Following the lead of learning theorists such as Bateson (1972), Argyris (1982) and Hedberg (1981), we may characterise organisational learning in two quite different ways. One is responsive and adaptive, triggered by negative feedback from a shift in the environment, that aims to restore a previous equilibrium. An example is the maintenance of an organisational output around a predefined operating point. This is what Argyris called *single-loop learning;* it is based largely on stimulus-response mechanisms. The other is the open system experience which entails reorganisation, or a repositioning of the environment itself, or a refashioning of the system's operating rules and behaviour repertoires. This is what Argyris called *double-loop learning;* or Hedberg (1981) called meta-learning; or Bateson (1972) called deutero-learning. It involves a change, not in the system's behaviour itself, but in the rules governing the system's behaviour.

Single-loop learning entails the storing and selection of adaptational responses in the tasks that the self-managing parts of an organisation accomplish. Teams of operators in cellular manufacturing, for example, take responsibility for producing one or more complete products with a set of machines dedicated to their use. In the process, they find ways to improve their operating methods—"learning-by-doing."[3] Provided they are given sufficient authority to make improvements on their own initiative (which is only possible with "knowledge workers"), they will be able to register improved operating methods, higher levels of skills, and greater adaptiveness—all of which can be characterised as operational improvement resulting from single-loop learning.

How then does double-loop learning occur? One form of "learning to learn" arises from collaboration between parts of the organisation, pooling experience so that each team does not have to "re-invent the wheel" every time an improvement is effected. This form of learning (or continuous adaptation) involves changes in a group's operating methods, or objectives, depending on the input received, and stored, from outside the group but within the organisation. An organisation that can efficiently spin off learning acquired in one division, and apply it in another, is a "double loop" learning organisation.

The literature on organisational learning tends to be somewhat anglo-centric. So let us look farther afield for examples of organisational learning. The Korean firms like Hyundai, Samsung and Goldstar are exemplary in this regard, spinning off their expertise in one product line to give them a flying start in a new product line.[4] One reason why Samsung and Goldstar could learn to produce world-class electronics products so fast is that they made liberal use of sources of expertise outside of their own resources. Samsung got its start in advanced electronics by importing technology from foreign companies, and adapting it to its own purposes, creating new routines that fitted with its own operational environment. It also drew heavily for its early inputs on the research and infrastructure support provided by public institutions, such as the national Korean research organisation KIET, and the macroeconomic management provided by the Economic Planning Board.

This extra-organisational source of organisational learning is not usually considered by organisational theorists such as Argyris—yet its reality is undeniable. The institutional framework within which firms operate is just as important as their own internal procedures in determining how fast they can "learn," i.e. adapt their procedures to changing circumstances.

We can picture a viable, responsive organisation in terms of its systems and sub-systems, all displaying twin features of autonomy ("self-management") combined with system dependence. Following the terminology introduced by Koestler (1967), we can describe such organisations as "holonic," and their component parts (which are "systems" or "sub-systems") as *holons*.[5] Then we can discuss organisational responsiveness or learning in terms of three levels. There is the responsiveness of the autonomous sub-systems themselves—the "learning-by-doing" of self-managing teams, for example. This is first-order learning; it is intra-holonic. Secondly, there is the responsiveness that comes from teams sharing information and experience, altering each other's rules and patterns of behaviour through sharing of organisational knowledge. This is second-order learning; it is inter-holonic. Thirdly, there is the organisational learning that comes from the firm's interaction with its environment, captured in its powers of "organisational imagination." A viable organisation, like any living organism, has to have powers of central co-ordination and intelligence that change the operating conditions for all internal parts and procedures. This is third-order learning; it is extra-holonic.

Holonic organisational architecture is illustrated in Figure 12-1, which shows four levels of a holonic system. The learning that takes place within holons, between holons and between levels of the system, is illustrated in Figure 12-2.

It is third-order organisational learning which appears to drive the rapid industrialisation efforts of latecomer nations like Italy and Germany in Europe, and latterly Japan, the Republic of Korea and Chinese Taipei in East Asia. It is the extra-organisational features of this learning, deriving from the institutional setting within which firms operate, that is of such interest. Let us call this "economic learning," by analogy with "organisational learning."[6]

ECONOMIC LEARNING

The concept of economic learning captures the notion that some economies seem to be able to accommodate changes (e.g. of products, technologies, markets)

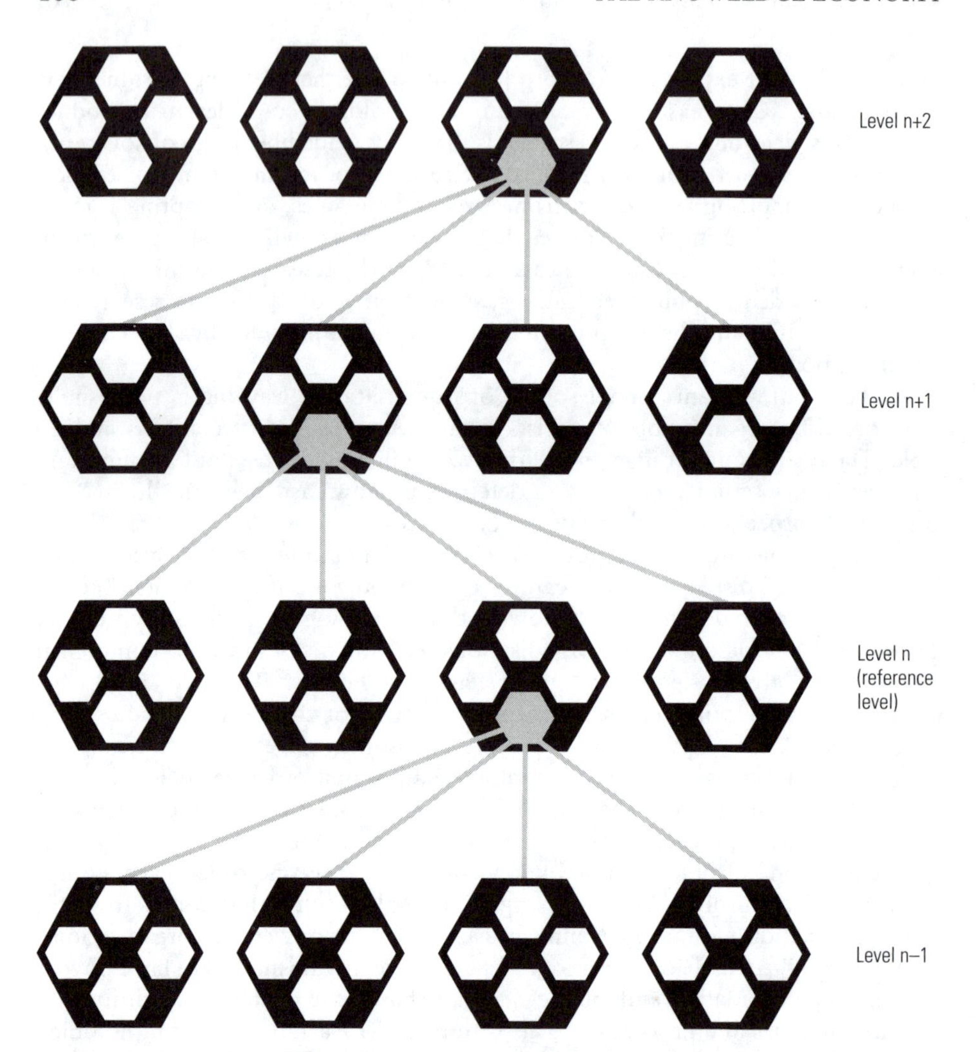

FIGURE 12-1 Scalar Holonic Chain: Four Levels

better than others. They do so partly through the flexibility of their firms themselves, but also through their capacities to promote inter-organisational linkages and collaboration and, above all, through the capacity of public institutions to imbibe, develop and disseminate innovations of various kinds to firms, thus accelerating the process of adaptation. We shall look at some examples in a moment.

Now exactly the same threefold pattern of learning can be seen to occur at the level of the economy itself. What we shall call first-order economic learning is that which takes place within organisations, through their own efforts. Second-order economic learning we may characterise as that which takes place between firms, in structured networks and clusters of collaboration (such as R&D consortia and joint ventures). Third-order economic learning is that which takes place at

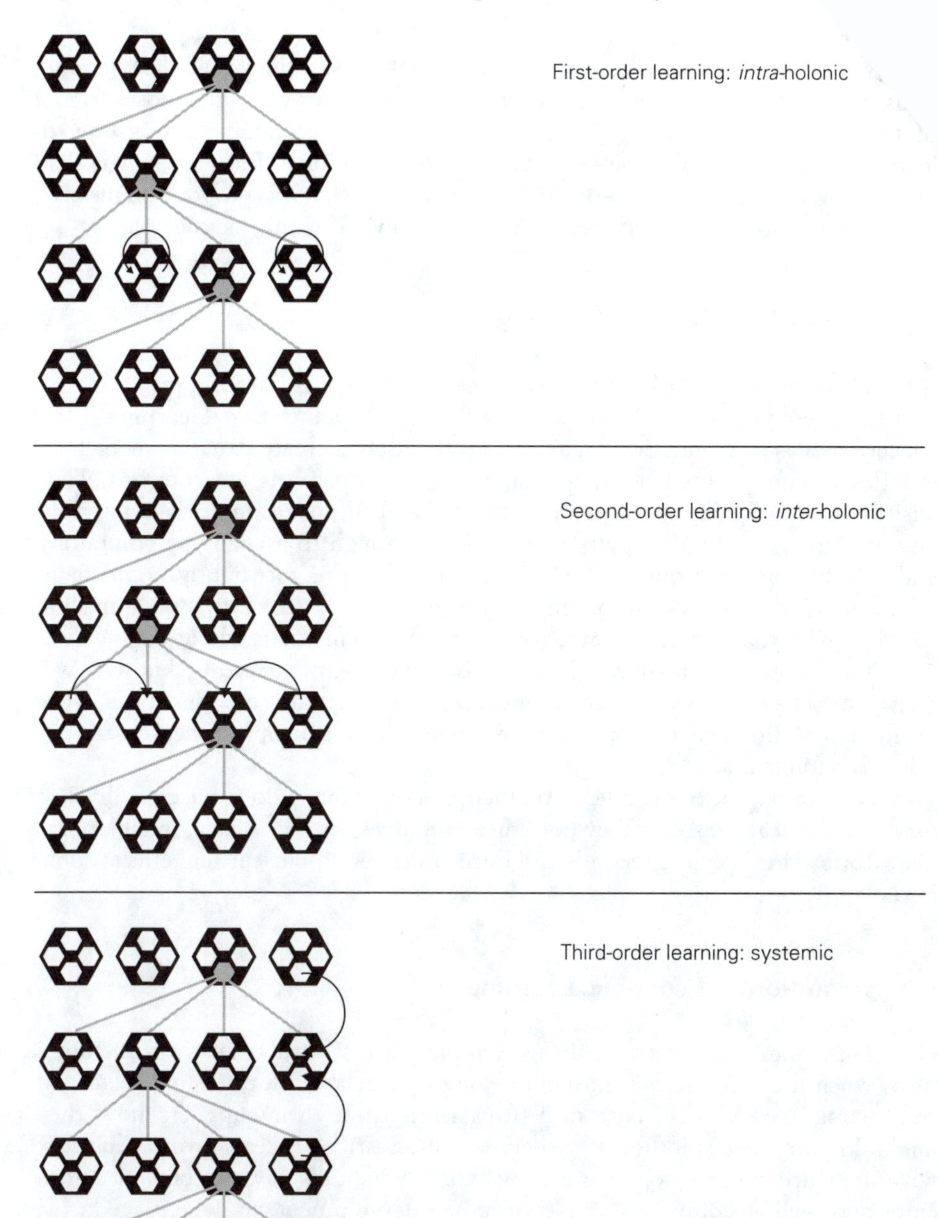

FIGURE 12-2 Three Orders of Learning

omy itself, through its public institutions and their interac-
etworks. Third-order economic learning is the most abstract
s concerned with how a whole economy "learns how to
ons clearly accelerate organisational learning better than
ers. This chapter is concerned with teasing out just what this proposition means.

Let us summarise the three orders of economic learning, as follows.

First-order Economic Learning

This takes place within firms (organisations), i.e. it is intra-organisational. It is in fact synonymous with what people refer to as "organisational learning." The concern here is to ensure that organisations themselves create structures which allow them to adapt intelligently to changes in their operating environment. They wish to bend and adapt—rather than shatter (as IBM, for example, is doing right now because it was not able to adapt quickly enough to a changing computing and information environment). Organisations that are too tightly coupled, in which there is too little autonomy in the parts, tend to shatter on impact—whereas those that are more fluid, are able to absorb impact without damage.

The knowledge acquired by organisations (their technical "know-how," their product portfolios, and their intellectual property assets) constitutes what we might call first-order economic knowledge. It is in principle a measurable national economic asset.

Now organisations can learn on their own, and many do so successfully. But they can also learn faster if they pool their resources, or knowledge, in collaborative efforts. This is where second- and third-order economic learning effects come into play.

Second-order Economic Learning

This takes place between firms. Supplier firms learn from their customer firms when they are brought into close, long-term relationships (as in "relational contracting").[7] Likewise, customer firms learn from their suppliers how they might do things better if they trust them. Producer firms can learn from each other when they are brought together into networks which display elements of co-operation as well as competition.[8] New product development can take place faster, and with reduced risk for individual firms, if they are brought together into collaborative R&D partnerships.[9] All of these are cases of what we are calling second-order economic learning.

Third-order Economic Learning

This takes place both outside and within firms but in such a way that their operating conditions are changed. It is "meta-learning," or learning how to learn;

it takes place at the level of the economic system as a whole. Its efficacy depends critically on the design and functioning of the economy's institutional framework. Examples include the case where a central institution attracts new product developments from foreign sources, and then establishes mechanisms through which these innovations are diffused to firms within the economy. Institutions which encourage adaptation on the part of firms can be designed. In this way the operating environment of the firms is changed; they are provided with an incentive to adapt, rather than simply being punished for not adapting (the market solution). These institutions are those which embody third-order economic learning.

Let us probe the collaborative structures that facilitate second- and third-order economic learning.

NETWORKS AND ORGANISATIONAL LEARNING

The past decade has seen significant advances in understanding the structures of co-operation and linkage between firms, and how they lend flexibility and competitive advantages to whole economies. Inter-firm networks have been discovered in fields such as marketing (e.g. export consortia), production (e.g. Italian industrial districts) and product and process innovation.[10] Indeed the linkages between firms, both domestically and internationally, are now seen to encompass a wide variety of forms, so that traditional atomistic market-mediated transactions, and internalised transactions within single firms, are seen merely as the extremes of a spectrum of co-operative inter-organisational arrangements.[11]

In networks, firms pursue their own interests but within an institutional framework that allows them also to pool resources or assets of one kind or another, achieving economies of scale or scope that would not otherwise be available. The advantages which such linkages confer on their participant members, their costs and benefits, and the different structures within which they can be supported and promoted, are now the subject of intensive scholarship.[12]

It is only recently that the economic and organisational literature has caught up with a fact that business people have known for years, namely that business is done with customers and through long-term contracting, rather than through "spot deals" in an open market. Obsessed as they have been by open "spot" markets, economists have in general been blind to the rich variety of collaborative arrangements that have been generated.

These arrangements include, in ascending order of intensity:

- sub-contracting—where a firm purchases services from another on a long-term contract;
- licensing—where a firm purchases another's product or technology, often with an arrangement to cover training in its use;
- consortium—where a group of firms join forces for a particular purpose, e.g. marketing some of their products in a specific region;

- equity partnership—where a firm goes beyond entering a contract for a service and actually purchases a small stake in the collaborating firm (short of a merger) to cement ties for the future;
- joint venture—where the equity participation between partners approaches the point where none of them is "dominant" and the venture takes on a life of its own.

Within each of these categories there are again numerous variations which we need not pursue here.[13] The point about all these forms of collaboration is that they bring together firms that would otherwise be head-to-head rivals, offering advantages to each of them and allowing them to do together what none of them could aspire to on their own.

Product innovation, and R&D more generally, constitutes an important field of economic activity where inter-organisational networking has been shown to bring substantial benefits to firms. Examples of innovation networks include such phenomena as strategic alliances in R&D; product development consortia; interfirm technology partnering; clustering of firms around public design or development facilities; and user-producer interactions.[14]

Most of these cases, from Italy, Germany, Japan and Chinese Taipei for example, depend for their success on structures and institutions within which the collaborative networks are embedded. Most of them also involve clusters of small and medium-sized firms, networking with each other or with larger firms. This "rediscovery" of the innovative role played by small-firm clusters, and their ubiquity in successful, technologically advanced economies, is one of the most striking findings of recent industrial research.[15]

How do network structures provide competitive advantage? Powell (1990*b*) argues that small-firm networks are "lighter on their feet" than large-firm hierarchies. In essence, he states, the parties to a network agree to forego the right to pursue their own interests at the expense of others. They derive substantial benefits in turn, due to their securing access to complementary assets, skills and markets.[16]

This is best seen through an example. The case of a small-firm innovation cluster in Australia, TCG, can be used to illustrate the general features of second-order economic learning through self-managing clusters.

TCG: INNOVATION THROUGH TRIANGULAR NETWORKING

In the inner Sydney enclave of Chippendale, a small group of firms called TCG (Technical and Computer Graphics) have been networking with each other and with the external world to become one of the largest privately-owned computer services operations in Australia.[17] TCG has perfected a form of commercial contracting between members of the group, combined with a "triangular" approach to new product development involving larger partners and customers, that leverages it into product areas and markets that would otherwise be well beyond the resources of a small group. This study examines the operations of TCG from the three-pronged perspective of its business strategy, linked to its networking structure, and its ability to embed its strategic alliances within the framework of public policy.

- TCG member firms exploit their network structure in the way that they leverage themselves into new markets and new product developments. Rather than seeking to "go it alone," TCG member firms identify the opportunities and then actively seek out partners for new developments, financing the whole maneuver through a major customer. In this way, TCG forms product-specific "triangles," which extend its network outwards into the global computer marketplace. Some examples give a flavour of this highly innovative approach.
- TCG has extended the product concept of its remote data terminals, originally developed for the retail market, into an aviation fuel monitoring terminal for use by airplane-refueling crews on tarmacs. A partner was found in the form of an existing manufacturer of (non-computerised) aviation fuel metering systems, and a major customer in the form of Mobil Oil. The result is a new system, the Rapid Aviation Refueling Information System (RARIS) in which all three partners have a stake and agreed channels for commercial development.
- TCG has developed the notion of electronic tags which can be applied to a wide array of products, from car engine numbers, through baggage tags, product serial numbers, identification cards, and animal markings. In the animal market it has lined up a manufacturing partner in the form of Trovan and leveraged itself into the animal ear tags market by forging an alliance with Leader, the world's largest supplier of non-electronic plastic ear tags. This is an example of technology "fusion" that has been identified as one of the strongest forces driving innovation in Japan.[18]
- TCG is developing a new field service terminal for use by maintenance crews. In this case the partner is a multinational computer giant (Toshiba) and the first customer who is driving the development is a major Australian utility organisation (Telecom). TCG gets some commercial advantages out of the arrangement, as well as alliances with major players that enhance its networking potential.

This then is a networking model of new product development, based on a foundational triangle of instigator (TCG), partner and major customer. It is a distinctive approach, that differs radically from the prevailing approaches followed in Australia that generally involve firms, large or small, working on their own.[19]

Second-order economic learning occurs within the TCG cluster through each member of the group being involved in the activities of the others, benchmarking its experiences, bringing new possibilities to their attention, and creating the openings within which product and technology "fusion" takes place.

Similar points are made by Johnston and Lawrence (1988) in their concept of Value Adding Partnership (VAP). These partnerships are networks under a different name, where the emphasis is on the competitive advantage that firms can reap by joining forces in a "partnership," in which each firm performs one aspect of a sequence of activities that together form a "value adding chain," and where each firm co-ordinates its activities with the other members of the chain. TCG can be seen as such a VAP, where the value adding chain is created by an order received from a customer, and member firms complete various phases of the order under the co-ordination of the firm which generated the order. The essential feature of the VAP for Johnston and Lawrence is that within its boundaries, companies form close and lasting ties with other members of the value adding chain.

Recently, Miles and Snow (1994) have also used the TCG example to illustrate their notion of a "network organisation" behaving like a "spherical" structure, with the network members playing the role of "bearings," on which the organisation turns to meet customers.

All of these conceptual innovations are seeking to capture the essence of the rapid, accelerated learning that takes place within these network structures.

Networks and Small Firms

One of the striking features of the scholarship on innovation networks is the emphasis it lays on the dynamic contribution made by small and medium-sized firms (SMEs). The essential advantages of SMEs lie not in their smallness as such, but in their responsiveness and diversity. A range of business strategies, technologies and organisational forms can be tapped through small firms, giving a robustness to an economy at a time when success is associated with innovation and market responsiveness. The industrial monoculture associated with large firms is in evolutionary terms a strategy likely to lead to industrial extinction. It actively inhibits the processes of experimentation that are fostered within small-firm networks, and which generate the industrial diversity that is coming to have such high survival value at a time of rapid economic adjustment.

The benefits of small-firm networks thus are felt at the most basic level in terms of their diversity, leading to their becoming the engines of innovation, and through this, the sources of future employment generation. Thus, their economic significance can hardly be over-estimated, both in their own terms and in terms of the links they establish with larger firms.

While clusters and networks enable firms to learn rapidly from each other, and thereby derive competitive advantages from their co-operation, the knowledge acquired remains within the network. A higher level of economic learning ensures that this knowledge is diffused across to other firms or networks, through institutions designed expressly for this purpose. This brings us to third-order economic learning.

THIRD-ORDER ECONOMIC LEARNING

What kind of institutional arrangements can be seen to accelerate the second-order learning of clusters and the first-order learning of firms themselves? Let us first look at some examples before discussing the general features. Let us look at some recent examples of collaborative learning in the knowledge-economy, in the case of one of the most technologically dynamic economies today, that of Chinese Taipei, to see how these processes work in practice in an East Asian context.

Collaborative Alliances in Chinese Taipei

Chinese Taipei has an economy populated by a few large firms and thousands of small firms. It has done extremely well in the fields of electronics and information technology, where the small and medium-sized firms have proven to be very flexible and market-adaptable.[20] Some of the medium-sized firms are rapidly growing to be very large, such as Acer and Tatung in PC's. Chinese Taipei thus offers a quite different model of economic development from that pursued by the Republic of Korea and Japan, where huge, diversified companies have dominated the industrialisation and innovation processes. As Chinese Taipei's previous comparative advantage based on low costs disappears, the issue for economic policy makers is twofold: can Chinese Taipei's small firms prove as good at innovation as they have done at production; and can the larger firms retain the flexibility in innovation they enjoyed when they were smaller?

In the 1990s, a series of experiments with inter-firm innovation alliances would appear to indicate that the answer to both questions is "yes"—at least tentatively. Chinese Taipei has developed a model of co-operative innovation clusters (or "strategic alliances") that exploits its mix of firms, and is accelerating its emergence as a leading manufacturer of advanced electronics and information technology products. Its experiences in the creation of inter-firm alliances for product innovation are therefore of great interest.

All the alliances in Chinese Taipei involve co-ordination by one of the government-funded research laboratories, such as CCL (Computer and Communications Laboratory) which is part of ITRI (Industrial Development Research Institute) and a trade association such as the Taiwan Electrical Appliances Manufacturers Association (TEAMA). All are directed towards innovation and flexibility, balancing competition by co-operation.[21]

All these phenomena may be viewed as forms of "third-order" economic learning, in the sense that the organisational learning that takes place is pooled between firms and held within public institutions. The institutional structures, organisational processes, economic rationale and strategic orientation of economic learning are of great current interest.

Personal Computer Alliances

In the early 1980s, Chinese Taipei established a strong position in PC manufacture, especially in peripherals such as monitors. Innovation at this early stage was limited; it was production efficiency that drove the country's competitive advantage. Towards the end of 1983, the Electronics Research and Service Organisation (ERSO) of ITRI joined with five local companies, including Acer, to produce an IBM-compatible PC, the PC-100. The alliance considerably shortened the time to bring the product to market, and ERSO's involvement ensured high standards were met. Next the PC-400 consortium was formed, involving ERSO and Tatung and two others; within a year, hardware design, production technique and BIOS were transferred to local manufacturers. This helped to lay the foundations for Chinese Taipei's consistent innovation in PCs through the 1980s.[22]

Notebook PC Strategic Alliance

In the late 1980s, the PC market was starting to show signs of fragmenting, with Notebook PCs becoming an important market trend. Firms like Acer and Tatung were able to respond to these trends on their own, just as Japanese firms like Toshiba were doing. But the economic policy makers in Chinese Taipei were keen to see new and smaller IT firms profiting from the new opportunities created by Notebook PCs, both in order to expand the market presence of national firms, and to replenish the supply of small firms into the electronics and IT industries.

Accordingly, ITRI's CCL (Computer and Communications Laboratories) and the industry body TEAMA (Taiwan Electrical Appliances Manufacturers Association) brought together a consortium of small PC firms to develop a commercial Notebook computer. The idea was to develop a standardised product and standardised components, to give smaller national firms a competitive advantage. For the PC firms, entry to such a consortium represented a cost-effective way of gaining access to a new product and new technology, as well as to marketing expertise.

The project was announced in April 1990, and was immediately met with an enthusiastic response. In all, forty-six firms signed up for the consortium, surprising CCL. These firms spanned the entire PC industry, from components manufacture to final assembly to marketing. Some of them were established firms, but others were start-ups.

The alliance made rapid progress and within only seven months had developed a 386 SX Notebook PC to mass production design stage. According to the rules of the consortium, this model was to be made available to the members. After displaying the initial product at the US COMDEX exhibition, some members of the consortium were eager to press on to further improvements, while others were interested only in marketing this product. Thus the alliance started to lose its common goals.

This early success created a problem for the individual members of the consortium: how were they to bring this common product to market? Essentially they were all bringing the same Notebook PC product to the same market, with only minor variations separating their offerings. The result was a fierce price war between the consortium members, which ended with some of them being bankrupted and others being forced out of the Notebook business. Thus, on both grounds, the alliance broke up after two years.

Although the Notebook alliance was organisationally a failure, it laid the foundation for spectacular success on the part of PC manufacturers in Chinese Taipei. In 1992, Chinese Taipei was world number three Notebook PC supplier; in 1993 it was number two; and in 1994 it has emerged as number one, toppling Japanese firms such as Toshiba.[23]

The TEAMA learnt many lessons from the Notebook PC experience and has structured innovation "strategic alliances" formed since along rather different lines. New alliances have been formed to develop HDTV, multimedia, and other consumer product applications. In these cases, fewer participant firms have been allowed to enter the consortium; they have been required to invest more in terms of finances and resources; and greater thought has been given to the procedures for the exploitation of the developed product. We describe these next.

Current TEAMA Co-ordinated Strategic Alliances

TEAMA currently convenes/co-ordinates 16 technology innovation clusters ("strategic alliances") covering such targeted electronic products as HDTV, videophone, laserfax, G4 ISDN computer fax, small size satellite TV receiving stations, smart cards, CD multiplex telephones, palmtop computers, and the "New PC" organised as a consortium around the IBM-Motorola "PowerPC" microprocessor.

Each of these clusters is formally constituted as a development consortium, with members being selected by TEAMA, and required to sign a development agreement, and pay upfront membership fees. Fundamental research services are contributed by ITRI, such as through its Computing and Communications Laboratory (CCL). Government co-ordination and audit is exercised by the Industrial Development Bureau of the Ministry of Economic Affairs.

High definition TV

Established in 1993, the HDTV consortium consists of leading Taipei electronics firms such as Tatung and Proton, together with some Taipei-Japanese joint ventures. The project is planned to proceed over five years, with new products coming out each year. The Taipei effort will be entirely digital, and designed to interface with world-wide digital standards. In 1994, the first step was accomplished with Tatung producing wide screen (16:9) sets and, later in 1994, a fully enhanced "advanced TV" (i.e. conventional TV with image enhancement). The third step will see a high definition fully-digital TV being developed in 1995. It will be built to match the standards that emerge in the United States, Europe and Japan (thus emphasizing Chinese Taipei's flexibility as a small player).

CCL has taken the initiative in forming a number of different consortia for the HDTV project, focusing on such issues as image capture, digital signal processing, TV projection, and flat screen displays. The companies involved have contributed around 70 top engineers to the project, while CCL has contributed around 30. Funds have been provided by the firms and by the MOEA. A Taipei chip designer and manufacture, United Microelectronics Corporation (UMC), is a member of each of the consortia, to develop new integrated circuits for digital HDTV. Thus the new product(s) will as far as possible be produced entirely in Chinese Taipei from Taipei components.

New PC

The world market for PCs in the second half of the 1990s will be divided into those powered by Intel's Pentium Microprocessor (and its strategic links with Hewlett-Packard) and those powered by the IBM-Motorola RISC-based PowerPC, which is feeding into all of Apple's products. One group of Taipei firms, including Acer, is siding with Intel. But another group, called the "New PC" consortium, is going with the PowerPC. Thus between the two groups, Taipei PC firms are set to continue their strong position in world microcomputer markets well into the 1990s.

The New PC consortium is structured in a much more sophisticated fashion than its Notebook PC predecessor.[24] Formed in November 1993, it was initiated by CCL/ITRI and TEAMA, and has the goal of establishing the PowerPC microprocessor as the new industry standard, and the "New PC" as a world-leading PC that exploits the full power of the new processor.[25] The consortium will develop "core" technology which member firms can then elaborate to their own specification. (This will avoid the "me-too" problems created by the Notebook PC alliance.) The consortium brings together upstream and downstream suppliers, thus ensuring that all components for the New PC will be manufactured in Chinese Taipei and will meet local performance standards.

A working model of the New PC based on the PowerPC version 601 was constructed and demonstrated at the Taipei Computex in June 1994. A more powerful model based on the PowerPC version 603 will be demonstrated at the Comdex Fall '94 in November in the United States. This model will form part of a range encompassing portable PCs, desktop PCs and servers. It is planned to produce even more powerful systems based on PowerPC versions 620 and 604, for workstations and servers. It remains to be seen how successful the "New PC" consortium members will be in bringing these products to market.

Economic Learning in Chinese Taipei Collaborative Alliances

Let us illustrate the first-order, second-order and third-order learning at work in these cases.

All involve both large and small firms in collaborative development consortia. These consortia enable firms to tackle development projects that would be beyond them.

Individually, the firms are brought rapidly to a point where they can commit themselves to projects that would otherwise be beyond them. This is the first-order learning.

The consortia also help to spread risk and reduce costs of innovation. Rapid commercialisation of carefully targeted "strategic" products is the key to these collaborative processes, which bring the flexibility of smaller firms, and the strengths of larger firms, together. Intellectual property rights and product exploitation rights are settled in advance, at the time of formation of the consortia. These generally accrue to the firms participating. Government in Chinese Taipei takes the view that the government benefits through the prosperity of the firms involved, collecting taxes and seeing employment expand. This is the second-order learning.

Fundamental research input is provided by a public sector research institute, or in the case of TSMC, a fundamental service is provided by a public sector firm which sparks the formation of dozens of small high-tech IC design houses. Thus the major cost and risk of entering a new technological sector is borne initially by the public sector.

Co-ordination is provided by government (e.g. the Industrial Development Bureau), by the public sector research labs, and by the industry itself (e.g. through TEAMA). This is entirely consistent with Chinese Taipei's history of state-led development through the 1960s, 1970s and 1980s. However once formed, the consortia are "self-managing," with the IDB of the MOEA providing audit functions only.

ITRI takes responsibility for acquiring and transferring necessary technology (e.g. in securing rights to the PowerPC for the New PC consortium). This again is a mechanism for spreading risk, for protecting smaller firms from the pitfalls of intellectual property litigation, and for establishing a structure within which it becomes possible for firms to enter closer long-term relations. Recall the comment made by Dalum, Johnson and Lundvall (1992), that "the capability to learn for the system as a whole or for sub-systems will depend upon the existence of environments where different kinds of knowledge, skill, competence and experience can be combined and allowed to generate new knowledge" (1992, p. 304). Clearly this Taipei case of a collaborative product development alliance provided such an environment. This is what is meant by third-order learning.

These new collaborative alliances, structured as they are as a result of the learning involved in poorer-performing earlier alliances (such as the Notebook PC case) promise to keep Chinese Taipei at the forefront of international competition in advanced electronics and high-tech products. They represent an innovative form in which government co-ordination has itself been "re-invented" for the new demands of the 1990s.

NATIONAL STRUCTURES OF INNOVATION

Our consideration of the institutional framework within which collaboration between firms takes place, in the cases of Australia and of Chinese Taipei, underscores the significance of national structures of innovation. Clearly, some economies learn faster than others because of differences in their national structures of innovation, or more generally, within the institutional frameworks that support third-order economic learning.

Let us highlight the effect that such differences can have, in the interesting case of the emergence of semiconductor industries in the major East Asian economies of Japan, the Republic of Korea and Taipei. All involved national projects to produce VLSI chips (Very Large-Scale Integration circuits). Here we have the same product—in each project one or two generations further along in its evolution—but three very different ways of co-ordinating private sector development through public sector involvement.

The Case of the Semiconductor Industry: VLSI Integrated Circuit Collaborative R&D Strategies in East Asia

The three major economies of East Asia—Japan, the Republic of Korea, Chinese Taipei—have been successful in developing a semiconductor industry, thus storming the bastion of the world's most technically demanding sector. In each case, they have used extensive collaboration between firms and government—but with some surprising differences in emphasis. In exploring these differences, we come up against the reality of distinctive national structures of innovation and the effects that they can exert.

In *Japan,* the famed MITI model was at work in the VLSI Project, where the major Japanese electronics and IT firms such as Hitachi, Toshiba, NEC and Fujitsu were brought together into a collaborative alliance (R&D consortium) to develop commodity memory chips—the 64K DRAM.[26] At that time US semiconductor companies like Texas Instruments and Motorola held near-total sway over the growing DRAM segment, which in the late 1970s looked set to expand rapidly as computers and other memory-hungry products were starting to expand in significance. MITI co-ordinated and orchestrated the entire VLSI Project, shifting government funds into the joint effort, and allocating different aspects of the work involved to different companies (e.g. circuit design features to one company; process technology improvement in lithography to another). The entire Japanese semiconductor industry was thereby leveraged to a new level of technological sophistication—and when the assault on the US DRAM market was launched in early 1980s (again a collaborative or orchestrated effort), it had swift and deadly results. By 1986, Japan had captured nearly 80 per cent of the US DRAM market.

In *Korea,* a similarly inspired VLSI project was mounted a few years later, from 1986 to 1987, as a means of bringing the fledgling Korean semiconductor industry up to world standard. Firms such as Samsung, Goldstar and Hyundai had invested heavily in becoming involved in semiconductors, focusing like the Japanese before them on standardized memory chips. From a standing start in 1983, these three firms invested huge sums in purchasing designs and process technology, largely from US start-up firms hungry for capital, and brought their early chips, such as 64K and 256K DRAMs, to the market in a small way in the mid-1980s. The Korean VLSI project focused on the prize of the 4M DRAM, which was set to be world market leader by the beginning of the 1990s.

As in the case of Japan, the Korean VLSI project was co-ordinated by the Ministry of Trade and Industry (MoTIE); it was backed by (relatively modest) government funds, expended in the government research labs, ETRI; and it involved only the existing large firms. But there the similarities end. In the Korean case, all the companies involved had access to basic design and process data acquired by ETRI, and secured through their own licensing efforts; each company (Samsung, Hyundai and Goldstar) developed its own version of the new product; and a "winner" was declared (in this case, Samsung) by the Ministry. State resources were then poured into backing the winning design, to help the company bring it to market first. The other companies were given the consolation prize of being given access to the winning technology, shortly after the winner was given a head-start; thus they were leveraged up to the best standard, and were enabled to enter the market with this product after only a short delay.

It was the 4M DRAM, launched as a mass market product by Samsung in 1989, that really provided the breakthrough for Korean producers into the US market, establishing them as a strong presence. On the basis of this success, Samsung set up a ULSI laboratory in its Kiheung plant, to work on the next generation 16M DRAM chip, developed in 1990, neck and neck with Japan. Korean firms currently hold around 40 per cent of the world market for 16M DRAMs—an astonishing result for an industry no more than a decade old.

In *Chinese Taipei,* a quite different approach has been pursued, but with equally impressive results. Again collaborative efforts were the centerpiece of the strategy, but the State played a much more direct role, in effect initiating the semiconductor industry itself through its public sector research institute, ITRI/ERSO. It was ERSO that as early as 1977 signed a technology transfer deal with RCA and developed its own IC fabrication Demonstration Lab—even before Korean firms like Samsung had made a commitment to the industry. But Chinese Taipei's development was gradual, building up its own expertise, and spinning off new companies from ERSO as the technology was mastered and was ready for commercialisation. In this way United Microelectronics Corp (UMC) was formed in 1980 as a public-private joint venture, and Taiwan Semiconductor Manufacturing Company (TSMC) in 1986, as an international public-private joint venture involving Philips as a major partner. By this time Chinese Taipei had a thriving IC design industry, a small but well-balanced and diversified IC fabrication industry, covering a range of logic and linear devices with specific applications—but not much of a presence in standardised memory chips.

Chinese Taipei's VLSI project entailed two phases. One was a government research effort within ERSO, over the three years 1984–86, designed to result in a working pilot plant and a design methodology and infrastructure, located within a Common Design Center thrown open to local design houses. The second phase was the launch of a spin-off company, Taiwan Semiconductor Manufacturing Company (TSMC), embodying the VLSI know-how acquired within ERSO. TSMC was indeed launched in 1986, but not as a conventional IC fabrication company. Instead it was a "silicon foundry," mandated to offer fabrication services to small IC design firms (as well as to large foreign customers) but not to produce products of its own. TSMC has been remarkably successful, both in its own terms, becoming one of the most profitable IC firms in the world but, even more significantly, in terms of sparking the formation of dozens of small IC design houses ("fabless" IC producers) around it on the Hsinchu Science-based Industry Park. Thus, by the end of the 1980s, Chinese Taipei had established a world-class and profitable VLSI IC industry, in which a flourishing cluster of IC design houses and conventional firms (five had entered the industry by 1989) had formed around the TSMC silicon foundry to leverage themselves into world niche markets. It was only at this stage that the challenge of DRAM production was taken up.

Based on the success of the Taipei VLSI project, the 1990s has seen a huge growth in design and manufacturing IC activities. By 1994 four companies had entered or were about to enter DRAM production—TI-Acer, Mosel-Vitelic, a new ERSO spin-off, WASC, and a new venture being founded by the Formosa Plastics Group, Chinese Taipei's biggest industrial conglomerate. By 1995, Chinese Taipei is likely to be the world's fourth largest IC supplier, after Japan, the United States and the Republic of Korea.

Which of the three national models has been most successful must remain a matter of judgement. But in many ways the Taipei effort must be judged as being most impressive, given the broad spread of products now produced by the industry, which attract customers in the form of the world's leading computing, communications and electronics firms, and given the usage made by the world's leading design houses of Chinese Taipei's many foundry services, led by TSMC. The Taipei national system of innovation has ensured the development of a balanced semiconductor industry—balanced in terms of product diversity; in terms of upstream and downstream activities; in terms of the involvement of small and large firms; and in terms of the co-operative relations co-existing with fierce competition amongst the firms clustered on the Hsinchu Science-based Industry Park.

On the other hand, the sheer ruthlessness of the Korean approach to new product development has ensured its major firms a rapid rise to world leadership in mass commodity memory chips; these firms, again led by Samsung, are now seeking to diversify their product offerings, to reduce their heavy dependence on DRAMs. Whether they can be successful in this endeavor remains to be seen, given the under-emphasis of the Korean national system of innovation on replenishing the supply of small firms. Meanwhile the Japanese semiconductor industry, which made the original breakthrough into the US market at the beginning of the 1980s, is going through a painful readjustment, and views with alarm the rise of the "Korean DRAM threat."[27] The Japanese national system of innovation is itself going through a period of profound readjustment, after its earlier exclusive emphasis on existing large firms.

For our purposes, the point is that all three countries have developed a successful semiconductor industry, rising respectively to second, third and fourth place in the world, through very different strategies and utilising very different institutional frameworks. In all three, the advantages of first-, second- and third-order economic learning are apparent.

- The companies themselves have rapidly acquired know-how, through technology imports, licensing, joint ventures, hiring of skilled personnel, and through the efforts of public sector institutions. Rapid first-order learning has been the key to success.
- Extensive inter-organisational collaboration, combined with intense competition, has been the hallmark of these industry development experiences. Collaboration has been effected particularly in the acquisition and diffusion of technology (product and process) and, in the 1990s, in the joint development consortia that have been formed for products or product areas such as flash memories. This has accelerated second-order learning.
- Third-order learning has been effected through the extensive reliance on public sector institutions for co-ordination of development efforts, for the reduction of risk, and for the diffusion of technology imported from abroad. But we have seen how the three countries developed quite distinctive forms of third-order learning arrangements, with distinctive results.[28]

This semiconductor example, and the previous cases of collaborative alliances in Chinese Taipei, underscore the need for collaboration to be extended also to research and scholarship on these pressing matters. The newly industrialised economies of East Asia constitute a rich field of inquiry in which to identify the forces and factors involved in successful economic learning, and in revealing the cognitive architecture of organisational learning. The success stories need to be analysed as well as the failures. International collaborative research that deepens our understanding of these processes is clearly warranted.

Public Policy to Support Economic Learning

Given the significance of national institutional frameworks in collaborative innovation, the role of public policy in shaping and feeding those institutions is critical.

It is in clustering and networking that small firms are able to capture economies of scale and scope that have previously been the province solely of large, integrated firms. Such networks emerge through the appearance of organised industrial markets, in geographically distinct districts, and in sectoral clusters. Hence public policy has been particularly concerned to encourage such clusters, e.g. through the formation of export consortia, innovation consortia and joint ventures, or local employment initiatives, sometimes backed by national and supranational finance (Bianchi, 1993).

A range of instruments is available to public authorities in this regard; they include provision of seed capital, formation of embryonic service centers, provision of small firm incubators, and, most importantly, changing the rules to allow public agencies such as telecommunications utilities to let contracts to consortia of small firms rather than to single, large-firm bidders. Policy need not seek to dictate how such clusters should form and on what terms; instead it tends to be concerned to ensure that small firms are not unnecessarily disadvantaged; that they are provided with some positive inducements to collaborate through clusters; and that unco-operative "opportunistic" behavior will be punished. In this way, public policy can be informed by the results of social science research, such as the now well-known case of "learned co-operation" in the iterated *Prisoners' Dilemma* game.[29]

From the perspective of innovation promotion, public policy in OECD countries is coming to be concerned with such issues as promoting and assisting the formation of small firms, allowing them to choose the technologies and markets where they seek to make a contribution, but ensuring that they are not disadvantaged in doing so, through lack of capital, lack of information, or through the excessive government regulation which has grown up in the large-firm sector.

Longer-term issues for policy concern the governance of inter-firm networks (e.g. ensuring that company law does not disadvantage "virtual corporations"), the enforcement of contracts within networks and organised markets (providing for more flexible legal instruments) and ensuring that competition policy (again directed at monopolies) does not stifle collaboration within small-firm networks. On the other hand, where collaboration occurs between large firms, it is equally important to ensure that such consortia do not constitute monopoly threats to the survival of existing and future small firms offering alternatives to the products or standards developed by the big-firm consortium.

The most important aspect of public policy with regard to clusters of small firms concerns its role in preventing the individual members from seeking a way out of their *Prisoners' Dilemma* by undercutting each other. Such an approach would have ripple effects that would eventually destroy the network—as has happened to some Italian small-firm districts that have sought to compete against low-cost imports by cutting their own prices and levels of quality. Public policy can play a significant role in raising the costs of such anti-network behaviour, such as by providing for minimum labor standards to be observed, and by setting standards to be met in the fulfillment of public contracts. In this way public policy can underwrite the collaboration that gives the networks their coherence, without destroying the competition that gives them dynamism.

NOTES

1. The OECD itself has played an important role in tracking these developments. For a summary and exposition of the major findings, see OECD (1991*a;* 1991*b;* 1992).
2. The term "learning organisation" has taken off, and now has considerable literature behind it. See the popular exposition by Peter Senge, *The Learning Organisation*

(1990), as well as the earlier work by Argyris (1982) and Argyris and Schon (1978). For recent overviews, see Pedler *et al.* (1991) and Huber (1991).

3. For an exposition of the significance of learning by doing for economics, see Arrow (1962).
4. For a description of the powerful organisational learning systems developed by the successful East Asian economies, see for example Amsden (1989) and her description of the Korean learning organisation, Hyundai. For the case of Japan, see Nonaka (1988).
5. The term "holon," coined by Koestler (1967), is derived from the Greek for "whole" (*holos*) and "part" (*on,* as in proton or neutron). Thus a self-managing team, for example, displays attributes of autonomy, yet it also depends for its effectiveness on the co-ordination provided by the total organisation; it is both "whole" and "part." For an exposition of holonic organisational architecture, see Mathews (1994b), and for its application to intelligent manufacturing systems (Mathews, 1994c). On the developments in organisational and management theory arising from a similar concern with new theories of co-ordination, see Wheatley (1992).
6. On the concept of the "learning economy," see Lundvall and Johnson (1994).
7. On relational contracting, see MacNeil (1978). On long-term supplier-customer relationships, see Lundvall (1985). For an application of the notion in marketing, as in "relational marketing," see Dwyer, Schurr and Oh (1987).
8. On the networks which bind an industrial economy, see Hakansson and Johanson (1988; 1993); Reddy and Rao (1990).
9. On such collaborative partnerships, see Teece (1989; 1992); Pisano and Teece (1989); Miles and Snow (1986); Snow, Miles and Coleman (1992); and Mody (1993).
10. On Italian industrial districts, see Pyke, Becattini and Sengenberger (1990); and Inzerilli (1990). For earlier works which probed the economics of their operation, see Brusco (1982); Piore and Sabel (1984); and for their embeddedness in state structures, see Weiss (1988). For a description of the district of Prato, see Weiss and Mathews (1991).
11. For further details of this perspective, see Thorelli (1986); Powell (1987; 1990a; 1990b); and Mathews (1993).
12. See Camagni (1993) for an exposition which looks at the costs and benefits of such networks; Hagedoorn (1990) for an estimate of their frequency; and von Hippel (1988) for an account of the sources of innovation arising within user-supplier networks. For a recent exposition of collaboration from the perspective of "time" in economic development, see North (1994).
13. See Imai (1985) and Imai and Baba (1989) for a particularly clear exposition of the structure of networks and their various manifestations. For a more sociological account, see Perrow (1991).
14. On innovation networks, see the special issue of *Research Policy,* Volume 20, No. 6. In particular, see the stimulating survey provided of the topic by Freeman (1991).
15. For an early exposition, see Piore and Sabel (1984).
16. Powell's treatment is very different from the conventional approach taken in industrial economics, which ever since Blois (1972), has regarded such arrangements as a surrogate for vertical integration, hence the term "quasi-vertical integration"; its essence is held to be the dominance of the smaller partner by the larger.

17. On TCG, see Mathews (1993; 1994a). For an exposition of the group's origins, by its founder, see Fritz and Ellercamp (1988). Since these studies were published, two companies in the TCG group have been listed on the Sydney Stock Exchange.
18. For the case of Japanese innovation by "technology fusion" see Kodama (1992).
19. Interest in Australia in the possibilities of networks as an alternative and superior form of industrial organisation, is growing. Recent papers from the Australian Manufacturing Council (1993) and the Bureau of Industry Economics (1991) have focused attention on the role that networks play in the successful economies of Japan, Italy and Germany, and have begun the task of identifying the scope for network development in Australia. The government announced a program of support for "enterprise networking" in its May 1994 statement, *Working Nation.*
20. For a comprehensive introduction to the Chinese Taipei economy, paying due regard to its institutional framework and industrial structure, see Wade (1989).
21. On these Taipei experiences, see the accounts by Taipei scholars: Chen (1993); Chen and Liu (1994); Gee (1991); and Wang (1993; 1994a; 1994b).
22. See Lin (1994), page 16.
23. None of the current top five Taipei Notebook PC suppliers participated in the development alliance—yet they have clearly benefited from its pathbreaking work.
24. Note that this in itself is an instance of economic learning, within the institutional framework itself.
25. The members of the consortium include major Chinese Taipei computer manufacturers such as Tatung, Mitac, DTK, FIC and Umax; UMC, as chip-set supplier, and Taiwan Auto-Design, as sytems solutions provider. The full complement of 32 companies has been allocated to four working groups (Platform Working Group, Add-on Card WG, Components WG and Software WG).
26. These acronyms are now universally used. A 64K DRAM is a memory circuit having 64,000 elements, termed a Dynamic Random Access Memory.
27. See the article (in Japanese) under this heading in *Nikkei Electronics,* March 1994.
28. See Weiss (1994) and Weiss and Hobson (1995) for a perspective on this issue that centres on the role of the state in governing the market in East Asian economies; the critical feature is "state capacity," which conceptually overlaps with the institutional framework of third-order economic learning.
29. See Axelrod (1984) for the original account, which shows clearly that co-operation is not a "natural" attribute, but is "learned" in the context of repeated exposures to structured outcomes. This is perhaps the key to harnessing co-operative energies in the "learning economy."

REFERENCES

Amsden, A. (1989), *Asia's Next Giant: Latecomer Industrialisation in Korea,* Oxford University Press, New York.

Argyris, C. (1982), *Reasoning, Learning and Action: Individual and Organisational,* Jossey-Bass, San Francisco.

Argyris, C. and D. Schon (1978), *Organisational Learning: A Theory of Action Perspective,* Addison-Wesley, Reading, MA.

Australian Manufacturing Council (1993), *Emerging Exporters,* report to the AMC by McKinseys, AMC, Melbourne.

Arrow, K. (1962), "The Economic Implications of Learning by Doing", *Review of Economic Studies,* Vol. XXIX, No. 80.

Axelrod, R. (1984), *The Evolution of Co-operative Behaviour,* Penguin, London.

Bateson, G. (1972), *Steps to an Ecology of Mind,* Ballantine, New York.

Bianchi, P. (1993), "The Promotion of Small-firm Clusters and Industrial Districts: European Policy Perspectives", *Journal of Industry Studies,* Vol. 1, No. 1, pp. 16–29.

Blois, K. (1972), "Vertical Quasi-Integration", *Journal of Industrial Organisation,* pp. 253–272.

Brusco, S. (1982), "The Emilian Model: Productive Decentralisation and Social Integration", *Cambridge Journal of Economics,* Vol. 6, pp. 167–84.

Bureau of Industry Economics (1991), "Networks: A Third Form of Organisation", Discussion Paper No. 14, Bureau of Industry Economics, Australian Government Publishing Service, Canberra.

Camagni, R. (1993), "Inter-firm Industrial Networks: The Costs and Benefits of Co-operative Behaviour", *Journal of Industry Studies,* Vol. 1, No. 1, pp. 1–15.

Chen, Tain-jy (1993), "Enhancing International Competitiveness through International Alliances (in Chinese), Report to the Industrial Development Bureau, Ministry of Economic Affairs, Chung-Hua Institution for Economic Research, Taipei.

Chin, Tain-jy and Meng-chun Liu (1994), "International Strategic Alliances and Taiwan's Industry", *Proceedings of the Conference on the Globalisation of Taiwan's Industry,* Chung-Hua Institution for Economic Research, Taipei.

Dalum, B., B. Johnson and B.-Å. Lundvall (1992), "Public Policy in the Learning Society", in B.A. Lundvall (ed.) *National Systems of Innovation: Towards a Theory of Innovation and Interactive Learning,* Pinter Publishers, London.

Di Bernardo, B. (1991), *Le Dimensioni d'Impresa: Scala, Scopo, Varieta* (The Size of Firms: Economies of Scale, Scope and Variety), Franco Angeli, Milan.

Dwyer, R., P. Schurr. and S. Oh (1987), "Developing Buyer-seller Relationships", *Journal of Marketing,* Vol. 51, April, pp. 11–27.

Freeman, C. (1991), "Networks of Innovators: A Synthesis of Research Issues", *Research Policy,* Vol. 20, No. 6. Reprinted in C. Freeman, *The Economics of Hope: Essays on Technical Change, Economic Growth and the Environment,* Pinter Publishers, London.

Fritz, P. and P. Ellercamp (1988), *The Possible Dream. TCG: An Australian Business Success Story,* Penguin Books, Melbourne.

Gee, San (1991), "Technology, Investment and Trade under Economic Globalisation: The Case of Taiwan", in W. Michalski (ed.), *Trade, Investment and Technology in the 1990s.* OECD, Paris.

Hagedoorn, J. (1990), "Organisational Modes of Inter-firm Co-operation and Technology Transfer", *Technovation,* Vol. 10, No. 1, pp. 17–30.

Hakansson, H. and J. Johanson (1988), "Formal and Informal Co-operation Strategies in International Industrial Networks", in F. Contractor and P. Lorange (eds.), *Co-operative Strategies in International Business,* Lexington Books, Lexington, MA.

Hakansson, H. and J. Johanson (1993), "The Network as a Governance Structure: Interfirm Co-operation Beyond Markets and Hierarchies", in G. Grabber (ed.), *The Embedded Firm,* Routledge, London.

Hedberg, B. (1981), "How Organisations Learn and Unlearn", in Paul Nystron and William Starbuck (eds.), *Handbook of Organisational Design, Vol. 1: Adapting Organisations to their Environments,* Oxford University Press, Oxford.

Huber, G. (1991), "Organisational Learning: The Contributing Processes and the Literatures", *Organisation Science,* Vol. 2, No. 1, pp.88–115.

Imai, K. (1985), "Network Organisation and Incremental Innovation in Japan", Discussion Paper No. 122, Institute of Business Research, Hitotsubashi University, Tokyo.

Imai, K. and Y. Baba (1989), "Systemic Innovation and Cross-border Networks: Transcending Markets and Hierarchies to Create a New Techno-economic System", in OECD (1991) *Technology and Productivity: The Challenge for Economic Policy,* OECD, Paris.

Imai, K. *et al.* (1985), "Managing the New Product Development Process: How Japanese Companies Learn and Unlearn", in K. Clark *et al.* (eds.), *The Uneasy Alliance: Managing the Productivity-Technology Dilemma,* Harvard Business School Press, Boston.

Inzerilli, G. (1990), "The Italian Alternative: Flexible Organisation and Social Management", *International Studies of Management & Organisation,* Vol. 20, No. 4, pp. 6–21.

Johnston, R. and P. Lawrence (1988), "Beyond Vertical Integration—The Rise of the Value-Adding Partnership", *Harvard Business Review,* Vol. 88, No. 4, pp. 94–101.

Kodama, F. (1992), "Technology Fusion and the New R&D", *Harvard Business Review,* July–August, pp. 70–78.

Koestler, A. (1967), *The Ghost in the Machine,* Hutchinson, London (Danube edition, with new preface, 1976).

Lin, O. (1994), "Development and Transfer of Industrial Technology in Taiwan, R.O.C.I.", in O. Lin, C.T. Shih and J.C. Yang (eds.) *Development and Transfer of Industrial Technology,* Elsevier, Amsterdam.

Lundvall, B.-Å. (1985), *Product Innovation and User-Producer Interaction,* Aalborg University Press, Aalborg.

Lundvall, B.-Å. (ed.) (1992), *National Systems of Innovation: Towards a Theory of Innovation and Interactive Learning,* Pinter Publishers, London.

Lundvall, B.-Å. and B. Johnson (1994), "The Learning Economy", *Journal of Industry Studies,* Vol. 1, No. 2, pp. 23–42.

MacNeil, I. (1978), "Contracts: Adjustment of Long-term Economic Relations under Classical, Neo-classical and Relational Contract Law", *North-western University Law Review,* Vol. 72, No. 6, pp. 854–905.

Mathews, J. (1993), "TCG R&D Networks: The Triangulation Strategy", *Journal of Industry Studies,* Vol. 1, No. 1, pp. 65–74.

Mathews, J. (1994a), *Catching the Wave: Workplace Reform in Australia,* Sydney, Allen & Unwin, Ithaca, New York, ILR Press, Cornell University.

Mathews, J. (1994b), "Holonic Organisational Architectures", *Human Systems Management,* (forthcoming).

Mathews, J. (1994c), "The Organisational Foundations of Intelligent Manufacturing Systems", *Computer-Integrated Manufacturing Systems* (forthcoming).

Miles, R. and C. Snow (1986), "Organisations: New Concepts for New Forms", *California Management Review,* Vol. 3, Spring, pp. 62–73.

Miles, R. and C. Snow (1994), *Fit, Failure and the Hall of Fame: How Companies Succeed or Fail,* The Free Press, Macmillan, New York.

Mody, A. (1993), "Learning Through Alliances", *Journal of Economic Behaviour and Organisation,* Vol. 20, pp. 151–170.

Nonaka, I. (1988), "Creating Organisational Order out of Chaos: Self-renewal in Japanese Firms", *California Management Review,* Vol. 30, pp. 57–73.

North, D. (1994), "Economic Performance through Time", *The American Economic Review,* Vol. 84, No. 3, pp. 359–68 (Nobel Prize Lecture, 1993).

OECD (1991a), *Technology in a Changing World,* Paris.

OECD (1991b), *Technology and Productivity: The Challenge for Economic Policy,* Paris.

OECD (1992). *Technology and the Economy: The Key Relationships,* Paris.

Pedler, M., J. Burgoyne and T. Boydell (1991), The *Learning Company,* McGraw-Hill, New York.

Perrow, C. (1991), "Small Firm Networks", Keynote speech, IAREP/SASE Conference "Interdisciplinary Approaches to the Study of Economic Problems", Stockholm School of Economics, 18 June.

Piore, M. and C. Sabel (1984), *The Second Industrial Divide: Prospects for Prosperity,* Basic Books, New York.

Pisano, G. and D. Teece (1989), "Collaborative Arrangements and Global Technology Strategy: Some Evidence from the Telecommunications Equipment Industry", in R. Rosenbloom and R. Burgelnan (eds.), *Research on Technological Innovation, Management and Policy,* Vol. 4, pp. 227–256.

Powell, W. (1987), "Hybrid Organisational Arrangements: New Form or Transitional Development?" *California Management Review,* Vol. 30, No. 1, pp. 67–87.

Powell, W. (1990a), "Neither Market nor Hierarchy: Network Forms of Organisation", in B. Staw and L. Cummings (eds.), *Research in Organisational Behaviour,* Vol. 12, pp. 295–336.

Powell, W. (1990b), "The Transformation of Organisational Forms", in R. Friedland and A. Robertson (eds.), *Beyond the Marketplace: Rethinking Economy and Society,* Aldine de Gruyter, New York, pp. 301–29.

Pyke, F, G. Becattini and W. Sengenberger (eds.) (1990), *Industrial Districts and Inter-Firm Co-operation in Italy,* International Institute for Labour Studies, Geneva.

Reddy, N.M. and M.V.H. Rao (1990), "Tbe Industrial Market as an Interfirm Organisation", *Journal of Management Studies,* Vol. 27, No. 1, pp. 43–59.

Sabel, C. (1992), "Studied Trust: Building New Forms of Co-operation in a Volatile Economy", in F. Pyke and W. Sengenberger (eds.), *Industrial Districts and Local Economic Regeneration,* International Institute for Labour Studies, Geneva.

Senge, P. (1990), *The Fifth Discipline: The Art & Practice of The Learning Organisation,* Doubleday/Currency, New York.

Snow, C., R. Miles. and H. Coleman (1992), "Managing 21st Century Network Organisations", *Organisational Dynamics,* Winter, pp. 5–20.

Teece, D. (1989), "Inter-organisational Requirements of the Innovation Process", *Managerial and Decision Economics,* Special Issue, pp. 35–42.

Teece, D. (1992), "Competition, Co-operation and Innovation: Organisational Arrangements for Regimes of Rapid Technological Progress", *Journal of Economic Behaviour and Organisation,* Vol. 18, pp. 1–25.

Thorelli, H. (1986), "Networks: Between Markets and Hierarchies", *Strategic Management Journal,* Vol. 7, pp. 37–51.

Von Hippel, E. (1988), *The Sources of Innovation,* Oxford University Press, Oxford.

Wang, Chien-nan (1993), "The Development and Strategy of Taiwan's Information Technology Industry", *Proceedings of the Conference on Information Technology Innovation and National Economy: Lessons for the Next Decade of Change, 8–9 October, KISDI, Seoul.*

Wang, Chien-nan (1994*a*), "Exploring Co-operative Opportunities between Taiwan and European Electronics Industries", in Chien-nan Wang (ed.), *Globalisation, Regionalisation and Taiwan's Economy,* Chung-Hua Institution for Economic Research, Taipei.

Wang, Chien-nan (1994*b*), "An Investigation of Industrial Strategies and Government Policies in International Industrial Co-operation" (in Chinese), Report to the Industrial Development Bureau, Ministry of Economic Affairs, Chung-Hua Institution for Economic Research, Taipei.

Wade, R. (1989), *Governing the Market: Economic Theory and the Role of Government in East Asian Industrialisation, Princeton University Press, Princeton, NJ.*

Weiss, L. (1988), *Creating Capitalism: The State and Small Business Since 1945,* Basil Blackwell, Oxford.

Weiss, L. (1994), "Government-business Relations in East Asia: The Changing Basis of State Capacity", *Asian Perspective,* Vol. 18, No. 2.

Weiss, L. and J. Hobson (1995), *States and Economic Development: A Comparative Historical Analysis,* Policy Press, Cambridge.

Weiss, L. and J. Mathews (1991), "Structure, Strategy and Public Policy: Lessons from the Italian Textile Industry for Australia", *UNSW Studies in Organisational Analysis and Innovation,* No. 5, Industrial Relations Research Centre, University of New South Wales, Sydney.

Wheatley, M. (1992), *Leadership and the New Science: Learning about Organisation from an Orderly Universe,* Berrett-Koehler Publishers, San Francisco.

13

Investing in Human Capital

Riel Miller and Gregory Wurzburg

The contribution of "human capital"—workers' know-how—to productivity goes largely unreflected in statements of companies' income and in their balance-sheets. The reason is simple: no one knows how to define and evaluate it. How then, can the costs and benefits of further education and training for upgrading it be measured?[1]

Many of the terms used to describe the economy today no longer reflect reality. Everybody knows that the lights would go out, the airplanes would stop flying, and the banks and many of the factories would shut down if the computer software that runs their systems suddenly vanished. Yet these crucial "intellectual" assets do not appear in any substantial way on the world's balance-sheets. Instead, they are full of "tangible" assets—buildings and machinery, stocks and financial reserves.

But important structural changes are occurring in the nature of economic activity, in the role of human resources as agents for such change, and in the role of public policy in facilitating the transition. And with increasing "knowledge-intensity," growth in employment must be sought through improved productivity in firms with a solid capacity to innovate and use technology effectively.[2] The initial qualifications of workers and the incentives for investing in further acquisition of knowledge show every sign of assuming more importance as determinants of performance, not only of individuals in labour markets, but of enterprises and national economies.[3]

So how does a government measure capital formation, when much new capital is intellectual? How does it gauge the productivity of the knowledge of workers whose product cannot be counted? And how then can it track productivity growth? And if it cannot do any of these things with the relative precision of simpler times, what becomes of the long-hallowed mission of government: guiding national economies? But even if some of these problems of measurement are solved, the phenomena they assess will be far more difficult to control than in the industrial economies of old.

National accounts and economic analysis frequently treat labour as a more or less homogeneous input to economic activity. But the simplifying assumptions about how "human capital" is measured and evaluated—the differentiated skills, knowledge and expertise of workers—are less readily tenable than ever because of shifts in economic output in the OECD countries away from goods towards services and other knowledge- and information-intensive forms of output. Because of these shifts, and the more competitive climate in which economic activity takes place, the economic survival of enterprises, and the employability and earning power of individuals, depend more and more on learning as the basis for agile adaptation. But the tools available to measure and attach economic value to human capital, and the "investment" in upgrading it, have not kept up with these changes.

The changes in the composition of output and employment have been dramatic. Between 1972 and 1992, the share of civilian employment in services increased from half to nearly two-thirds, as output in the OECD countries tilted increasingly towards them. Employment shares in knowledge- and information-intensive service sectors grew especially quickly. In the United States, for example, employment in financing, insurance, real estate and business services grew nearly four times faster than overall employment, and more than twice as fast as employment in community, social and personal services. In France, employment in financing, insurance, real estate and business services grew twice as fast as overall employment. Simultaneously, manufacturing employment fell from 36% to 29%, and agriculture employment fell by nearly half to less than 7%.

But the changes in output tell only part of the story, because the requirements of qualifications within sectors—manufacturing included—were also rising. As these changes occurred, the occupational composition of employment was also changing. Between 1981 and 1991, the blue-collar share of employment declined by an average of 3 percentage points, while the white-collar share rose by more than 6 points. The fastest-growing of the occupations were those in professional, technical, administrative and managerial activities. These occupations are expected to continue to be the fastest-growing, if one judges from the countries for which occupational forecasts are available. In the United Kingdom, for example, they are the only jobs in which significant growth is expected by the year 2000. In Japan, employment in professional and technical occupations is expected to grow by more than 40% before the end of the century, nearly four times faster than the next fastest-growing group, clerical and related occupations. In the United States, employment in professional and technical occupations is expected to grow by 36% by the year 2005, nearly three times faster than craft and skilled manual occupations.

Yet, for all the importance of the knowledge and skills of the workers as factors in performance, not only are the means for measuring them remarkably crude; they are also rigidly determined by certifying institutions.[4] The challenge for policy-makers is to consider ways to improve the signals used to indicate the constantly changing productive capabilities of the labour force.

THREE BARRIERS

Three substantial barriers stand in the way of more efficient approaches to measuring and valuing human resources in more knowledge- and skill-intensive economic activities.

One is a lack of transparency in the costs of labour, and particularly of upgrading the qualifications of experienced workers. As continuous upgrading becomes a routine part of human-resource management, labour costs expand beyond the usual wage and non-wage expenses (social charges, pension and health costs), to include the direct costs of training (course fees, training material) as well as indirect costs (such as the value of production forgone while workers are off the job, and that lost as workers practice and perfect what they have learned).

Yet the definition and measurement of these attendant costs, and the extent to which they are reported for statistical or tax-reporting purposes, are highly variable. Sometimes the salary costs of people participating in training are not counted. The costs of production forgone when people leave the workplace to participate in training are difficult to measure and rarely captured except in detailed case-study analysis. It is even more difficult to evaluate the costs of the initial lower productivity of workers when they return from training, and start applying the content of their training.

Remedies to this problem take a number of forms. The Australian authorities, for instance, in co-operation with the OECD and with support from a number of other OECD countries, are engaged in the preparation of a manual intended to improve the consistency of definitions and measures used in the collection of training statistics. In another vein, Finland and Sweden considered introducing changes to financial accounting and reporting practices by requiring enterprises to provide details of training costs on their statements of income and loss.

A second problem is the difficulty of measuring the productive capacity—the knowledge, skills and abilities—that workers acquire through further training and/or experience on the job. Methods and institutions for undertaking this type of in-progress assessment remain underdeveloped, although advances are being made in a number of countries. Some, such as the *Bilan des Compétences,* established through cooperation between education and labour-market authorities in France, aim at evaluating what knowledge and skills individuals have acquired, as an aid in job-search and placement. Others, such as the Assessment of Prior Learning, in Canada, are carried out by institutions of higher education to assess what individuals have learned for the purpose of placing them at an appropriate point in institutions of formal education. Still others, such as the National Qualifications Framework in New Zealand and the National Council of Vocational

Qualification in the United Kingdom, are intended to relate formal education and training achievement to a national structure of vocational qualifications that correspond to practical requirements of qualifications in the labour market.

Although some of these approaches, such as those found in France, New Zealand and the United Kingdom, are better adapted to meeting the immediate demand for precise information on qualifications that are required in the workplace, all of them move towards fulfilling basic requirements for individualised assessment of qualifications acquired outside the context of formal education and training institutions.

Even when qualifications can be measured, there is a third problem in reflecting a realistic economic value for them. The barriers here are found in a number of forms. Enterprises cannot capitalise training costs or the stream of benefits from upgraded qualifications of workers, to carry them on the balance sheet of their financial reports, and to allow them to be depreciated over the useful life of the skills involved.

The reasons are derived from the fact that workers—and their qualifications—are not owned by enterprises, and from the absence of institutional arrangements, such as bonding arrangements or insurance, that would allow firms to exercise a claim on their value. This prevents them from spreading the costs of training over the period of time during which they enjoy the benefits of the qualifications acquired by it. This, in turn, distorts the rate-of-return analysis by which investment choices (tangible v. intangible) might be evaluated. It underestimates the apparent rate of return to training by counting all of the costs, but only those benefits which are expected in the year in which training expenditure is made.

Nor can individuals count on a predictable return to improved qualifications because wage- and salary-setting does not usually take systematic account of upgraded qualifications, even where they are reliably measured. Payment for ability—wages fixed on the basis of what workers know and can do—is still rare; instead, wages are typically linked to the jobs for which they are hired.

The absence of more sophisticated means for measuring and valuing human resources, particularly the qualifications acquired through experience and training, can heighten the risk of mis-allocation of resources. In the firm, the lack of data can reduce the importance of rate of return as a criterion in management decisions on training and human resources. As a result, criteria for investments in employees' skills get crowded out by other considerations, such as government-imposed training levies or even "training targets" established by corporate headquarters, but which do not necessarily have any bearing on the strategic and tactical requirements of an enterprise.

For workers the already risky and expensive decision to invest in the acquisition of skills becomes even more difficult without transparent and reliable evaluation and recognition of their current capacity. In general, in circumstances in which information about qualifications is so incomplete, where the likelihood of benefiting from upgraded qualifications is so uncertain, and where insurance is not possible, it is probable that the qualifications acquired in training will be under-valued, yet another reason that resources will be allocated inefficiently.

INNOVATIONS IN ASSESSMENT

The OECD Jobs Study, in urging national authorities to address factors that interfere with more effective practices for developing human resources, suggested that they consider innovations in financial accounting and reporting practices (such as reporting the costs of developing human resources and workforce qualifications) and in systems for the measurement and recognition of skills and abilities (like those found in Canada, France, New Zealand and the United Kingdom).

Such changes are consistent with developments in business thinking. Companies like Dow Chemical, the Canadian Imperial Bank of Commerce and Hughes Aircraft are introducing new methods for evaluating and recording the knowledge assets of their workforces.[5] These practices fit well with the shift to quality and teamwork where sharing ideas and generating new knowledge are essential for success. Firm-based financial accounting and reporting practices, although rooted mostly in an era in which knowledge was easier to manage, are making progress. For instance, there is experimental use of human-resource satellite accounts—which provide detailed information on the development costs of human resources in income statements, and breakdowns of qualified staff on balance sheets—to accompany audited financial statements, and a growing interest in requiring fuller disclosure of information on human-resource development and workforce qualifications. Yet the durability of these innovations remains uncertain without agreed rules or a broader base upon which to spread risk and collect relevant experiences.

The increased emphasis on life-long learning has brought forward a number of policy responses. The Canadian government, for instance, is organising a National Conference on Prior Learning Assessment for the autumn to accelerate the implementation of initiatives already underway in most provinces. The New Zealand Qualifications Authority has reached agreement with higher-education institutions under which the qualifications they award are now accommodated within the national framework for qualifications. These innovative initiatives to assess learning beyond the traditional certifying establishments point towards a growing demand for more detailed information for human-resource management.

For policy-makers the goal is clear. More transparent information about workers' productive abilities (their investments in knowledge) is required in order to improve hiring and training practices and, ultimately, increase economic growth. Policies that facilitate efforts to reconceptualise the management of human capital is one way of improving decisions both on the uses of the asset (stock) and the incremental investments that either maintain or add to it (flow). New systems of information about human capital and decision-making are required to address a number of pressing questions. What form of human capital should attract investment? How does one set the proper incentives? Is there a way to determine the extent of over- or under-investment? Is the existing stock of knowledge embodied in people being properly and efficiently used? Providing the information that can answer these questions more accurately and at a lower cost for individuals, firms and governments will go a long way towards encouraging the growth of knowledge and learning—and the vital innovation that will flow from them.

NOTES

1. Riel Miller, "Investment Knowledge and Knowledge Investment: The Need to Rethink Human Capital Information and Decision Making Systems." *OECD Publications,* Paris, 1995.
2. "The OECD Jobs Study: Facts, Analysis, Strategies." *OECD Publications,* Paris, 1994.
3. "The OECD Jobs Study: Evidence and Explanations." *OECD Publications,* Paris, 1994.
4. See pp. 12–15.
5. Thomas A Stewart, "Your Company's Most Valuable Asset: Intellectual Capital," *Fortune Magazine,* 3 October 1994.

Part Five

Society and Public Policy: Government, Education, and Training in the Knowledge-Based Economy

14

An Era of Man-Made Brainpower Industries

Lester C. Thurow

THE DISAPPEARANCE OF CLASSICAL COMPARATIVE ADVANTAGE

The classical theory of comparative advantage was developed to explain the geographic location of industry in the nineteenth and twentieth centuries. In the theory of comparative advantage, location of production depended upon two factors—natural resource endowments and factor proportions (the relative abundance of capital and labor).[1] Those with good soil, climate, and rainfall specialize in agricultural production; those with oil supply oil. Countries that were capital-rich (lots of capital per worker) made capital-intensive products, while countries that were labor-rich (little capital per worker) made labor-intensive products.

In the nineteenth and for most of the twentieth century, the theory of comparative advantage explained what needed to be explained. The United States grew cotton in the South because the climate and soil were right; it made cloth in New England because New England had the water power to drive, and the capital to finance, textile mills. New York was the biggest city in America since it had the best natural harbor on the East Coast and the capital to build a water connection (the Erie Canal) to the Midwest. Pittsburgh was the iron and steel capital, since given the location of America's coal, iron ore, rivers, and lakes, it was the cost-minimizing place to be. In an age of railroads, Chicago was destined to be America's transportation capital and hog butcher to the world. Texas was oil, and the availability of electricity dictated that aluminum be made on the Columbia River in the state of Washington.

Consider this list of the twelve largest companies in America on January 1, 1900: the American Cotton Oil Company, American Steel, American Sugar Refining Company, Continental Tobacco, Federal Steel, General Electric, National

Lead, Pacific Mail, People's Gas, Tennessee Coal and Iron, U.S. Leather, and U.S. Rubber.[2] Ten of the twelve companies were natural resource companies. The economy at the turn of the century was a natural resource economy.

But something else is interesting about that list. Bits and pieces of each of these companies exist inside other companies, but only one of those companies, General Electric, is alive today. Eleven of the twelve could not make it to the next century as separate entities. The moral of the story is clear. Capitalism is a process of creative destruction whereby dynamic new small companies are continually replacing old large ones that have not been able to adjust to new conditions.

The same picture was true outside of the United States. Before World War I more than one million workers toiled in the coal mines of Great Britain—6 percent of the total workforce.[3] Coal was king. It was the motive force that powered the world. Today less than thirty thousand workers toil in those same coal mines.

In 1917 manufacturing was on the rise but thirteen of the twenty largest industrial enterprises ranked by assets were still natural-resource-based companies: United States Steel, Standard Oil, Bethlehem Steel, Armour and Company, Swift and Company, Midvale Steel and Ordnance, International Harvester, E. I. du Pont de Nemours and Company, United States Rubber, Phelps Dodge, General Electric, Anaconda Copper, American Smelting and Refining, Singer Sewing Machine Company, Ford Motor Company, Westinghouse, American Tobacco, Jones and Laughlin Steel, Union Carbide and Weyerhaeuser.[4]

In the late nineteenth and early twentieth centuries, those with natural resources, such as Argentina and Chile, were rich while those without natural resources, such as Japan, were destined to be poor.[5] Everyone who became rich in the nineteenth and twentieth centuries had natural resources.

Once a country became rich, it tended to stay rich. Having a higher income, it saved more; saving more it invested more; investing more it worked with more plant and equipment; working with more capital its productivity was higher; and having higher productivity it could pay higher wages. For those who grew rich, there was a virtuous cycle leading them to more riches. As they became rich, they shifted to capital-intensive products that generated even higher levels of labor productivity and even higher wages.

In contrast, consider the list made in 1990 by the Ministry of International Trade and Industry in Japan speculating as to what would be the most rapidly growing industries in the 1990s and the early part of the twenty-first century: microelectronics, biotechnology, the new material science industries, telecommunications, civilian aircraft manufacturing, machine tools and robots, and computers (hardware and software).[6] All of them are man-made brainpower industries that could be located anywhere on the face of the earth. Where they will be located depends upon who organizes the brainpower to capture them.

Natural resource endowments have fallen out of the competitive equation. Modern products simply use fewer natural resources. Bridges and cars have fewer tons of steel embedded in them, and devices such as the computer use almost no natural resources. Modern transportation costs have created a world where resources can be cheaply moved to wherever they are needed. Japan is a good example, having the world's dominant steel industry yet having no coal and no iron ore. That could not have happened in the nineteenth century or for most of the twentieth century.

After correcting for general inflation, natural resource prices have fallen almost 60 percent from the mid-1970s to the mid-1990s.[7] Bet on another 60 percent fall in the next twenty-five years. Raw materials are going to be pouring out of the old Communist world but, even more important, the world is on the edge of a material science revolution that will be turning out made-to-order designer materials. Biotechnology is going to be speeding up the green revolution in agriculture. Few will become rich in the twenty-first century based simply on their possession of raw materials.

Capital availability has also fallen out of the competitive equation. With the development of a world capital market, everyone essentially borrows in New York, London, or Tokyo. Today an entrepreneur in Bangkok can build a plant as capital-intensive as any in the United States, Germany, or Japan despite his living in a country with a per capita income less than one tenth that of those three countries. Effectively, there simply is no such thing as a capital-rich or a capital-poor country when it comes to investment. Capital-intensive products are not automatically made in rich countries. Workers in rich countries won't automatically work with more capital, have higher levels of productivity, or enjoy higher wages.

In an era of man-made brainpower industries capita/labor ratios cease to be meaningful variables, since the whole distinction between capital and labor collapses. Skills and knowledge, human capital, are created by the same investment funds that create physical capital. Raw labor (the willingness to sacrifice leisure) still exists, but it has become much less important in the production process and can, in any case, be bought very cheaply when there is an entire globe of poor underemployed workers to draw upon.

Today knowledge and skills now stand alone as the source of comparative advantage. They have become the key ingredient in the late twentieth century's location of economic activity. Silicon Valley and Route 128 are where they are simply because that is where the brainpower is. They have nothing else going for them.

With the invention of science-based industries in the twentieth century—the first being the chemical engineering industries of Germany—the deliberate invention of new products became important. Those who invented new products would produce those products during the initial, high-profitability, high-wage, stages of their life cycle. Eventually production would move into the third world but by then the product would have become a labor-intensive, low-wage commodity with low profitability. Textiles were the classic example. They fueled the industrial revolution in both Great Britain and the United States but are today a standard third-world-manufactured product.

But what came to be called "the product cycle" no longer exists. The art of reverse engineering along with the growth of multinational companies interested in employing their technologies wherever production costs are lowest has led to a world where new product technologies flow around the world almost as fast as capital and natural resources. Proprietary new product technologies aren't necessarily employed where they are invented or by those who financed them.

Think of the video camera and recorder (invented by Americans), the fax (invented by Americans), and the CD player (invented by the Dutch). When it comes to sales, employment, and profits, all have become Japanese products despite the Japanese not inventing any of them. Product invention, if a country is also not the world's low-cost producer, gives one very little economic advantage. Technology has never been more important, but what matters more is being the leader in process technologies and what matters less is being the leader in new product technologies.

Being the low-cost producer is partly a matter of wages, but to a much greater extent it is a matter of becoming the masters of process technologies, having the skills and knowing how to put new things together, and the ability to manage the production processes. To be masters of process technologies a successful business must be managed so that there is a seamless web among invention, design, manufacturing, sales, logistics, and services that competitors cannot match. The secret of being the best is found, not in being either labor- or capital-intensive, or even in being management-intensive, but in having the skills base throughout the organization that allows it to be the low-cost integrator of all of these activities.

The classical theory of comparative advantage is often taught as if everyone benefits from trade. Technically that is not true. The total income of every country that takes advantage of comparative advantage grows, but there will be individuals within each country who lose. What the theory holds is that those who gain from international trade receive enough extra income from their activities that they could compensate those who lose when international trade commences. If that compensation isn't actually paid (and it almost never is), then those who lose are quite rational to oppose international trade.

But in the classical theory the losses usually will be quite small. First, full employment is assumed to exist. Free trade does not push anyone into unemployment. Second, transition costs are assumed to be zero. There is no region-, industry-, or firm-specific physical or human capital that is destroyed when workers are forced to shift between regions, industries, or firms. Third, returns are assumed to be everywhere equal. Each industry has the same rate of return on human or physical capital. Each firm and industry pays the same wage rate for a worker's being willing to give up an hour of leisure. As a consequence, being forced to shift jobs doesn't change wages very much, if at all.

In the classical theory of comparative advantage, there is no role for government in determining the location of industry. There was a "right" place to do everything given by natural resource endowments and factor proportions. If everything was done in the "right" place, the world would maximize its total production. Wise governments know that any attempt to alter private location decisions would simply burden the economy with the inefficiency costs of having economic activities located in the "wrong" places.

This set of beliefs led to what are now the immortal words attributed to the chairman of President George Bush's Council of Economic Advisers, Michael Boskin: "It doesn't make any difference whether a country makes potato chips or computer chips."[8]

But none of these assumptions is of course true. Trade can cause unemployment. Those who lose their jobs when imports expand often remain unemployed for long periods of time. Theoretically, governments could stimulate their economies to prevent higher unemployment but they often don't. There are transition costs in moving people between regions, industries, or firms. Empirically, wages and rates of return on capital do not equalize in even rather long periods of time.

In 1992 average American wages ranged from $20.68 per hour in cigarette manufacturing and $19.70 per hour in malt beverage manufacturing to $5.94 in women's dress manufacturing and $5.29 in eating and drinking establishments.[9] If fringe benefits are included, these differentials expand by one fourth.[10] Average rates of return on common equity ranged from 27 percent in pharmaceuticals to minus 26 percent in building materials in 1992.[11] Looking at returns by firm rather than industry, the differences are even larger.

Such differences persist over long periods of time. Real-world economies are dynamic and never settle down into an equilibrium world of equal wages or equal rates of return. Pharmaceuticals have become a hot political issue precisely because they have yielded the highest rate of return on capital for essentially the entire post–World War II period. Petroleum has paid wages above the mean (plus 29 percent) and household services wages below the mean (minus 36 percent) consistently.

Wages don't just depend upon individual productivity. Ph.D. university-based economists playing on the American team make a lot more money than their equivalents who play on the British team. Their knowledge is not less than ours, but they generate less revenue with their activities because of the productivity of the other team members with whom they work. The value of any individual's knowledge depends upon the smartness with which it is used in the entire system—the knowledge absorption abilities of both the buyers and other suppliers.

These realities do not change the conclusion that there are net benefits from international trade, but they do mean that the aggregate losses and the number of losers can be very large. If the winners actually compensated the losers, the winners could lose most of their gains. Losers are often very numerous and lose large amounts of their income. Fighting hard to prevent such losses is not irrational.

Another layer of complexity is added when man-made brainpower industries that depend upon research and development and human skills dominate the system. Investors don't just respond to a fixed set of investment opportunities. Research and development investments create a set of industrial possibilities. Countries don't have the same set of investment opportunities.

The industries of the future have to be invented. They don't just exist. In the era ahead countries have to make the investments in knowledge and skills that will create a set of man-made brainpower industries that will allow their citizens to have high wages and a high standard of living. By way of contrast, natural resource industries were essentially a birthright. One was born in a country with a lot of natural resources or one wasn't. Man-made brainpower industries are not a birthright. No country acquires these industries without effort and without making the investments necessary to create them.

The theory of comparative advantage still holds but a country's comparative advantage is created by what it does—more precisely by what investments it makes. If a country has not generated the necessary skill base, Ph.D.s in microbiology, it cannot have a biotechnology industry.

American observers often worry about the excessive growth of the service sector with its lower than average wages. While understandable these are not the right worries. Historically, our statistical data have divided industries into agriculture, mining, construction, manufacturing, and services, where services is a heterogeneous category that includes everything not counted in the other four categories. Services is simply too heterogeneous to be an interesting category. On average, the services industries pay wages one third less than those in manufacturing, but some service industries, such as finance or medicine, pay the highest wages in the economy.

The real issue is not the growth of services but whether the economy is making a successful transition from low-wage, low-skill industries (some of which exist in each of our standard statistical categories) to high-wage, high-skill industries (some of which exist in each of our standard statistical categories). Two of the largest twelve companies in America in 1900 (Pacific Mail and People's Gas) were service companies and two of the industries that the Japanese identified as most desirable ninety years later (telecommunications and computer software) were also service industries. Success or failure depends upon whether a country is making a successful transition to the man-made brainpower industries of the future—not on the size of any particular sector.

In an era of man-made brainpower industries, the global economy is a dynamic one always in transition. There aren't lengthy periods of time without technical change where competition can equalize wages and rates of return on capital investment so that all activities are equally lucrative, so that it doesn't matter what one does. While there certainly are long-run market forces equalizing returns, specific firms and industries maintain above-average wages and above-average returns on capital for long periods of time. They do so by moving from product to product within technological families so fast that there is almost no chance for those not in the industry to enter it quickly enough (it takes time to develop the necessary brainpower and skills) to drive down above-average returns on these new activities. As others enter, they are in fact phasing out these new activities to replace them with other, even newer, higher-return activities.

Cost barriers to entry are high and the time necessary to catch up with market leaders is lengthy. To catch up with the American aircraft manufacturing industry, for example, Europe's Airbus Industries required more than two decades and more than $26 billion in public funds.[12]

The economist's concept of equilibrium is useful, since it identifies the long-run direction of economic forces, but it is not a useful concept for describing economic reality at any moment in time. At every instant of time the economy is operating in a period of short-run dynamic disequilibrium, moving toward equilibrium, but with dynamic change coming so fast relative to the time lags that would be necessary to reach equilibrium that periods of short-run disequilibrium never have a chance to become periods of long-run equilibrium.

During such periods of disequilibrium there are often very high wages to be earned and very high rates of return on capital investment to be had. By keeping one generation ahead in making microprocessors, Intel's profits were 23 percent of sales and its net return on assets 17 percent despite having to set almost $500 million aside to cover the costs of correcting a flaw in the Pentium chip.[13] Keeping one jump ahead in software, Microsoft's net income was running at 24 percent of sales in 1995.[14] These above equilibrium returns made Bill Gates into America's wealthiest person with $15 billion in net worth before he was forty.[15]

Such returns will not last forever (in economics they are known as disequilibrium quasi-rents), but they can last for many years—Intel's profits have run far above average for more than a decade. These profit opportunities are the modern equivalent of finding El Dorado—the city of gold. They are very nice to have while they last and they generate permanent wealth that doesn't disappear after the gold mine has yielded its last ounce of gold. Of such events are personal and national fortunes made.

If a firm or a country wants to stay at the leading edge of technology so that it can continue to generate high-disequilibrium wages and profits, it must be a participant in the evolutionary progress of man-made brainpower industries so that it is in the right position to take advantage of the technical and economic revolutions that occasionally arise. The costs of being forced out of such industries are not just the costs of having to move people and capital from one industry or geographic location to another, or of the lower wages that laid-off workers will receive upon reemployment. In the short and medium term the real costs are the lost high wages and profits that one could have had if one had stayed at the leading edge of the wave of new technologies. In the long run the costs are those of getting shut out of future developments and not being able to be a player in new high-wage, high-profit opportunities that will arise. Countries that have not made random access memory chips won't make microprocessors.

If natural resources have ceased to dominate economic activity in a world of man-made brainpower industries, if factor proportions have dissolved in a world of global capital markets and worldwide logistics, if new product introductions come so fast that there is never time enough for equilibrium to develop in labor or capital markets, if transition costs are very large, if high and persistent unemployment is a worldwide fact of life, then the real world is far removed from the classical theory of comparative advantage. Trade still yields great net benefits, but how those benefits are distributed, who receives the benefits and the losses, becomes a much more complicated problem.

SKILLS: THE ONLY SOURCE OF LONG-RUN SUSTAINABLE COMPETITIVE ADVANTAGE

With everything else dropping out of the competitive equation, knowledge has become the only source of long-run sustainable competitive advantage, but knowledge can only be employed through the skills of individuals. As with everything else, knowledge and skills will move around the world—but slower than anything else. Education and training take a long time to complete, and many of the relevant skills are not those taught in formal educational institutions but the process skills that can only be learned in a production environment. The theory of semiconductor design is relatively easy to learn. Actually building semiconductors to the tolerances that are required (less than half a micron) is very difficult.

Today's transportation and communications technologies mean that skilled workers in the first world can effectively work together with the unskilled in the third world. Skilled components can be made in the first world and then shipped to the third world to be assembled with low-skill components that have been made there. Putting the first world's skilled together with the lower-waged third world's unskilled cuts costs, allows profits to rise, and permits some of the first world's skilled workers to have higher wages than they would have if they were still working with the higher-waged unskilled workers of the first world.

Research and design skills can be electronically brought in from the first world. What sells can be quickly communicated to the third world factory and retailers know that the speed of delivery won't be significantly affected by where production occurs. Instant communications and rapid transportation means that markets can be effectively served from production points on the other side of the globe.

Multinational companies are central in this process, since their decisions as to where they will develop and keep technological leadership are central to where most of the very good jobs will be located.[16] Multinational firms will decide to locate their high-wage leadership skills in the United States not because they happen to be American firms but only if America offers them the lowest costs of developing these technological leadership skills. The countries offering companies the lowest costs of developing technological leadership will be the countries that invest the most in research and development, education, and the infrastructure (telecommunications systems, etc.) necessary to exploit leadership positions. National wealth will go to those countries that build the constellations of skills that reinforce each other.

Organizations with global skills will have to be built and managed. Those with the skills to put the necessary worldwide webs of skill together are apt to be the highest paid of the knowledge workers—the elite of the elite.

In the past, first world workers with third world skills could earn premium wages simply because they lived in the first world. There they worked with more equipment, better technology, and more skilled co-workers than those with third world skills who lived in the third world. These complementary factors effectively raised their productivity and wages above what they would have been if they had been working in the third world. But that premium is gone. Today they will be paid based on their own skills—not based upon the skills of their neighbors. Put bluntly, in the economy of the future those with third world skills will earn third world wages even if they live in the first world. Unskilled labor will simply be bought wherever in the world it is cheapest.

If one looks at the breakthrough firms of the early 1990s, it is clear that there is a lot of productivity to be gotten by tearing down traditional functional walls between areas such as R&D, design, manufacturing, or sales and by pushing decision making much farther down into the organization to cut out layers of management hierarchy. But all of those actions require a much better educated and skilled workforce at the bottom. Those down at the bottom of the organization have to be capable of understanding the firm's strategy so well that, because of their intimate local knowledge, they will make decisions better than the decisions that the "boss" would have made under the previous system.

If the person on the unloading dock runs a computerized inventory control system wherein he logs delivered materials right into his hand-held computer and the computer instantly prints out a check that is given to the truck driver to be taken back to his firm (eliminating the need for large white-collar accounting offices that process purchases), the person on the unloading dock ceases to be someone who just moves boxes. He or she has to have a very different skill set.

Factory operatives and laborers used to be high school graduates or even high school dropouts. Today 16 percent of them have some college education and 5 percent have graduated from college. Among precision production and craft workers 32 percent have been to or graduated from college.[17] Among new hires those percentages are much higher.

In an era of man-made brainpower industries, individual, corporate, and national economic success will all require both new and much more extensive skill sets than have been required in the past. By themselves skills don't guarantee success. They have to be put together in successful organizations. But without skills there are no successful organizations.

The hallmark of the industrial revolution has been the slow replacement of the unskilled by the skilled. But for most of its duration, public investments in education have raised the supply of skills at least as fast, and perhaps faster, than the market demanded. That did not occur by accident. Mass universal compulsory public education was invented by the textile mill magnates of New England, who needed better-educated workers in their factories. Their motives were partly altruistic and partly economic. They were willing to pay taxes to help finance that education, but they did not want to pay the entire cost. They wanted the help of other taxpayers.

By nature the education investments of democratic governments tend to be egalitarian. Historically, those investments of government have allowed the unskilled to gradually become skilled—first by free grade schools, then free high schools, and finally free (the GI Bill—$91 billion in grants and $103 billion in loans in today's dollars), low-cost (public), or subsidized (private scholarships) university educations.[18] Without government investments in education, education would undoubtedly have remained the preserve of the rich as it has in every country where the investments have not been made. Government investments in education created the middle class.

Ahead lies a period not of slow evolution but of punctuated equilibrium when the skill sets required in the economy will be radically different from those needed in the past. This rising need can be seen in the recent studies showing rates of return on skill investments to be more than twice those of investments in plant and equipment.[19] But support for public egalitarian skill investment is being slashed—loans are replacing private scholarships, tuitions are rising sharply in public universities as taxpayer funds are withdrawn, federal loans replace what used to be federal scholarships, and public educational spending is being cut more than proportionally at both state and federal levels whenever budget reductions are made.

The necessary supply of skills will undoubtedly arise in the era ahead, but those additional supplies need not come, and probably will not come, from the unskilled workers who currently live in the first world. With the ability to make anything anywhere in the world and sell it anywhere else in the world, business firms can "cherry pick" the skilled or those easy (cheap) to skill wherever they exist in the world. Some third world countries are now making massive investment in basic education. American firms don't have to hire an American high school graduate if that graduate is not world-class. His or her educational defects are not their problem. Investing to give the necessary market skills to a well-educated Chinese high school graduate may well look like a much more attractive (less costly) investment than having to retrain an American high school dropout or a poorly trained high school graduate. As the data on falling wages indicate, the unskilled in the first world are on their way to becoming marginalized.

In a global economy what economists know as "the theory of factor price equalization" holds that an American worker who does not work with more natural resources than a South Korean (and none can, since there is now a world market for raw material to which everyone has equal access), who does not work with more capital than a South Korean (and none can, since there is a global capital market where everyone borrows in New York, London, and Tokyo), who does not work with more skilled complementary workers than a South Korean (and none can, since multinational companies can send knowledge and skills to wherever they are needed around the world), and who does not work with better technology than a South Korean (and few will, since reverse engineering has become an international art form whereby new product technologies move around the world very fast, South Korea is making R&D investment at rates higher than those of many developed nations, and multinational companies will use their new technologies in South Korea if that is the cheapest place to do so) will find that at each skill level he or she has to work for wages commensurate with the pay found for that skill level in South Korea. Adjusted for skills, South Korean wages will rise and American wages will fall until they equal each other. At that point, factor price equalization will have occurred.

Until the early 1970s a truly global economy did not exist and unskilled Americans were awarded a wage premium simply because they were Americans. They would automatically work with more raw materials, employ more capital-intensive processes, have workmen with more skills, and use better technology than would workers in South Korea. But this premium is vanishing—and will ultimately disappear entirely.

None of the brainpower industries listed by the Japanese has a natural home. Where these seven industries will be located depends upon who organizes the brainpower to capture them. Organizing brainpower means not just building an R&D system that will put a nation on the leading edge of technology in each of these seven areas, but organizing a top-to-bottom workforce that has the brainpower necessary to be masters of the new production and distribution technologies that will allow them to be the world's low-cost producers in each of these seven areas.

In today's global economic game, technology strategies have become central. Americans will face others with strategies for conquering the key strategic industries of tomorrow. Europe's Airbus Industries is the best current example of this reality. In 1994 it received more orders for new planes than Boeing. What is the American answer to Airbus Industries? Whatever arguments Americans advance to prove that Europe has "wasted" too much of its money in developing the Airbus, it exists and isn't going away. America will have to develop defensive industrial policies to deal with situations where the rest of the world targets one of America's key industries—even if Americans decide not to have offensive industrial policies. But what is true in sports is equally true in economics: If one plays defense all of the time and is never on offense, one never wins.

A technology strategy does not mean that a government has to pick winners and losers. The European Common Market picks what it thinks are hot technologies and then announces that it has matching funds in programs such as JESSI, ESPIRIT, or EUREKA, where if at least three companies from two different countries come through the door with a good project and half the money, these private funds will be matched with government money. Government is not picking winners and losers, but it is expanding time horizons and the scale of operations and making it cheaper for firms to play tomorrow's game.

A country's technology policy is its industrial strategy. It determines where that country will play the game. Technological investments conversely require an industrial strategy. What is strategic and what is not?

To make the right R&D investments, America must analyze its skill and technological strengths and weaknesses, as well as those of its principal competitors. It has to understand where the keys to achieving economic success are located. Is leadership in the telecommunications industry of tomorrow to be gotten by strengthening America's laboratory leadership in key technologies or in building a fiber optics test bed such as the one that is now being built in eastern Germany?

BRAINPOWER TECHNOLOGIES AND THE NATURE OF THE FIRM

New communications technologies such as cheap, high-quality video conferencing are transforming, and will continue to transform, the internal communications, command, and control functions (what the military calls C^3) of the business world. When reporting has to be person-to-person, how many people can physically report to any one other person—twenty? thirty? Whatever the number, divide that number into the total number of people in a firm to determine the levels of hierarchy necessary. When those reporting to each other had to be located together so that they could physically meet, the necessities of communications, command, and control dictated many levels of management and the existence of a large corporate headquarters.

In an era of electronic interactions, however, the issues of who reports to whom, how many people report to each supervisor, and where the reporters and the reportees are located are not determined by physical necessities. Learning the corporate gossip (who's up and who's down) and finding a godfather to help advance your career (traditionally probably the two most important reasons for wanting to have an office at the corporate headquarters) don't require a physical location at corporate headquarters anymore. Geographically fluid C^3 systems replaced fixed C^3 systems.

As JoAnne Yates, a professor at MIT, has demonstrated in her excellent book on corporate communications, to a surprising extent the C^3 systems of the modern corporation are still directly modeled on the patterns set by the nineteenth-century railroads.[20] They were the first firms that needed communications, command, and control systems that could operate across large geographic areas. They also had a peculiar problem. Being invented before the telegraph, trains were the fastest known method of communication. How was one to coordinate two things, often on a single track where they could run into each other, when the things to be coordinated were faster than any other method of communication?

The answer was a hierarchical organization run by the timetable, the rule book, and the stopwatch. Downward coordination through written rules and orders; upward communication of experience by reporting progress in meetings. The system was designed to optimize the detailed transmission of orders down through the corporate hierarchy, since orders down were more important than information up if trains were to be safely run.

To a surprising extent our modern corporations are still run along the same lines even though they have very different problems and very different methods of communication.

Almost by definition hierarchical chains of command are poor transmitters of information up through the organization. Amorphous information tends to get lost as it moves up from one person to another. Underlings don't like to tell their bosses bad news (one almost always gets blamed) and bosses don't like to feel that they are simply information-transmission belts upward from their underlings. Deliberately vague reports of potential disasters become ever more vague as they move up the organization.

Giving orders to subordinates that can be made to look as if they come directly from you, and not your boss, is very different from telling one's boss what your subordinates told you when he will hold you responsible for the failures being reported. Information only flows up a chain of command when one is delivering very good news or when something has gone very wrong and cannot be hidden.

Modern communications systems make today's corporate organizations relics of the past. What is the best way to organize a modern corporation? It probably has not yet been invented. Business is in a period of stripping out layers of management (some of them will probably be put back in) and experimenting with different reporting and information systems. But what we do know is that a very different communications, command, and control system will lead to very different forms of business organization.

If knowledge is power, and it is, the possessors of knowledge are going to be radically different in the future, and with that difference will flow changes in power relationships. This is already visible in retailing, where the bar codes and the knowledge that goes with them have shifted economic power from national manufacturing companies with famous brand names to retailers who control shelf space and know what is or is not selling much better and faster than those who make the products.

Best practice currently calls for breaking down divisions into functional areas such as marketing, manufacturing, R&D, and design and pushing decisions down the hierarchy as far as possible. While that requires very different workers at the bottom, people smart enough to make the right decisions, it also requires very different people at the top, those who can communicate the companies' strategies so well that those at the bottom will make the decisions that those at the top would have made if they had had all of the information possessed by those at the bottom.

Walk into any office building today and count the number of offices with no one in them—idle space, computers not turned on (9 percent in active use), telephones unused.[21] The normal occupant is away doing something else—meetings, travel, selling, whatever. With today's technology all of this idle space and equipment is unnecessary. Employees could walk into their company building, sit down at the first vacant desk, plug in their personal telephone number, call up their computer's files, order the flat-screen TV set on the wall to show pictures of their family, and instantly be in business in their own personal offices. The problems are not technological—all of the necessary technology exists—but learning what will and will not work sociologically. One's office is one's cave. Just ordering people to give up their personal offices would cause a revolution. The winners will be those who find a way to change the sociology to make the temporary office seem as if it is a personal physical cave to which the worker can retreat. They will cut office overheads by startling amounts and be the new cost leaders.

While no one knows for certain the shape of the business organization of the future, we do know with certainty that the business organization of the future will be very different.

VALUES IN AN ELECTRONICALLY INTERCONNECTED GLOBAL VILLAGE

The same new technologies are producing a world where values and economics reverberate back and forth with each other creating something brand-new. Human culture and human values are for the first time being shaped by a profit-maximizing electronic media. Never before have societies left it almost completely to the commercial marketplace to determine their values and their role models. Both in its depth (the amount of time spent watching it) and breadth (the percentage of the human population who watch it), TV creates a permeating cultural force that has never before been seen. Movies are the modern art form. The head of the Boston Pops resigns to write and play background music for movies because he believes that is where the mass audience is to be found.

TV and the movies have replaced the family in generating values.[22] The average American teenager watches twenty-one hours of TV per week while spending five minutes per week alone with his or her father and twenty minutes alone with his or her mother.[23] By the time the teenage years have arrived, he or she will have seen eighteen thousand murders.[24] The average American over the age of eighteen watches TV not much less than the average teenager—eighteen hours per week—and is probably equally under its influence.[25] One can argue about the exact extent to which TV violence causes real violence and what happens when the number of TV murders per hour doubles, but no one can doubt that values are heavily influenced by what we see on TV.[26] Perhaps it isn't surprising that the total murder rate is down while that among the young is up.

While on a safari across the Saudi Arabian desert in early 1995, my oldest son and I came across some bedouin camel herders with an encampment of tents, miles from the nearest roads and electrical lines, but with a satellite dish pointed at the heavens and an electrical generator to power it. They were watching on TV what you and I watch on TV. That is the modern world.

The world of written communications, the world that has existed since the onset of widespread literacy, stresses linear logical arguments that move from one point to the next with each point logically building on the last point. Emotional appeals are certainly possible, but they are harder to make on a piece of white paper than face-to-face. A visual-verbal media in many ways moves us back to a world of illiteracy. What counts is the emotive visual appeal to feelings or fears and not the logical appeal to abstract rigorous thought.

Logical appeals can be made on the electronic media, but it is a far better medium for stirring emotions than for transmitting logical information. One has to learn to read. It requires work, time, and investment. One does not have to learn to watch the TV set. It requires no effort. That difference is a big difference. As the vocabularies of those on TV shrink, as they are, the vocabularies of those who watch TV shrink along with them. Moving from the written word to a visual-verbal media is going to change the very ways we think and make decisions. The famous speakers and speeches of ancient Greece and Rome are no more. Neither are those famous American speakers and speeches. The great debates between Webster and Calhoun over slavery or the Gettysburg Address are simply impossible today.

Writing replaced oratory slowly since writing's full impact required the existence of widespread literacy and that only slowly happened over thousands of years after writing had been invented. The electronic media will have effects as powerful as those of writing, but they will come much more rapidly since one does not have to "learn" how to watch TV or the movies. The new medium is more verbal and more emotive, but it is also not the direct face-to-face environment of the illiterate village, either. This is a verbal and emotive environment not controlled by the village elders and families but by those who want to make money—something very different.

In the United States negative political advertisements neatly illustrate the clash between rational thought and emotion. The public says that they dislike negative political advertising. They believe it corrupts the political process and it leaves them cynical about all politicians. But negative political advertisements work—they win elections for those who use them. What the public logically rejects, it emotively accepts. Not surprisingly, politicians use what moves the public to change their voting behavior and don't listen to what the public tells them about their thoughts. Yet both are real. Negative advertising can both work (win elections) and can at the same time create cynical citizens who believe that every politician is corrupt and ripping off the system.

With the television cameras there to record Gorbachev's visit, Tiananmen Square lingers on in the world's memory. Cut off from the world of television coverage, the horrors of Cambodia and Burma did not exist until they were made into movies—*The Killing Fields* and *Beyond Rangoon.* Bosnia could never be completely ignored by the world's leaders, since it has never disappeared from the TV screens.

In a TV culture what one believes to be true is often more important that what is actually true when it comes to understanding and predicting human actions. Nothing makes this power more evident than the fact that in recent years murder rates have been falling in America's cities (in some cities such as New York dramatically), and in some cases (Boston, for one) are now as low as they were thirty years ago, yet the reporting on murder has convinced almost everyone that murders are dramatically rising.[27] Feelings that a crime wave is under way caused demands to arise for the authorities to do something tangible. By referendum, California in 1994 passed its three-strikes-and-you're-out prison-sentencing reform. What is seen on TV is more real than reality.[28] That unreal "reality" has led to such a concern about crime that California's university budgets are being shrunk to expand prison budgets. Yet, viewing the situation rationally, there are no old perpetrators of street crimes. A three-strikes-and-you're-out law is essentially a pension system for old criminals. Student numbers shrink; prison populations soar. By 1995, California's prison budgets were double those of its universities, with state expenditures per person in prison four times as high as expenditures per person in its universities.[29]

In movies such as *Jefferson in Paris* or *Pocahontas*, people lose track of what is historically real and what is theater.[30] Did Jefferson have a black mistress? How old was Pocahontas? Were American Indians natural environmentalists? Since everyone knows that what these movies portray will come to be seen as historical facts, even if they aren't, and even if the makers are not even pretending to represent historical facts, they become controversial.[31]

The media becomes a secular religion essentially replacing shared history, national cultures, real religions, families, and friends as the dominant force creating our mental pictures of reality. But the media are not Rasputin with a covert or overt political agenda. It is not left or right. It has no overarching ideology or agenda.

One can denounce it as Republican presidential candidate Bob Dole did ("We have reached the point where our popular culture threatens to undermine our character as a nation [producing] nightmares of depravity"), but the denunciations are irrelevant because the media are not controlled by any one individual or group of individuals.[32] The media simply provide whatever sells—whatever maximizes profits. If right-wing radio talk show hosts get high ratings, they will be the ones on the air. If left-wing radio talk show hosts got higher ratings, the right-wing hosts would be off the air.

What sells is excitement. The same citizens who applaud Senator Dole's attack on the values portrayed in popular movies and music buy both. If they didn't buy what they say they don't like, it would not be produced. It is simply not exciting to watch Senator Dole's role models and values of the past.

What sells is speed and instant gratification—TV shows have to be completed in thirty to sixty minutes, movies in two hours; both have to move very quickly from episode to episode. Individual consumption is glorified (as in *The Lifestyles of the Rich and Famous*) as the only focus for private ambition—individual fulfillment the only legitimate goal. For the TV hero, death and all real limitations are abolished; there is no duty or sacrifice, no role for the community, no common good; all behavior is depicted as legitimate; feelings, not actions, are supposed to demonstrate values. Emote, don't think. Communicate, but don't commit. Be cynical, since all heroes will ultimately be shown to be fools. "Freedom from" does not imply an "obligation to." All social organizations, including government, are voluntary and they exist only to give the individual the means to pursue his or her own private ends. When the viewer doesn't like it (whatever it is), the media message is, he/she should exit and drop out.[33]

Under the pressure of a medium that does not believe the willingness to wait has any value, the percentage of those who believe in the value of hard work fell from 60 to 44 percent in just ten years.[34] The destruction of the past and the elimination of the social mechanisms that link one's experience with those of earlier generations is an "eerie phenomenon" of the late twentieth century.[35]

In today's world the neighbor most often invited into your home is not a real neighbor. It is a TV family far wealthier than the real average American family (about four times as wealthy), which leaves the real American family with a very misleading, exaggerated notion of how wealthy the average American really is. Comparing themselves with that mythical family, everyone ends up with feelings of relative deprivation.

In the media world no one with the exception [illegible] works. The TV world is a world of consumption [illegible] has to be done in the past to generate consumption i[illegible] done in the present to guarantee consumption in th[illegible] ture simply does not occur. Yet capitalistic economi[illegible] ture if they are to survive.

Capitalistic culture and TV culture fit togethe[illegible] ested in making money. Yet their values are not cong[illegible] to have some focus on the future; the other sees no future that requires sacrifice.[36] One can only change the content of the media by persuading the citizenry that something that is now regarded as dull is exciting, and that is very hard to do. It is hard even to imagine how one would make an exciting TV show about individuals patiently not consuming so that they can invest in the future.

At mid-century, books were written (for example George Orwell's *1984* and Aldous Huxley's *Brave New World*) about how modern communication technologies would permit authoritarian thought control, but they got it exactly backward. Modern electronic technologies promote radical individualism, and mass culture controls national leaders much more than national leaders control the mass culture. The electronic media is changing values and those values will in turn change the nature of our society.

The wired village will inevitably lead the world in the direction of more direct rather than representative democracies. One can argue that representatives have more time to think about the issues; but those in favor of direct democracy can respond that they are also much more subject to lobbyists. And if one looks at places such as Switzerland or California with a tradition of direct democracy, it is difficult to argue that they are a worse form of government. But it is a different form of government. Like or dislike it, direct democracy is on the way. What the technology permits, our ideology will require.[37] Why should voters filter their beliefs through elected representatives if that is no longer a physical necessity?

What is expected to be our most rapidly growing, profitable industry, an as-yet-unnamed industry at the intersection of telephones, television, computers and media arts, is having an enormous influence on how old activities (for example, home shopping) are done, the new activities (video games) upon which the consumer is willing to spend his or her money, but most importantly on the values that are brought into both our consumption and production activities.

NOTES

1. Paul A. Samuelson and William D. Nordhaus, *Economics* (New York: McGraw-Hill, 1989), pp. 901–910.
2. This list was sent to me by a reader of my *Head to Head* (New York: Morrow, 1992) and supposedly appeared in the *Wall Street Journal* at the turn of the century, but I have been unable to locate the exact citation.
3. B. R. Mitchell, *British Historical Statistics* (New York: Cambridge University Press, 1933), pp. 104, 253.

Chandler, Jr., *Scale and Scope: The Dynamics of Industrial Capitalism* ...dge, Mass.: Harvard University Press, 1990), pp. 638–43.

...er C. Thurow, *Head to Head* (New York: Morrow, 1992), p. 204.

...bid., p. 45.

7. Eduardo Borenstein et al., *The Behavior of Non-Oil Commodity Prices,* International Monetary Fund, August 1994, p. 1; International Monetary Fund, *Primary Commodities: Market Development and Outlook,* July 1990, p. 26.
8. Professor Boskin denies that he ever made any such remark but it will go down in history as his most famous remark regardless of whether he did or did not actually make it.
9. U.S. Department of Labor, *Employment and Earnings,* March 1993, pp. 93, 99.
10. Lawrence F. Katz and Lawrence H. Summers, *Rents: Evidence and Implications,* Brookings Economic Papers, Microeconomics 1989, pp. 209, 220.
11. Fortune, *The Fortune 500,* April 19, 1993, p. 254.
12. "Put Away Childish Things," *The Economist,* July 8, 1995, p. 14; "Survey: The European Union," *The Economist,* October 22, 1994, p. 1.
13. Brent Schlender, "Why Andy Grove Can't Stop," *Fortune,* July 10, 1995, pp. 90, 94.
14. Lawrence M. Fisher, "Microsoft Net Is Stronger Than Expected," *New York Times,* July 18, 1995, p. D4; Michael A. Cusumano and Richard W. Selby, *Microsoft Secrets* (New York: Free Press, 1995).
15. "Oh What a Difference a Day Makes," *Fortune,* September 4, 1995, p. 21.
16. Office of Technological Assessment of U.S. Congress, *Multinationals and the National Interest,* 103d Congress, Washington, D.C., p. 2.
17. John Holusha, "First to College, Then the Mill," *New York Times,* August 22, 1995, p. D1.
18. William L. O'Neill, *American High: The Years of Confidence, 1945–1960* (New York: Free Press, 1986), pp. 9–10.
19. Peter Applebome, "Study Ties Educational Gains to More Productivity Growth," *New York Times,* May 14, 1995, p. Y13.
20. JoAnne Yates, *Control Through Communications* (Baltimore: Johns Hopkins University Press, 1989).
21. John Koomey, *Report for the Department of Energy on Usage of Computers* (draft).
22. Daniel Yankelovich, "How Changes in the Economy Are Reshaping American Values," *Values and Public Policy,* ed. Henry J. Aaron, Thomas E. Mann, and Timothy Taylor (Washington, D.C.: Brookings Institution, 1994), p. 46.
23. National Issues Forum, *Kids Who Commit Crimes* (New York: McGraw-Hill, 1994), p. 24.
24. Ibid., p. 26.
25. Suzanne Hamlin, "Time Flies, but Where Does It Go?" *New York Times,* September 6, 1995, p. C1.
26. Elizabeth Kolbert, "Television Gets Closer Look as a Factor in Real Violence," *New York Times,* December 14, 1994, p. 1, D20.
27. Ruben Cataneda, "Homicides in D.C. Fall," *Washington Post,* March 30, 1995, p. B1.

28. Fox Butterfield, "Many Cities in U.S. Show Sharp Drop in Homicide Rate," *New York Times,* August 13, 1995, p. 1.
29. Martin F. Nolan, "California Sees Prisons Filling As Colleges Decline," *Boston Globe,* August 28, 1995, p. 3.
30. "Republic of the Image," *New Perspectives Quarterly,* Summer 1994, p. 25.
31. Richard Bernstein, "'Jefferson' Turning Rumor into Movie Fact," *International Herald Tribune,* April 13, 1995, p. 20.
32. Bernard Weinraub, "Dole Sharpens Assault on Hollywood," *International Herald Tribune,* June 2, 1995, p. 3.
33. Robert H. Bellah et al., *Habits of the Heart* (New York: Harper and Row, 1985), p. 279.
34. Shlomo Maital, *Minds, Markets, and Money* (New York: Basic Books, 1982), p. 39.
35. Eric Hobsbawm, *Age of Extremes: The Short Twentieth Century, 1914–1991* (London: Michael Joseph, 1994), p. 3.
36. Robert L. Heilbroner, *The Nature and Logic of Capitalism* (New York: W. W. Norton, 1985), p. 109.
37. "The Future of Democracy," and "Democracy and Technology," *The Economist,* June 17, 1995, pp. 13, 21.

15

High School—The Neglected Majority: Whose Mid-Kids Are on Track for the Global Economy?

Hedrick Smith

If they're not on the college-bound track, they're on the never-never track. . . . They cannot present themselves to employers and say: "I have the skills and aptitudes that are necessary in order to be a competitor in a global economy." They don't leave high school with a certificate that has any currency[1]

—Bert Grover, Former Wisconsin School Superintendent

The German secret weapon is the education of the high school graduate who doesn't go on to university. . . . After you get through a German apprenticeship training program, you're simply the best-educated person in the world at your level.[2]

—Lester Thurow, MIT Economist

The future now belongs to societies that organize themselves for learning. . . . Our most formidable competitors know this.[3]

—Ray Marshall and Marc Tucker, *Thinking for a Living*

For the average young people at American high schools, the educational system is stuck in the past, in a time warp.

Back in 1980, the American educational system fit the needs of the then-modern economy. But today, that system is as outmoded for many students, and as behind the competitive curve in education, as the mass-production system at General Motors has been behind the curve in making automobiles.

The two went hand in hand—GM's production system and the old-fashioned "general education" program of most U.S. high schools. They were products of the same mind-set. GM mass-produced cars; it wanted workers who took orders and did assembly-line jobs by rote. American high schools mass-produced semiskilled human labor. Both did well enough—until their world changed.

Today, the old American educational model no longer fits the new competitive game. Old-style "general education" does not deliver enough thinking employees for tomorrow's economy. There is a serious mismatch between what the educational system tries to produce and what the job world needs, and the heart of the problem is a mind-set that ignores realities.

The curriculum and the educational priorities at most American high schools are geared to the college-bound; the dream of college sets the main agenda for American high school education. Yet economists assert that 70 percent of the jobs in the American economy do not require a four-year college degree, and educators report that 70 to 75 percent of American teenagers will not actually finish four years of college. Despite these numbers, the non-college-bound student—the average American high school student—is low priority in most American high schools.[4]

"The neglected majority." This is the term that Bert Grover, Wisconsin's state school superintendent for twelve years, gave to average American high school kids.

By "the neglected majority," Grover does not mean the dropouts or the troubled youngsters of the inner cities, or the better students, who are headed for America's university system, the best in the world. America leads the world at both the top and the bottom of the educational ladder—graduate schools and dropouts.

What worries Bert Grover and a growing body of experts is the great American middle. The young people in the middle, America's mid-kids, will be the backbone of our workforce. They will provide the human resources for every business from high-tech electronics to manufacturing to banking to a multitude of service industries. Or else they will be a drag on the economy, doomed to lower living standards because they are no more qualified—or even less qualified—for modern business and industry than mid-kids in Malaysia or Mexico.[5]

What Bert Grover says is echoed by educators, state governors, and the heads of major corporations: Preparing mid-kids for high performance in the new work world is the key to whether America's standard of living will rise in the twenty-first century or continue to stagnate for the majority.

To see how well America is doing for its mid-kids in comparison to its global rivals, I visited three high schools in America, Germany, and Japan—and I focused on three average eighteen-year-olds at Blue Springs High outside Kansas City, Missouri; Yutakano High in Toyota City; and the Career School and the Mercedes Apprenticeship Center in Sindelfingen, Germany.

AMERICA: "PROGRAMMATIC ANARCHY" FOR THE AVERAGE TEENAGER

Jason Fuller is a typical mid-kid from the heart of America: clean cut and crew cut, he likes all the things American teenagers are supposed to like—girls, cars, fast food, parties, and cash in his wallet. When I met Jason Fuller during the spring of 1993, he was in the final term of his senior year at Blue Springs High School in a suburb of Kansas City, Missouri. Jason has a soft-spoken, mid-South drawl, but he was husky enough to play tackle on the football team and to throw discus in track. He was friendly and talkative and seemed capable, but school bored him.

Rich Shatswell, Jason's stepfather since he was two years old, had long worked as an assembler at the General Motors plant in Fairfax, Kansas; his mother, Rosa, was an audit manager for Texaco. The family lived in a nice two-story home in a new housing development, and they kept the lawn neatly manicured.

In 1980, when Kansas City was a thriving factory town, high school seniors such as Jason Fuller could follow their fathers into factory jobs at the GM plants in Fairfax or in Leeds, Missouri, at the Ford plant at Claycomo, or at Armco or Allis Chalmers. Those jobs were their ticket to a good middle-class life. The standard high school course, "general ed," qualified them; any specific skills could be learned on the job.

Global competition changed all that. The GM plant at Leeds, Armco, and Allis Chalmers have all shut down; GM Fairfax has cut back from two shifts to one; other big plants and even most smaller companies want only people with special qualifications. Seniors such as Jason Fuller can no longer move right from high school into well-paying jobs, and many of them don't know how to cope.

Blue Springs High School, one of America's best, was rated triple A by the state of Missouri and cited by *The Wall Street Journal* in 1992 as one of the twenty top public high schools in America.[6] In 1992, its football team won the state championship, its band went to the Rose Bowl, and its choir sang at Carnegie Hall over Thanksgiving. Roughly 60 percent of Blue Springs' graduates went to four-year colleges and another 10 percent-plus to two-year community colleges.[7] That is above the national average: Only about half of America's eighteen-year-olds start college and half of those don't finish four years.

Yet Blue Springs High lacked an effective program for average non-college-bound students. It had bits and pieces, but, like America generally, Blue Springs had no integrated strategy for teenagers such as Jason Fuller.

In his senior year, Jason was taking four classes: a study hall, a tech course in electricity, a reading lab, and a class in marketing—the centerpiece of his program.

The big attraction of the marketing class was that it enabled Jason and his classmates to get out of school at 11:11 a.m. to work at what were close to full-time jobs. In short, Blue Springs High left Jason with a watered-down hodgepodge of courses and no purposeful path into the future.

According to many American educators, Jason Fuller's predicament, with minor variations, is typical of hundreds of thousands of American high school students. "When it came to dealing with the needs of the non-college-bound—the neglected majority," declared former Wisconsin state school superintendent Bert Grover, "we had institutional and programmatic anarchy."[8]

One major reason is that the American way is to leave it to the individual student, supported by his family, to find a path into life. And yet, without giving young people clear guidance and providing an organized structure, the adult world is often just abdicating its guiding role in education to the uncertain whims of teenagers.

Jason Fuller's guidance counselor, Joellen Lightle, who had responsibility for half of the 650-member senior class, remembered that at the start of the senior year, Jason had been eager, as he put it, to "get out of high school and get on with my life." To Jason, she said, "That didn't mean more education. That meant a job, a real job."[9]

Boredom with seemingly irrelevant courses was one big impetus. Breaking away was another. But hidden beneath those symptoms, Mrs. Lightle suggested, was a deep fear about suddenly facing adult life and a feeling of inadequacy about making the big choices. "There's almost a panic to get a job and become independent," she said. "They want very much to feel that they're in control."

What Jason had really needed most was strong school support, direction, firm requirements, and an integrated, purposeful course structure. Blue Springs High provided that to students who were on its college prep track, but it was not geared to provide that same structure to the non-college-bound students. For them, it had a menu of electives.

One option was "Vo-Tech": three hours a day at a regional Vocational Technical Center, which offered courses in thirteen different crafts (auto mechanics, business computing, drafting, electronics, health care, and so on). But an older friend of Jason's had tried Vo-Tech, and it had not helped him get a good job; Mrs. Lightle did not recommend Vo-Tech on the ground that the center's equipment was badly out of date because industry was changing so rapidly.[10] The center's director, Walter Kennon, shared that worry.[11] Bill Oakes, an auto mechanics instructor, suggested another problem—a communication gulf between the guidance counselors and Vo-Tech. Oakes reported that the only time guidance counselors ever came to the Vo-Tech Center was to get their cars fixed cheaply by the students. "I've yet to see a guidance counselor come into my shop," Oakes bristled, "so how do they know what we have?"[12]

Jason found greater appeal in marketing class, which gave him a chance to make some money after school to keep his beat-up old 1970 Chevrolet Monte Carlo in gas and insurance. Like 700 other students at Blue Springs High (out of 2,000), Jason was driving his car to school every day. To support the car, Jason had been working for nearly two years after school, flipping hamburgers and waiting on customers at the Sonic Drive-in, and marketing class enabled him to keep that job.

It was the classic American teenage ritual: Get a car and become an adult. The problem was, Jason wasn't driving that car, the car was driving him. It was a distraction. While the car was literally taking him to school every day, it was actually taking him away from education. Jason was putting in thirty to thirty-five hours a week at the drive-in—much longer hours than he was putting in at school. The car and the job had diverted Jason from the real business of his high school years.

Jason represents a nationwide phenomenon. Two thirds of American high school sophomores, juniors, and seniors take jobs during the school year; seniors work the most—an average of twenty hours or more per week, according to Professor Laurence Steinberg of Temple University.[13] Steinberg and other scholars warn that while a modest amount of work may foster maturity and motivation, there is a serious danger when the job load gets too heavy. Ten hours is the break point; less than ten hours of work, and grades typically rise, Steinberg's studies show; more than ten hours, and schoolwork and grades suffer; at twenty hours or more, the falloff is dramatic.[14]

Jason Fuller was far above the danger point, but no one at Blue Springs High stopped him or warned him off. In fact, marketing class made it easy for him to arrange those long hours.

Steinberg contends that excessive after-school work is a big reason why American high school students compare poorly against other countries on international tests. "Everybody worries why Japanese and German and Swedish students are doing better than we are," Steinberg says. "One reason is, they're not spending their afternoons wrapping tacos."[15]

FOR JASON FULLER, THE PIECES DON'T FIT TOGETHER

The test of Blue Springs High's approach was whether the marketing class and Jason Fuller's after-school job fit together as parts of a coordinated program that was helping Jason build long-term skills and develop a career path. This approach is taken at the high school level in several European countries, and very effectively in Germany, as we shall see. An effective work-study program requires a close working relationship between the school and the employer, to ensure that the academic program and the on-the-job training dovetail. Experts say that there also need to be firm performance standards for both the work-site training and the classroom work. At Blue Springs High, the connections were loose and standards were lax.

The central figure of the work-study program was Jerry Keister, the marketing teacher, a veteran of twenty years' experience in the classroom. Keister was supposed to be teaching the students about the world they were all eager to join as young adults—the world of work. Yet, from what I saw, his course stirred little interest. One morning, as Keister described how to extract tax information from a pay stub, three of the twenty-seven students were reading newspaper want ads, one was balancing his checkbook, a couple were dozing, and no more than eight or nine were bothering to take notes. Tests were mostly multiple choice, announced a week in advance, and Keister gave the class a day off beforehand so that students could bone up. The answers to essay questions were only about a paragraph long, he said.

The co-op jobs that Keister approved for his students, and in some cases helped them obtain, were limited in career potential. They were mostly low-skilled, entry-level jobs in restaurants, drive-ins, and retail shops. The tie-in between these jobs and his marketing course was tenuous; in Jason Fuller's case, there was no effort to coordinate his work with his electricity course. In fact, Keister told me that he accepted almost any job students could find. Jason said that there was little connection or discussion between Keister and his managers at the Sonic Drive-in, and he thought that was typical.

Even continuity of work did not seem to matter. Jason got into an argument with an assistant manager at the Sonic Drive-in; he quit and took a job filing and clerking for his aunt, who ran a tax counseling service from her home. Jason needed the new job to qualify for his midday release from school; Keister gave his permission.

In spite of Jason's job jumping, Keister asserted that Jason was laying the basis for a career after graduation.

"In what career?" I asked.

"Well, right now, we talked about the police." Keister replied. "He's interested in law enforcement."

Not having heard that before, I blurted out my skepticism: "He's been doing short-order cooking. He's now working for a tax accountant. How does that build a police career?"

"I get back to the basic skills," Keister replied. "We have so many students here that you can't have thirty-five different programs for every student. But, you know, you've got to learn how to work first of all. He knows he has to go to work on time, he knows he has to work so many hours, he knows he has to be loyal to that employer. And when he becomes a police officer, hopefully he'll say, 'Well, I remember that from class.' "[16]

Mrs. Lightle, the guidance counselor, was dubious about the career value of entry-level fast-food jobs for seniors. Instead of giving students serious training, she said, the businesses were using them to meet immediate needs. At best, she said, Jason Fuller and other Blue Springs seniors were getting some "job awareness," but no skills training.[17]

As Jason Fuller neared graduation, he himself suddenly had qualms about having dabbled aimlessly at minimum-wage jobs. I asked him whether anyone—Keister, Mrs. Lightle, or other teachers—had tried to help him develop a career or skills that would be useful after graduation.

"No, nobody really pushed me towards one," Jason answered. "It was pretty much my decision of what I wanted to do."

"And how do you feel about the decisions you made?" I asked.

"I feel like maybe somebody should have pushed me a little bit harder," he said. "Maybe I should've had somebody with a little bit more authority, such as my mom or dad or guidance counselor or teacher, help me out."[18]

Feeling at a dead end, Jason had gone to see an Army recruiter, hoping the Army would pick a career for him. His idea was to join the Army Reserves, but the reserves would give him only a few weeks on active duty after boot camp for job training—hardly enough to develop career skills. In the end Jason decided to join the Marines, and he landed in the infantry, much to his parents' dismay.

I went to see Ted Lewman, the principal, a good-looking man in his forties who is articulate about the importance of high standards, a good work ethic, and instilling the proper values. He was understandably proud of Blue Springs' twenty-eight honor students with straight-A, 4.0 grade point averages. Lewman had less to say about the school's programs for non-college-bound seniors, and I asked him specifically whether he felt the combination of marketing class and working after school at a drive-in constituted a well-organized program for students such as Jason Fuller.

"Well, I wouldn't think that the high school's responsible for the fact that he's a short-order cook," Lewman replied.

"Do you think that kid is going to compete with a Japanese and a German eighteen-year-old?" I asked.

Lewman flushed. After a pause he said ruefully, "That may be the toughest question you've asked. Because the school then becomes totally responsible for providing all the opportunities and the skills necessary for a young person to be competitive in the world market, and I'm not sure we're equipped for that to happen."[19]

In terms of the new competitive game, that response not only casts tens of thousands of Jason Fullers adrift, unprepared for the world beyond high school, but leaves them at a disadvantage to their peers in other countries. Jason Fuller was the victim of an old educational mind-set.

The fault lies not with Blue Springs High alone or with one misguided program. It lies with a general failure of American society and its educational institutions to develop programs and commit adequate resources to prepare American mid-kids for world-class jobs in a new competitive era. That failure deeply troubles such educators as Wisconsin's Bert Grover.

"If they're not on the college-bound track, they're on the never-never track," Grover declared passionately. "They're in an educational wasteland. They cannot present themselves to employers and say: 'I have the skills and aptitudes that are necessary in order to be a competitor in a global economy.' They don't leave high school with a certificate that has any currency."[20]

GERMANY: "DUAL EDUCATION"—THE SMOOTH TRANSITION FROM SCHOOL TO WORK

The Germans take a radically different approach to preparing their average teenagers for the global economy. They see each young person's skills as a social asset to be developed for the common good, as well as for individual fulfillment. In the German view, each teenager's growth is too important to society to be left just to the individual. The Germans believe the passage from school to work—one of life's most difficult transitions—has social ramifications; society, therefore, has a stake in seeing that this transition goes smoothly.

In Germany, many groups have come together to devise a workable national strategy. Whereas Americans compartmentalize the process—schools prepare students, businesses hire and train workers, and everyone trusts the market to sort things out—by contrast, the Germans have forged a system of partnerships and connections to ensure that both the individual's needs and the needs of business and industry are met. German schools, families, businesses, trade associations, chambers of commerce, labor unions, state governments, and the federal government all get into the act—all sharing the German conviction that it is essential to invest in people.

For centuries, one hallmark of the German economic system has been the apprenticeship tradition. It dates back to the medieval guilds and the practice of master craftsmen, or *Meister,* taking on young apprentices and fashioning them into qualified journeymen. Because the Germans put great stock in achieving high standards of craftsmanship, they set high qualifications for their workforce.

Alan Watson, a British author, observed in his book *The Germans* that "the very idea of entering a job untrained or employing somebody not specifically prepared for the work . . . is so alien in Germany" that everyone sees the necessity of a well-organized, well-run training and educational system for German youths.[21]

The sheer sweep and scale of the German program are impressive. Some 500,000 companies, professions, and public employers work closely with the public education system to operate a system of "dual education"—a combination of classroom courses and on-the-job apprenticeships in 400 different vocations. These range from modern electronics to journalism, from baking and bricklaying to marketing and office management, from hairdressing and health care to insurance and law.[22] Nearly two thirds of all Germans between the ages of sixteen and nineteen—or 750,000 a year—enter apprenticeship programs after tenth grade.[23] Typically, apprenticeships last three years; afterward, many apprentice graduates decide to go on to technical colleges or institutes for engineering degrees or advanced technical training. Apprenticeships are so highly regarded that even university-bound Germans often spend a couple of years in an apprenticeship program, to gain skills, self-confidence, and maturity. Many German firms now prefer up-and-coming managers to have both kinds of education—in an apprenticeship program and at a university.

What is striking about the German mind-set is its realism about the life prospects for youth. Germany, America, and Japan each winds up with roughly the same proportion of its young people graduating from college or university—around 30 percent. What distinguishes the Germans is their recognition in advance that most teenagers will *not* finish university. As a result, they take steps to provide good training and education for these young people, rather than letting them drift after an aimless high school education or after dropping out of college.

Instead, at age sixteen, all German high school students are given a tough set of exams, and two thirds are then channeled into the dual-education system of training for crafts, industry, and professions. That system, while not without its problems in matching every youngster to a desired career and to the changing needs of industry, has helped Germany avoid America's "neglected majority" of mid-kids. It has provided German teenagers with solid job skills and clear pathways into the mainstream economy and has historically given West Germany the lowest youth unemployment rate in Europe.[24]

The core of the German dual-education system is the heavy engagement of business and its close partnership with education. In the 1990s, West Germany's industries and crafts have been spending roughly $15 billion a year on apprenticeship training, and the program has been extended into the eastern states.[25] America, with nearly four times West Germany's population, would have to spend $60 billion a year to match the German effort.

The depth of German industry's engagement in this enterprise flows from Germany's high-performance strategy. One key to Germany's strong long-term export performance is its class of skilled workers; many German plant managers say that well-trained workers can do many things that Americans turn over to engineers. High wages and a high standard of living are taken as a given in Germany, even with the wage reductions of the past two recession years. To pay such high wages, German CEOs build their ability to compete globally on high quality—and that quality rides on a high-performance workforce and a superior educational and training system.

Training youth is accepted as a price of doing business in Germany, even in hard times, such as the past two years. As a practical matter, German businesses are required by their chambers of commerce and trade associations to provide training, or to pay the costs instead.[26] Most of German industry jealously watches over the dual-education system: Industry develops training courses, sets standards, does most of the training, runs the examinations, and certifies that apprentices meet Germany's tough quality standards.

Apprenticeship training, which takes place in many tiny shops and stores, is often big business. Siemens, the electronics giant, has a $15 million, six-story industrial building for training 600 apprentices in machining and electronics—from freshmen apprentices in dark blue coveralls laboring at industrial workbenches to senior class apprentices using state-of-the-art computer-programmed machine tools.[27] Near Stuttgart, Mercedes has two even more spacious and modern apprenticeship centers to train 4,000 apprentices.

To German companies, sound apprenticeship training is not only necessary for recruiting top-quality workers but a social responsibility, as I heard from Hartmut Welzel, former personnel chief at Ford Motor Company in Cologne. And it is smart marketing. German consumers regard good training as an indicator of high-quality products, Welzel told me. They will trust in a company's products only if the company has a reputation as a good trainer.[28]

In short, guaranteeing high-quality training to German youth has been woven into the fabric of German economic life.

FOR ROLAND WACKER, THE PIECES FIT TOGETHER

Roland Wacker, a German eighteen-year-old, was in many ways a dead ringer for Jason Fuller, except that he was thinner and his hair was swept up into a high wave. Like Jason, Roland had been bored with schoolwork, he had no interest in college, and he was itching to get his hands on something practical. Like Jason's stepfather, Roland's father had worked in an auto factory and was now working for a parts supplier for Mercedes; his mother worked, too. The Wacker family lived in a modest two-story brick German row house in a blue-collar suburb of Stuttgart. Also like Jason, Roland had wheels; he proudly drove me in his little green 1979 Volkswagen Polo to the neighborhood café and bar where he met his friends.

But the parallels to Jason Fuller end there. Roland Wacker was on track to a mainstream job; he was in a high-quality apprenticeship program that paid him 900 marks, or $600, a month, during his training. Roland's academic program was demanding, and it dovetailed with the high-tech job training he was getting at Mercedes-Benz as an apprentice. The apprenticeship had actually stimulated him to work harder and take more interest in academics than he had when he was in school full time—because he had finally grasped how theoretical work improved his ability to learn his job.[29] For Roland, the pieces fit together.

At the Mercedes technical training center in Sindelfingen, Roland was taking an apprenticeship in industrial electronics. The training course was a fast track into a high-tech adult job. The Mercedes training center was absolutely up to date on technology, in stark contrast to the Vo-Tech Center near Blue Springs High.

Mercedes and its instructors were sparing no cost or effort to maximize what they were teaching Roland and his generation of apprentices. One afternoon, for example, Roland and two other senior-year apprentices were given a test by the *Meister,* the master craftsman who was their instructor: Find and fix the error the instructor had programmed into the electronic circuitry of the $1 million robot they had been using. The problem was like the real repair problems they ran into on the days when they were assigned to work in the Mercedes plant. To Americans, spending so much money on equipment to train high school–age apprentices might seem foolish; to the Mercedes instructor, it was only good sense. "We're training tomorrow's workers," he said.

A simple idea, and it testified to the high priority Mercedes placed on state-of-the-art training for its apprentices. They were not second-class citizens who were given worn-out equipment; they were important to Mercedes' future, to Germany's future.

The same purposefulness drove Roland's academic courses. Like all German apprentices, Roland divided his time between job training at Mercedes and classes at an academic center, called a *Berufsschule*—in his case, 3½ days a week in training, 1½ days in class. Unlike Jason Fuller, Roland was not getting watered-down academics. His physics course in electricity was a quantum leap above Jason's tech course in electricity. An instructor, Reinhold Wendel, commented that it was an old-fashioned idea that industrial work is mainly manual labor, because in the new economy technology plays a greater role. "These apprentices have to learn more theory because they're doing less with their hands," Wendel said. "But they're comfortable with that—they like it."

The Mercedes program was light-years ahead of the old American "general ed" course. Ironically, there was more "mind training" in this industrial program than in the classrooms of many full-time American academic high school programs.

"We teach them how to set goals," Wendel said. "That includes how to work in a team, how to get along with others. Second, we teach them certain methodological approaches to learning so that *they learn how to learn* about new subjects. We make sure that they don't simply become skilled workers who have to be told how to do everything. We want a worker who thinks on the job and has suggestions on how to improve things."[30]

The German program also had a heavy dose of pure academics—calculus, German language, economics, and a social studies course that gave Roland Wacker not only grounding in the German political system but a detailed discussion of the German tax system and how it finances the social security net. Somehow, the Germans were cramming a five-course load into a part-time classroom education, and Roland Wacker was taking it seriously, especially the final exams that loomed at the end of his apprenticeship.

"In technology, circuitry, in mathematics, economics, German, and social studies—the tests are pretty hard because it's a total of three and a half years of learning," Roland said. "You're tested on what you've learned during the whole apprenticeship program."[31]

Still, I wondered, was Roland Wacker, or any German youngster, ready at sixteen to pick a career path for life?

His parents described how at fourteen and fifteen, Roland and his classmates had begun talking with their families and teachers about careers. They had been taken by their schools to the career information and counseling centers that exist in every town and city. The one in nearby Stuttgart was a huge building, a fund of information—books, videos, pamphlets, and rotating job fairs and demonstrations. Young people were told how to get proper training, where to find jobs, what each job was like. They were stimulated to think about the possibilities and then helped to make a choice. Various trades offered tryout internships and job shadowing—or watching adult workers do their jobs. Roland tried an internship in sales, but he didn't like it—not enough action. Then he gravitated toward industrial electronics. His mother had seen the clues all along: the strobe light system and electrical gadgetry he had made as a boy; the computer and stereo system he had hooked up in his bedroom.

Roland's father, an apprentice in auto mechanics in his own youth, backed Roland's choice. He had pushed all three of his sons into apprenticeships. "It's definitely an advantage," he said, "a requirement for the future."[32]

Roland himself felt good about his choice. Instead of being bored in class, he was now stimulated as never before. "Back then I didn't do too much for school," he admitted. "But here, if you don't pay attention and get good grades, then you could get passed over and then you don't have a job. The pressure is there. . . . I do more for school now than I did before. The school and work complement each other. You need the knowledge you get from school in order to get ahead in the plant."[33]

Part of Roland's motivation in class was that he knew Mercedes would look over his whole transcript—academics as well as job training—before making a decision to hire him permanently after he finished his apprenticeship. This is an important feature of the German dual-education system—there is no job guarantee at the end, just as the company has no assurance that the apprentice will choose the company. Each has to impress the other during the apprenticeship. And the lack of a guarantee is a spur to do one's best.

One important question remained—did the Mercedes management believe it was getting its money's worth from its investment in its apprentices?

Mercedes reckoned the full cost for each apprentice—his or her pay, training facilities, new equipment, teachers' salaries, everything—at about 100,000 deutsche marks (over $60,000). "If you accept that this is an investment into possibly a lifetime's work, then it's an excellent investment," asserted Helmut Werner, chairman of the Mercedes management board. "When they are through with that, you have a real first-class specialist."[34]

Hilmar Kopper: From Apprentice to Head of Deutsche Bank

The apprenticeship system in Germany permeates the economy—not just in blue-collar careers that Americans associate with vocational training but in such professional careers as banking, law, journalism, insurance, management. The formula is always the same—academic work integrated with practical on-the-job training; theory and practice together—dual education.

At a commercial vocational school, I met Nicole Rose, at eighteen finishing a banking apprenticeship and ambitious eventually to become a bank manager like her mother. Not only had Nicole taken courses in German and social studies as well as accounting, finance, economics, and banking, she had worked in the branch of a regional bank as a teller, doing computer work in the back office, and advising new customers. She had even been to Britain to learn about foreign banking.[35] The bank's chief training officer said that it was quite realistic for Nicole Rose, as an apprentice, to aspire to become a bank manager and to reach middle management—without a college education. Three of the bank's managing directors, he said, had risen from apprenticeships.[36]

In fact, I met quite a few German executives who had been apprentices; the highest ranking among them was Hilmar Kopper, the speaker or chairman of Deutsche Bank, one of the richest, most powerful banks in the world.

Kopper, who as a boy had made money on the black market after World War II selling scrap metal and used ammunition, had become an apprentice because his father could not afford to send Kopper to college. A family friend advised a banking apprenticeship on the grounds that knowing finance would always be useful. Kopper decided to give it a try, hoping later to make his way to university. But before that happened the bank offered him a job in New York, and his career at Deutsche Bank was under way.

Kopper had educated himself with reading and travel. At his home in the hilly suburbs outside Frankfurt, he had a personal collection of paintings and abstract sculpture by Scandinavian, Russian, and German artists.

I asked him whether, in the German system, having been just an apprentice without a university degree had been a handicap.

"Well, as a matter of fact, whenever I had time, I went to the university—for three years, I spent almost every evening there," he replied. "I never took an exam, but I think I've picked up quite a bit. . . . Still, I have no professional academic education."[37]

Kopper's career was testimony to the effectiveness of the German dual-education system and to the competitive advantage that Germans derive from their ability to fit the education and training of youth to the world beyond school.

"The German secret weapon is the education of the high school graduate who doesn't go on to university," asserts Lester Thurow, former dean of the Sloan School of Business Management at MIT. "At that level, after you get through a German apprenticeship training program, you're simply the best-educated person in the world at your level. They turn out an absolutely world-class worker, and it allows them to make very sophisticated products, use very sophisticated machine tools, and just operate technologies at levels that the rest of the world finds impossible to operate."[38]

JAPAN: "A POWERHOUSE OF EDUCATION"

What characterizes the Japanese high school system is the intensity of the educational effort, the high demands set for all students—including those who are headed for the work world—and the unusual role of teachers in arranging job placements for their students.

Japan, like America, has nothing to compare with the German apprenticeship system at the high school level. In Japan as in America, companies prefer to do specific job training; high schools concentrate on completing a stiff core academic program. Since the early postwar period, the Japanese have had vocational high schools, but they are gradually being converted into regular high schools.

Like the Germans, however, the Japanese believe that putting young people onto a secure track into the mainstream economy is too important to society to be left to the individual. They have developed a strong support system for placing all high school students after graduation, including those not bound for college. In order to ensure a seamless transition from school to work, the Japanese system has forged closer ties between business and schools than exist in America. Recruiters from Japanese industry come right into the high schools during the last several months of the senior year, to get their pick of the graduating class for their blue-collar, clerical, or technical workforce. As a result, an extremely high percentage of non-college-bound Japanese high school seniors have lined up permanent jobs *before* they graduate.

The stakes at this stage of a Japanese teenager's life are extremely high. Japanese society is highly stratified, but it is also a meritocracy. Academic performance can lift a young person's fortunes or forever tarnish his or her destiny. How well a Japanese teenager does in high school sets the path for the rest of his or her life—whether that young person gets into university and how good a university, or what kind of company he or she will work for. One harsh reality of Japanese society is that not too many people get a real second chance if they do badly in high school. Most Japanese stick to their career paths—often with one employer for their entire lifetime—and therefore their initial point of entry into the adult world is crucial. It fixes their status and their standard of living.

Even getting into high school is serious business in Japan. High schools have their own entrance exams, and junior high school students compete citywide to get into the best high schools, public as well as private. In every city and province, high schools are academically ranked by the Ministry of Education, and the rankings are made public. The top schools attract the top students, offering them the best opportunities for getting into the top universities, which become pedigrees for the choice jobs in government, industry, and academic life; and so on down the line. Hence, all Japanese junior high school students slave to get as far up the ladder as they can. The competitive pressures are fierce. By junior high, even moderately affluent Japanese parents in Tokyo and other big cities send their children to *jukus,* or private cram schools, which hold evening and weekend classes, to prep for high school entrance exams. In big cities, half of the seventh-, eighth-, and ninth-graders take these cram courses, often at a cost of several thousand dollars a year.[39] In provincial centers, such as Toyota City, *jukus* are far less prevalent and are attended by only about 10 percent of the students.[40]

Everywhere, the pressure is on to perform, even at an average school such as Yutakano High School, ranked fifth out of nine high schools in Toyota City. Like Blue Springs High School in America, Yutakano High takes great pride in getting more than half of its senior class of 460 into regional four-year universities. One quarter of the class went to two-year colleges, and more than a hundred students were headed for technical training courses or into the job market.[41] To motivate students, the teachers had stretched a large white banner from one end to the other of the corridor outside the senior classrooms; it bore the names of last year's graduating class and where each had gone to college or to work. The idea was to spur the current year's seniors to go all out.

High school in Japan is a far cry from elementary school. Gone are the freedom and the ebullient spontaneity of second-graders. The teenagers at Yutakano High show that same youthful energy as they chat and joke in the hallways or out on the baseball or soccer field, but, when the bell rings for class, they become subdued, focused, attentive.

"A powerhouse of education" is how Tom Rohlen described Japan's high schools. Rohlen, a Stanford University sociologist who for many years has benchmarked high schools in Japan and America, pointed out that all Japanese high school seniors are taking their second year of science, their sixth year of math, and their sixth year of literature since seventh grade. The math includes calculus, which is important in industry; almost every Japanese student takes calculus, compared to one third of the German students and only about 6 percent of American teenagers.[42] Because the Japanese school year is 240 days, compared to 180 days in America, Rohlen reckoned that Japanese teenagers finish high school with the equivalent of four more years of time in school than their American peers. Not surprisingly, their work is usually at the American college level.

"Whatever subject we're looking at, the amount that the students are doing here and the level they're going to reach is higher," Rohlen asserted. "It's almost not comparable. We're talking about kids in the middle of Japan getting a level of education that's maybe at the top five to ten percent of the American student population."[43]

Every high school in Japan has to meet the same rigorous standards, set by the Ministry of Education in Tokyo. So, even at Yutakano, a week's spring vacation includes homework. One homeroom teacher, for example, urged students to plan their vacations "so that you can get your homework done easily. Finish early, and then think about the areas that you are not strong in."

The teachers at Yutakano High pack information into their students. One senior math class was deep into number sets and probability theory. In English, a woman teacher was drilling her students in grammar and punctuation and having them repeat passages of English conversation after her. In political economics, a tall, angular instructor was setting out the various forms of corporations and the provisions of "The Law Regarding the Prohibition of Monopolies and the Preservation of Fair Trade," writing furiously on the blackboard in impeccably formed Japanese *kanji,* or ideographs. The heavy emphasis on lecturing and note taking in Japanese high schools is patterned after the German and American universities of the nineteenth century, according to Tom Rohlen.

The Japanese also take the opposite view from Americans in their theory of personal development from childhood to maturity. Whereas Americans think that young children need to be taught self-discipline and teenagers should be given independence and autonomy as they approach adulthood, the Japanese in contrast believe in allowing freedom in the early years and then gradually reining children in, so that discipline is imposed in the high school years as adult responsibility looms on the horizon. "The funnel narrows and narrows," said Rohlen. "We give adolescents their freedom. In Japan, they say adulthood is serious business and now you're expected to really settle down, master an enormous amount of information, work hard."

A pragmatic economic mind-set is also at work. With methods that smack more of drill than of creative learning, Japanese high schools are training and hardening a work team for global competition.

"It seems very stifling to me," Rohlen commented. "It's far more information, by far, than American kids are used to having to field at this age. Whether they like it or not—and I would say that most [Japanese] students do not like this part of their life—they are being shaped as citizenry and as future workers in a way that makes them highly disciplined, well informed, and skilled in many of the kinds of things an economy can use."[44]

For Yasuteru Iyoda, the Teacher Makes the Pieces Mesh

At Yutakano High, Jason Fuller's counterpart was Yasuteru Iyoda, clean cut and crew cut, good looking, soft spoken, and rather serious. In his dark blue wool uniform, worn by Japanese high school students since the last century, Yasuteru looked like a Japanese naval cadet. His father, like Jason's stepfather, worked on the assembly line in the auto industry—for a supplier to Toyota. Like Jason, he was an average student. But there the parallels between the young American and the young Japanese ceased.

Even though Yasuteru Iyoda had no intention of attending a university, he had to take the full regular course load and the same exams as his college-bound classmates. No study halls, remedial reading, or watered-down tech courses for Yasuteru. He had to grind his way through courses on probability theory, Japanese corporate law, and the history of Chinese dynasties. Japanese companies, like universities, pay attention to academic results.

Employers in Japan are looking for dedicated hard workers, and they want new recruits who have shown they can learn. What is more, almost all companies require students to take the employers' own rigorous qualification tests, and Yasuteru Iyoda had to bone up for those. So he felt much more pressure than Jason Fuller did to get the most out of his senior year and to do his best academically.

Yasuteru Iyoda had neither the distraction of a car nor the competing demands of an after-school job. Like other students, he could take part in the wide variety of clubs, sports, and extracurricular activities that were popular with students at Yutakano High. But typically, students taper off their extracurricular activities in their senior year, in order to concentrate on studies—and that is what Yasuteru Iyoda did. Too much was riding on his senior-year academic performance for him to take time away from his studies to play on a sports team or be active in a club.

Yasuteru Iyoda's lack of a car typified the lifestyle of Japanese high school students. In fact, the most visible symbol at Yutakano High of the different lifestyles of American and Japanese teenagers was the ubiquitous presence of bicycles in Toyota City, of all places. Whereas the parking lot at Blue Springs High was jammed with seven hundred student cars, the area around Yutakano High was crammed with bike racks, and the bicycles were not fancy ten-speeds but basic utilitarian three-speeds showing plenty of wear.

"Japanese kids just don't have cars," Tom Rohlen remarked. "Their parents are expecting them to spend their high school years really studying hard."

What is more, that careful process of socialization in primary school, which is powerfully reinforced by the social order and conservativism of Japanese society, paid off. Japanese high school teachers spend very little time coping with disciplinary problems or worrying about dropouts. Yutakano's principal, Minoru Ogiso, said the dropout rate was only 1.1 percent in all of Aichi Prefecture, including Toyota City. He mentioned only two persistent discipline problems—smoking and motorcycles. Motorbikes and motorcycles were legal, but the school had barred them from its grounds.

"We've found out that when you get caught up in riding motorcycles and motorbikes, you lose any desire to study hard," Ogiso explained. "So we as educators have agreed with parents that we should prevent and correct this problem."[45]

The most striking feature at Yutakano High was that the teachers, instead of worrying about discipline, took on the task of ensuring that their students made a smooth transition from high school to the next stage of their lives, whether at a university, at a technical institute, or in a job. In the case of Yasuteru Iyoda and about fifty other students headed into the work world, responsibility for brokering the job hunt fell to Hiro Imai, a mild-mannered teacher of Japanese literature in his early forties. In Japan, as in America, Imai-sensei said, part of his job was preaching realism to Japanese parents who counted mistakenly on Yutakano High to get their children into some university. At first, he said, students felt the burden of their parents' expectations; but over time they would change their goals and decide to go after a job at some good company right out of high school.

Imai-sensei coached the students on their personal options and how the job market worked. In a career room, he displayed photos and personal letters from some of last year's seniors, reporting on how they liked their jobs. He urged the students to study company recruiting pamphlets. In one guidance session with eighteen students, he handed out a glossy brochure circulated by Toyota Tekko, a supplier firm in the Toyota family of companies. The brochure not only showed the company's vacation spa, gymnasium, and worker dormitories, it spelled out what the firm wanted in new workers.

"Please look," Imai-sensei instructed. "It says, 'We look for curiosity.' The brochure discusses the value of questioning. The company says they want their workers to stand up and question things."

Imai-sensei did not mince words about the recent hard times. Normally, with a nationwide labor shortage, Japanese companies aggressively hunt for new workers. By early 1993, in the midst of recession, Imai-sensei warned Yutakano's seniors that things would be tough; Nippondenso, the auto electronics giant, was cutting its new hires in half. "This recession will continue for one or two more years," Imai-sensei warned, "and what companies tighten up on most in order to survive is hiring."[46]

Later, he interviewed the students one by one. It was April, the start of the new school year in Japan, and student career plans were vague. Some girls talked of clerical jobs at big corporations. One boy wanted to go into banking. Like Jason Fuller, Yasuteru Iyoda thought he wanted to be a policeman. Imai-sensei checked with the students periodically, and he talked with their homeroom teachers about their interests. He did not want to put his credibility or the school's reputation on the line until he was sure that a student's intentions were firm. But once assured, he made contacts with the appropriate companies.

"I go to the personnel department directly to find out if there's a position open," Imai-sensei told me. "I'm the one who confirms this with the company."[47]

In Japan, with its tradition of slow consultation and consensus, such negotiations last several months. The companies want to follow the students' performance in school and to test them. Students may change their minds. Imai-sensei shepherds both sides. His strong suit is continuity: he nurtures long-term relationships with scores of companies, mostly in the region around Toyota City. He keeps track of the work records of previous Yutakano graduates at various companies and makes a point of mentioning their records to corporate recruiters as he pushes the career ambitions of the new seniors.

By July, the fourth month of the senior year, the academic pressures were intense and the tempo of the job hunt was picking up. Yasuteru Iyoda had changed his mind. He no longer wanted to be a policeman; he wanted to try for a job at the auto upholstery plant where his father worked. It was still not midyear, and the hallway outside Imai-sensei's career office became a waiting room for company recruiters. Imai-sensei, the literature teacher, was bargaining with industry: Give me more jobs for my students, and I'll send you my best prospects.

But jobs were tight. When the recruiter from Nippondenso said how few openings he had, Imai-sensei groaned. But the man from Sango, which makes mufflers and other components for Toyota, needed quite a few workers. Throughout the fall and into early 1994, Imai-sensei kept trying to match students to jobs. Students kept changing their minds, including Yasuteru Iyoda, who eventually decided to go for a job in the printing trade at a company called Kojima Press—and he got it. Like other students, Yasuteru felt an obligation to do well, not only for the honor of his family but for the school and next year's seniors.

"If graduates at some company work very hard and do really well there," he said, "then the company will think highly of the school and try to recruit more from the school. So for the sake of younger students, we must do our best."[48]

His point was telling. The school's track record was Imai-sensei's trump card in placing his seniors in good jobs. An implicit bargain was struck: The school pushed its students hard academically and prepared them well; employers took the school's guarantee; and the graduates protected the school's reputation.

A month before graduation in March 1994, Imai-sensei had met his goal. For the fifth year in a row, his batting average, as he put it, was "one hundred percent."[49] Even in recession times, he had lined up a job for every single student who wanted to go into the work world after graduation. That record was actually a bit better than that of the teachers who were coaching the university-bound students, some of whom had flunked the entrance exams and were planning to try again in a few months.

In Toyota City, some high schools did better and some did worse. But the performance at Yutakano High, an average high school, was no fluke. Nationwide, Tom Rohlen reported, the normal rate for placing high school graduates in universities, junior colleges, training programs, or jobs *prior to graduation* is 90 percent or better. A stunning benchmark for Americans.

THE HIGH PRICE OF AN OBSOLETE MIND-SET

By comparison with their peers in such countries as Germany and Japan, many average American young people have been held back not primarily by the poor performance of high schools but by an obsolete mind-set.

One of the harshest indictments of our system, as a system, came from a national bipartisan commission that included former labor secretaries from the Carter and Reagan administrations, corporate CEOs, and union leaders. The commission declared in 1990 that "America may have the worst school-to-work transition system of any advanced industrial country." Students not on the college track, it asserted, get "watered-down courses" and very little opportunity "for acquiring relevant, professional-level qualifications for occupations. The result is that typical high-school graduates mill about in the labor market, moving from one dead-end job to another until the age of 23 or 24. Then, with little more in the way of skills than they had at 18, they move into the regular labor market, no match for the highly trained German, Danish, Swedish or Swiss youth of 19."[50]

One root cause of the problem is that through the 1970s and '80s and even into the '90s, much of American industry treated average workers as a disposable resource, while America's global rivals saw training their workforce as an essential competitive advantage—a source of high quality and productivity. There are notable exceptions in American industry, and their number is growing. But, in comparison with other countries, most American businesses have not regularly made large investments in time and money in upgrading the skills of their frontline workers. According to one study, American employers in the 1980s spent about $30 billion a year on the education and training of their employees. Two thirds of that money was spent on college-educated employees, and 90 percent of the funds were spent by fewer than 1 percent of America's firms.[51] The classic American high-volume, low-cost, mass-production economy did not demand much from the mass of high school–educated workers. And the general education curriculums at many American high schools left large numbers of non-college-bound graduates without the skills needed to be competitive and world class in today's global economy.

The human price of that strategy has been high. Its consequences surfaced forcefully in the 1980s. When American businesses found that Koreans, Mexicans, Chinese, or Puerto Ricans could do semi-skilled as well as low-skilled work just as well as American workers but for less money, American plants closed and hundreds of thousands of American jobs went abroad, and the Jason Fullers of America could not find good, steady work when they got out of high school. American families stayed afloat financially by having a second wage earner, usually the wife, join the workforce. While the American economy continued to grow in the 1980s, the living standard of the working middle class stagnated or went down.[52] And while the number of jobs in America has continued to rise into the mid-1990s, the quality and pay of the jobs of those with only a high school education have dropped.[53]

In short, the earnings gap has been growing between college-educated Americans, who generally have the skills to compete globally, and high school–

educated Americans, most of whom do not. By focusing its resources on the college-bound, America's public school system has unintentionally become undemocratic, elitist. Among others, Thomas Kean, Republican governor of New Jersey from 1982 to 1990 and now president of Drew University, warns that this trend is creating a dangerous divide in America—the divide between the college-educated minority and the 70 to 75 percent who do not graduate from a four-year college.

"You follow them [the 70 percent] through, and their earnings haven't even kept pace with inflation, so they're losing—they're losing every day—and they see the vision of the new house and the new car disappear," Kean asserted. "You take the kids who go to college, they're all exceeding the rate of inflation. So you've got seventy percent of the kids going this way [his hand points down] and thirty percent going the other way [his hand points up], and you're not going to have that exist very long before this democracy is going to be in trouble. The seventy percent isn't going to allow the thirty percent to do that for very long."

As Kean and others see it, the disparity in earning power—and, behind it, in skills and the quality of education—is an issue threatening not only to America's capacity to compete economically but to the stability and cohesion of American democracy. "We cannot have unequal opportunity in this country," Kean has argued. "We have to go back to what Jefferson and Lincoln and everybody talked about—equal opportunity. And kids aren't getting it."[54]

Quite obviously, a keen sense of the perilous consequences that Kean cites and a growing awareness of foreign educational models for average high school students have spurred a new burst of educational reform in America in recent years. At the national level, both the Bush and Clinton administrations have promoted a campaign to raise America's national educational standards through the Goals 2000 legislation passed by Congress in 1994. At the state and local levels, there are scores if not hundreds of effective experiments at educational reform—important pioneering efforts, though still a tiny fraction of America's 110,000 schools in the nation's 15,000 school districts. So far, there is no national strategy being implemented.

One important theme among educational reformers has been to make American high school education more relevant to the world outside school. Some reformers have sought to reach out to minority students, who will be an important component of the American workforce in the year 2000 but who are currently dropping out of inner-city high schools at an alarming rate. Other reform efforts have focused on delivering modern job training and a classroom education to match, patterned after the German dual-education system. It is to these reform efforts that we now turn.

NOTES

1. Bert Grover, interview with the author, May 18, 1993.
2. Lester Thurow, interview with the author, Mar. 8, 1993.

3. Ray Marshall and Marc Tucker, *Thinking for a Living: Education and the Wealth of Nations* (New York: Basic Books, 1992), p. xiii.
4. Ibid., p. 64; Bert Grover, interviews with the author, Oct. 18, 1992, and May 18, 1993.
5. *America's Choice: High Skills or Low Wages!* Report of the Commission on the Skills of the American Workforce (Rochester, N.Y.: National Center on Education and the Economy, 1990), pp. 3, 14.
6. Williams C. Bainbridge and Charles Harrison, "How Are the Schools?," chart in special section, "Retooling the Schools," *The Wall Street Journal,* Mar 31, 1989, p. R30.
7. Joellen Lightle, interview with the author, Mar. 2, 1993.
8. Grover, interview, May 18, 1993.
9. Lightle, interview, Mar. 2, 1993.
10. Lightle, interview, Mar. 3, 1993.
11. Walter Kennon, interview with Kathleen McCleery, Jan. 26, 1993.
12. Bill Oakes, interview with the author, Mar. 3, 1993.
13. Laurence Steinberg, telephone interview with Steve Johnson, Mar. 3, 1994.
14. Laurence Steinberg and S. M. Dornbusch, cited in Steven Waldman and Karen Springen, "Too Old, Too Fast," *Newsweek,* Nov. 16, 1992, p. 80.
15. Waldman and Springen, ibid., pp. 80–88, especially p. 81.
16. Jerry Keister, interview with the author, Mar. 2, 1993.
17. Lightle, interview, Mar. 3, 1993.
18. Jason Fuller, interview with the author, Mar. 4, 1993.
19. Ted Lewman, interview with the author, Mar. 3, 1993.
20. Grover, interview, May 18, 1993.
21. Alan Watson, *The Germans: Who Are They Now?* (Chicago: Edition Q, 1992), p. 165.
22. A. Hoffmann, ed., *Facts About Germany* (Frankfurt am Main: Societäts-Verlag, 1992) pp. 342–344.
23. Watson, op. cit., p. 169.
24. Ibid., p. 170.
25. German embassy, research data, Mar. 29, 1994.
26. Lester Thurow, *Head to Head* (New York: William Morrow, 1992), pp. 273ff.
27. Werner Rebham, interview with the author, Mar. 11, 1991.
28. Hartmut Welzel, interview with the author, Mar. 4, 1991.
29. Roland Wacker, interview with the author, Mar. 30, 1993.
30. Reinhold Wendel, interview with the author, Mar. 30, 1993.
31. Wacker, interview, Apr. 5, 1993.
32. Gerhard and Erika Wacker, interview with the author, Apr. 1, 1993.
33. R. Wacker, interview, Apr. 5, 1993.
34. Helmut Werner, interview with the author, Mar. 31, 1993.
35. Nicole Rose, interview with the author, Mar. 29, 1993.
36. Helmut Walker, interview with the author, Mar. 29, 1993.

37. Hilmar Kopper, interview with the author, Apr. 8, 1993.
38. Thurow, interview with the author, Mar. 8, 1993.
39. Steven R. Weisman, "How Do Japan's Students Do It? They Cram," *The New York Times,* Apr. 27, 1992, p. A1.
40. Teacher Suzuki, interview with the author, Jan. 29, 1993.
41. Deputy Principal Takei and Dean Kawai, interview with the author, Jan. 29, 1993.
42. Vance Grant, U.S. Department of Education, interview with Anne Lawrence, Mar. 31, 1992.
43. Tom Rohlen, interview with the author, Apr. 27, 1993.
44. Rohlen, interview, Apr. 27, 1993.
45. Minoru Ogiso, interview with the author, Apr. 27, 1993.
46. Hiro Imai, class, April 26, 1993.
47. Imai, interview with the author, Apr. 27, 1993.
48. Yasuteru Iyoda, interview with Steve York, July 1, 1993.
49. Imai, interview with Miho Kometani, Mar. 9, 1994.
50. *America's Choice,* pp. 4, 47, 46.
51. Marshall and Tucker, op. cit., p. 69.
52. *America's Choice,* pp. 24–26.
53. Labor Secretary Robert Reich, speech, Washington, D.C., Mar. 3, 1994.
54. Tom Kean, interview with the author, Oct. 15, 1993.

16

Recognising Skills and Qualifications

Danielle Colardyn and Marianne Durand-Drouhin

Against a background of technological innovation, economic restructuring and keener competition, the improvement and renewal of skills and qualifications are critical to economic development and competitiveness. So the focus on adapting skills, broadening qualifications and inventing new methods and means for life-long learning must be constant.[1]

What determines the educational, social and professional value of a diploma? What are the mechanisms and institutions that ensure the certification of initial and further education? Has there been a shift in the roles and responsibilities of government, business, unions and professional associations? Are the systems and practices in OECD countries drawing closer together? Above all, what is at stake for workers and enterprises when different approaches are recommended?

Multiple and continuous learning processes must be developed to respond to technological and economic change, and to the diverse requirements and interests of learners. The mechanisms used to assess, certify and recognise knowledge and expertise must also be updated. To facilitate the accumulation of recognised skills[2] and qualifications, equivalences for skills and qualifications have to be continuously defined and redefined, whether acquired in school, at work, or elsewhere. A "common language" and negotiating institutions are necessary to "evaluate" and adjust such skills and qualifications to demand and conditions in the labour market.

Most OECD countries should now be developing qualification systems that are more flexible, open and coherent. They should display three basic features:

transferability within the education system, "visibility" for business and professional associations, and portability on the labour market.

TRAINING AND TRANSFERABILITY

The skills and abilities acquired in the education system are validated by a range of certificates, from diplomas for full courses to credits certifying the assimilation of a specific "module" or part of a course. A major problem in most OECD education systems lies in the non-recognition and therefore non-transferability of such certificates from one sector of education to another—between apprenticeships, technical education and general education, for instance, or between initial and further education. In practically all the OECD countries, young people with initial vocational training at secondary level or adults with qualifications gained in further education still have no access to higher education, or have to struggle to be accepted. Furthermore, it is often hard to change subjects or vocational areas within a sector without beginning the whole cycle over again (changing trades in an apprenticeship, for instance, or switching to other studies).

These obstacles are a legacy of the past, when vocational qualifications were gained almost exclusively through initial education or apprenticeships, and when distinctive, watertight educational tracks reflected the relatively stable division of labour and social hierarchy in the world outside.

By overhauling or re-organising their certification systems, most OECD countries are now trying to link together the various sectors and levels of initial teaching and training to make the pathways of skill formation more flexible and effective, providing improved opportunities to acquire high-level qualifications. By the same token, unified systems of certification aim at integrating the skills acquired by adults, in some cases during their working or social lives, into a coherent and open system of initial and life-long education and training.[3] The aim is to build bridges from one sector to another and one level to another, without compulsory detours for candidates to "re-learn" what they already know and have mastered.

In Germany and Switzerland, for instance, first bridges between school-based education and apprenticeships aim to improve transferability: the university-entrance diploma can in some cases be obtained at the same time as a recognised vocational qualification. This kind of "twinning" allows both routes to be followed simultaneously, thus avoiding long and costly itineraries. In Canada the assessment of prior learning, formally acknowledged in a Portfolio, allows people to build up a capital of recognised and certified skills and qualifications, regardless of where they were acquired. The Portfolio is the foundation upon which individuals can develop a training strategy and build a path for their careers. The recognition of a variety of skills may thus give access to specific courses or programmes in higher education. It is a way of adding knowledge and know-how to conventional education while at the same time making the education system smoother and more efficient.

THE VALUE OF VISIBILITY

To be of use in the workplace, the achievements of life-long learning should be visible to business and professional associations, especially employers. For young people in search of their first job and with nothing to show but an initial education certificate, such visibility is crucial. It is equally important for adults to be able to indicate the skills acquired in the education system and elsewhere so that they can be put to full use in the workplace.

To ensure the visibility of skills and qualifications, some OECD countries have developed co-ordinating and negotiating institutions where together government, industry and occasionally professional associations (particularly those of engineers) co-operate. There are several modes of co-ordination. Some, like the Dual system (in German-speaking countries and Denmark), leave it to institutions concerned to decide together on the contents and structure of the qualifications they require, to provide guidance on the different sequences of an apprenticeship and the standards to be achieved, and to negotiate the value of the qualifications on the labour market. In other countries, where initial vocational training is provided mainly in schools, the principal aim of such institutions (such as consultative occupational committees in France[4] or school boards in Sweden) is to provide information and guidance for schools on how to adapt the supply of training. More recently, less elaborate co-ordination systems have been set up (in the United Kingdom and Australia, for instance) to identify corporate requirements and endorse the standards derived from them (respectively the National Council of Vocational Qualifications and the National Training Board).

PROMOTING PORTABILITY

Once they are known to all the individuals and institutions in the labour market, skills and qualifications must be put to use, that is, they should serve as a benchmark when hiring or promoting people. Certificates help to make qualifications more portable from one job to another, or from one enterprise or sector to another. In some countries, collective agreements provide a formal framework for such portability.

In Germany, for instance, certificates of initial vocational training are highly valued because of the benefits they bring: conditions and salaries drawn up by collective agreement, access to advanced vocational training, and unemployment benefits. On the other hand, only some further training programmes available have been awarded formal recognition (the *Meister* and *Techniker* certificates), the majority of courses being worth whatever value is attached to them by individual enterprises.

More or less formal links between diplomas, remuneration and working conditions also exist in other countries on the European continent, in some cases with explicit reference to the skills acquired through further training (France, Sweden). In English-speaking countries, on the other hand, the portability of a qualification is more often a local affair, negotiated within a firm and possibly bolstered by the prestige of the institution awarding the certificate or recognising the skill or qualification. But there are exceptions, and in several of these countries efforts are being made to strengthen the links.

The mechanisms determining the value of skills and qualifications within the education system or on the labour market, and the channels through which the various "actors" consult one another, are far from identical from one country to the next. To see how diverse traditions and institutions are, one only has to look at European attempts to harmonise qualifications and introduce mutual recognition. How do the implications of different approaches for both young and adult workers vary from one country to the next? To answer that question, one must take a closer look at the meaning of "qualification" and "competences" in different countries.

COHERENCE V. FLEXIBILITY?

Since the 19th century, countries in the north of continental Europe have been setting up national systems of vocational qualification and certification based either on centralised government (as in France) or on self-regulation or co-regulation by economic "actors" (chambers of commerce, trade associations and unions in German-speaking countries and Scandinavia).

In this part of the world, a "vocational qualification" (*qualification professionnelle*) is traditionally defined as the ability to carry out complex, multidimensional and interdependent tasks. It is based on the traditional image of a "trade" and so refers to mastery of an entire "occupational field." The belief is that to develop such qualifications young people have to follow and complete formal, structured programmes of vocational education and/or training. At secondary level, these range from two to four years in duration.

Vocational qualifications, assessed and certified through theoretical and practical examinations, are then recognised by diplomas that may be national, regional, local or specific to a particular branch (say, metallurgy or banking). Qualifications can then be matched to job classifications following negotiations with industry and trade associations.

The systems prevailing in those continental European countries have undergone substantial reform over the past few decades. An overhaul of Germany's Dual system, for instance, has led to the modernisation and broadening of the programs and regulations in initial training and related qualifications. Of the 900 apprenticeship trades that were listed in 1970, only some 370 remain. With more multidisciplinary content and more emphasis on theoretical knowledge and reasoning, the aim is to arm young apprentices more thoroughly to deal with the growing abstraction, complexity and interdependence of most jobs. These reforms have been accompanied by massive investment in research, negotiations with business, unions and public authorities, and by experimentation in teaching methods.[5]

Similar consultation- and negotiation-based objectives and approaches have guided reforms elsewhere in continental Europe, such as the development of *alternance* (alternating learning periods at school and at work) and the *baccalauréat professionnel* in France. Sweden and Finland have opted for the creation of an "integrated" cycle of upper-secondary education offering broad vocational qualifications, grouped into a small number of tracks (14 in Sweden, 22 in Finland), with increased emphasis on general education and work experience.

The main objectives are the same everywhere: to open up education systems further and make them more flexible, improve the quality of skills and make them more relevant so as to respond to changing labour demand and to re-orient the development of jobs towards higher skills and economic performance. In all of these countries, the certification of initial education is not confined to indicating the content and level of what is learnt. It also provides guidance for the pedagogical organisation of learning processes and helps to motivate young people to complete their training.

The English-speaking countries, by contrast, do not have a strong tradition of formal vocational training, either in schools or in the workplace. Since the 1980s some of them, like Australia and the United Kingdom, have been endeavouring to define vocational qualifications and have set up unified qualifications systems (the National Framework for the Recognition of Training, or NFROT, and the National Vocational Qualifications, or NVQs, respectively), run by the Council and Board mentioned above. These unified systems are meant to assess and certify vocational qualifications based on the idea of "skills" or "competences," defined as the proven ability to accomplish concrete tasks, identified by or in cooperation with employers. The recognition of such "competences" is based on standards, also drawn up with the help of employers and setting out the degree of difficulty, and hence the ability, required.

Unlike the traditions in continental Europe, these new approaches try to avoid any systematic reference either to education and training programmes or job classifications. They attempt to measure "competences" in a way that is neutral (regardless of institution or place of learning), relevant and flexible, of use to actors on the labour market, and adaptable to changing requirements for skills. They tend to divide programs and qualifications into "modules" and "credits." The diploma crowning a prescribed and prestructured period of formal learning gives way to the recognition of more partial skills, accumulated in an order and at a pace that suit the individual rather than those laid down by the education system (though it is true that most of this competency-based modular training continues to be provided in, or in close association with, colleges and other such institutions).

The originality of this approach lies in the strict separation between the certification of a skill or "competence" and the place/time of acquisition, which might be the school or the workplace, during initial schooling or further education. The idea is to accredit precisely defined knowledge and know-how, acquired "somewhere, at some time." This approach focuses on outputs; it is not related to educational inputs, such as the process, pathways or quality of teaching and learning.

SHARING RESPONSIBILITY

There is indisputable proof that this new approach, now being developed by most English-speaking countries, can be beneficial to adults engaged in further education. In their case, recognition of "prior achievements" is a way of sorting out and clarifying their educational, vocational, cultural and social experience.[6] These achievements can subsequently be taken into account when negotiating salaries and conditions of employment.

But what happens when the approach is applied to young people in initial training? A number of concerns are being voiced. First, the young are faced with educational choices but do not have a clear idea of their implications. In such a context it is hard to establish a social and occupational identity that is easily recognisable in the world of work. The recognition of that identity does—or should—entail a genuine commitment on the part of industry (especially through collective agreements) and of adults more generally to acknowledge the efforts the young person has invested in initial education.

Second, the division of programmes into modules and partial "competences" may perhaps foster flexibility in the education system to the detriment of coherent pathways. It could encourage young people to drop out of the education system early and leave school with a patchwork of abilities. They would therefore be deprived of a sound educational foundation which would subsequently allow them to pursue a qualifying career path.

Third, in regulating training supply by subjecting it to the educational choices of young people (and their parents), such an approach discharges government of any responsibility. In the end, it makes the "clients" of the education system responsible for the quality of training and its relevance to economic activity.

The many developments generated by economic and technological change mean that school systems, and public authorities, can no longer take sole responsibility for the initial and further training of the workforce. But over-hasty conclusions would put the qualification of future generations at risk. Ways must be found to share responsibility in a manner that, allowing for specifying and differences across countries, both the quality and flexibility of education and training can be maintained. Of the innovations now being implemented in both groups of countries, an outstanding requirement is to differentiate between training for young people and training for adults, while preserving the internal coherence of national training systems and improving their ability to respond to demands and opportunities on the job market.

NOTES

1. "Assessment, Certification and Recognition of Occupational Skills and Competences in Vocational Education" and "Assessment and Recognition of Skills and Competences in Initial and Further Training." *OECD Publications,* Parts, forthcoming 1995.
2. The notion of "competence," in the sense of "a capacity to accomplish concrete tasks," is now frequently associated with the idea of "skills."

3. "Continuing Professional Education of Highly Qualified Personnel." *OECD Publications,* Paris, forthcoming 1995.
4. "Assessment and Recognition of Skills and Competences: Developments in France." 1990 (available free of charge from the OECD Directorate for Education, Employment, Labour and Social Affairs).
5. "Vocational Training in Germany: Modernisation and Responsiveness." *OECD Publications,* Paris, 1994.
6. Danielle Colardyn, "Certification in Adult Education," in T. Husén and T. N. Postlethwaite (eds.). *The International Encyclopedia of Education.* 2nd edn. Vol. 2, Elsevier Science, Oxford, 1994.

17

Human Resource Development in the Knowledge-Based Economy: Roles of Firms, Schools and Governments

David Stern

LEARNING-INTENSIVE PRODUCTION

Increasingly rapid mobility of information and capital forces firms to become ever more nimble. Constant change within organisations, and mobility of workers among firms, require everyone to keep learning all the time. Learning includes transfer of existing information, knowledge, and skill from those who have them to those who need them. It also includes the discovery of previously unknown facts and principles. Within firms, the accumulation of many small new discoveries is vital to the continuous improvement of products, services, and methods of production. This is a knowledge-based economy, but more importantly it is learning-based, because the success of companies and individuals depends especially on information flows.

More rapid change in markets and technologies makes it relatively more efficient to locate the creation and acquisition of productive knowledge close to the actual productive process. Knowledge and skill developed outside the work situation are increasingly likely to become obsolete before they can be put to use. Firms and schools alike are displaying greater interest in how work itself generates productive competence (Lave and Wenger, 1991; Berryman and Bailey, 1992). Growing evidence points to the cost-effectiveness of work-based compared to school-based training (Middleton *et al.*, 1993; Elias *et al.*, 1994). This paper describes how these shifts are altering the roles of firms, schools, and governments in preparing individuals to acquire knowledge and create new ideas.

FIRMS

Business enterprises have traditionally considered training as an expense to be minimised. They would generally prefer to hire ready-trained workers—or buy or affiliate with another company that possesses the desired expertise—than provide the training themselves. Significant exceptions are the dual system for initial vocational training in German-speaking countries, the French system for continuing education of employees, and the Japanese system of long-term employment contracts for core employees; but in each of these cases special economic incentives have been created to override firms' natural reluctance to provide training (Soskice, 1994; Berton *et al.,* 1991; Koike and Inoki, 1990).

A basic reason why firms generally prefer to minimise their outlay for training is that they lose their investment when employees leave (Lynch, 1994; Stern and Ritzen, 1991). Increasing mobility of employees among firms should therefore tend to strengthen employers' reluctance to offer training.

On the other hand, the more rapid obsolescence of work-related knowledge and skill makes it more difficult for employers to find exactly what they need on the open market. They must somehow develop it themselves. Furthermore, as firms offer less employment security, they may try to compete for the most qualified people by offering instead greater "opportunity for self-improvement" on the job (*Business Week,* October 17, 1994, p. 43). The opportunity to acquire skill and knowledge that may be useful in a future job becomes more valuable for employees as there is less assurance of remaining with the current employer for a long time. A good case in point is the temporary help industry itself. One firm that has grown as a direct result of the trend toward more short-term employment is Manpower, Inc., which in 1992 employed a larger number of people than any other US company. Manpower, Inc. provides temporary staffing to other companies, and has created a highly structured method for enabling its employees to consolidate and develop their skills and knowledge as they move from one assignment to another (Seavey and Kazis, 1994).

Enterprises can minimise their training cost and at the same time promote employee development through the strategy of just-in-time learning. This means acquiring skill or knowledge at the time and place where it is needed, instead of learning it ahead of time and in a different place. Learning that is embedded in the work process inherently entails less opportunity cost than learning off the job. Like just-in-time inventory control, just-in-time learning avoids unnecessary investment and minimises deterioration of knowledge and skill from non-use. The need to solve an immediate problem also provides both a motivation to learn and a context that makes new information meaningful.

Firms are developing new practices to promote just-in-time learning. There is no systematic evidence about which arrangements are most effective, but we can characterize some of the emerging practices as follows:

- *Cross-training by co-workers* involves creating teams whose members have complementary skills and knowledge, which they teach to one another. Such arrangements have become commonplace in manufacturing, spurred by the diffusion of the Japanese model of "lean production" (Womack *et al.*, 1990). Firms in service industries are also increasingly organising employees into teams, and encouraging members to share knowledge and information. For example, customer service representatives who formerly carried out highly fragmented tasks are now more often grouped into teams with responsibility for a broader range of functions. The reorganisation requires team members to train one another in their respective specialties. One insurance company has created a written list of all the separate tasks a team should perform, and pays individual team members additional salary if they master more of these tasks; managers have observed that employees now use idle moments to exchange work-related information instead of talking about other things (Brown *et al.*, 1993).

- *Job rotation* gives individuals an opportunity to broaden or deepen their skills through exposure to a planned sequence of tasks. This is a hallmark of human resource development in Japanese firms, where employees normally remain with the same employer for a long time (Koike and Inoki, 1990). The long career in one firm makes it possible to broaden knowledge and deepen skill by moving workers through a sequence of related jobs over the course of many years. It is not unusual to find, among the information posted in a work area, a chart displaying the level of competence of each worker in performing the jobs done there, and a plan for the next set of assignments designed to increase everyone's competence.
- *Skill-based pay,* or pay for knowledge, is a major departure from traditional practice in Europe or North America. Standard compensation practice makes an individual's pay for a given period depend on the job classification to which the person was assigned. Skill-based pay adds a salary increment that depends on the individual's demonstrated mastery of certain knowledge or skills, independent of the job the person actually performs during the pay period. To the extent that salary depends on competence rather than position, employees become more willing, even eager, to accept reassignment to different jobs. A recent survey in the United States by Osterman (1994) found that 30 per cent of establishments awarded skill-based pay to at least some of their employees. This is remarkable, given that the idea was unheard-of in the United States until 20 years ago. The principle that pay follows the person, not the job, is also a feature of the compensation system in large Japanese companies.
- *Formal or informal groups* (e.g. quality circles) may be created to discuss problems, develop new procedures, or codify current knowledge or skill. These are well-known as a method for involving employees in solving problems related to quality and efficiency (Cole, 1989; Applebaum and Batt, 1994). In France, small groups of workers in newly emerging jobs have been formed for the purpose of writing down the knowledge and

skill required (Barbier *et al.*, 1992). An additional effect of these group activities is to keep employees' minds engaged in thinking about what they are doing, a basic prerequisite for learning.

- *Suggestion systems* reward the contribution of ideas by groups or individuals to improve products or work processes. Incentives may be provided for continual discovery of problems and solutions. Like quality circles, suggestion systems help to engage workers' minds even if the work itself is largely repetitive. Along with quality circles, suggestion systems are used extensively in Japanese firms, some of which elicit an average of one or two suggestions per employee per week; workers are paid a small amount of money for each suggestion, and a larger amount if the suggestion has substantial value to the company.

Off-the-job training may incorporate "doing by learning" (Stern, 1992a). That is, problems originating in the work itself are analysed in the course of classroom instruction, resulting in ideas for solutions that can be implemented in the work setting. For example, a class may introduce the concept of cycle time, or five-step problem-solving, then ask participants to apply the concept to real problems in their own work. Just-in-time learning is achieved by bringing the work process into the classroom.

Certain employees may be designated as *mentors* or *tutors* for co-workers. This role has been formally developed to the greatest extent in German initial vocational education, where an apprentice must be supervised by a qualified *meister.* The French have also created the role of *tuteur,* who supervises young trainees in the workplace (Brochier *et al.*, 1990) or who guides regular employees through the requirements to obtain a vocational qualification (Kirsch, 1990).

Written analysis of work problems may be assigned as a condition for promotion or advancement. This is another common practice in Japan, where candidates for promotion may be asked to write a 20- to 50–page paper proposing a solution to a particular problem or a set of improvements to current methods. The higher the position, the more substantial the essay.

Job aids may be provided in such forms as computerised "help" menus, databases, and expert systems. The spread of computers in workplaces has made it possible to replace printed manuals, which are clumsy to update, with on-line help functions that can be updated continuously (US Congress Office of Technology Assessment, 1990). From computer controlled machining to health care to banking, computer application software, databases, and expert systems increasingly offer on-the-spot guidance and information for workers.

Groups or networks may link different workplaces with similar problems. Billboards and listservers on computer networks provide the means for fast exchange of information. Potentially, this could be an important tool for communicating solutions to problems in different workplaces. However, such communication may be blocked by companies' proprietary interests.

While these and similar arrangements move learning closer to the production process, work itself is also changing. Because firms must continually seek improvements in their products, services, and methods of operation, employees are increasingly expected not only to adapt to change but also to initiate it, by proposing their own ideas. Increasingly, employers must rely on ideas offered by employees. But what kind of incentive can elicit new ideas? Coercion is out of the question. Monetary rewards can induce people to submit large numbers of written suggestions, but the Japanese experience indicates that the changes proposed tend to be tiny. Bigger ideas arise only out of genuine interest. The father of creativity is curiosity.

SCHOOLS

To prepare individuals for work that demands curiosity and continual learning, many employers now call for education that promotes thinking for all students, not just for the elite as in the past. Vocational education, which traditionally has offered practical training for students who were considered to possess relatively low academic ability, is now being reformed and in some places radically reconstituted. Reforms include strengthening the academic content of vocational classes and making it easier for vocational graduates to pursue further studies at university level. These changes are intended to attract more intellectually-talented students into vocational programmes, to give them sufficient theoretical grounding to deal with changing technology, and to prepare them for continual problem solving. As change proceeds in this direction, the line between vocational and academic education becomes indistinct. Instead of serving as an alternative to general education, vocational education becomes a method for promoting it. The blending of vocational and academic education mirrors the convergence of working and learning in the workplace.

Developments along these lines are occurring in many OECD countries. For example:

In the *United States* there is now a proliferation of new programmes designed to integrate academic and vocational education (Grubb *et al.,* 1991; Rosenstock, 1991). This follows revision in 1990 of the federal law that subsidises vocational education programmes run by states and localities. Prominent spokesmen for employers in the 1980s had complained about the poor preparation of vocational graduates from secondary schools (National Academy of Sciences, 1984; Committee for Economic Development, 1985; Kearns and Doyle, 1988). Since employers had traditionally provided decisive political support for vocational education as a separate track, their complaints had a major impact. The 1990 law requires that all federal money for vocational education must be spent on programmes that integrate academic and vocational instruction. Examples include career academies, which organise the core curriculum of the high school around an occupational theme such as health careers, electronics, or computer-related occupations. Graduates from career academies may enter the workforce full time, or they may pursue further studies at a college or university, where they may continue in the same field or change to an entirely different one. Evaluations have found that students in career academies achieve higher grades and are more likely to complete secondary school compared to similar students (Stern, Raby, and Dayton, 1992). Another recent innovation is "tech prep," which combines the academic and vocational curriculum and also links the last two years of secondary school with the first two years of post-secondary education (Hull and Parnell, 1991). These and related innovations have received additional impetus from passage of the 1994 School to Work Opportunities Act, which is described further below.

A new "integrated" vocational-academic high school curriculum has just been created in *Japan*. Until 1994, high schools offered either a prescribed general curriculum as preparation for university, or a specialised vocational curriculum. However, the proportion of students attending vocational high schools had fallen from 40 per cent in 1955 and 1965 to 26 per cent in 1992. Therefore, beginning in 1994 high schools were permitted to offer an "integrated" curriculum focusing on career development. Students in the integrated programme have fewer required subjects and are given career guidance to help them design their own course sequence. As of 1994, only seven schools had introduced the integrated curriculum, but it was expected that the idea would catch on and promote "convergence of vocational and general education" (Yoshimoto, 1994, p. 5). This convergence already has occurred to some extent at the post-secondary level, through the growth of special training colleges offering higher diplomas in industrial, commercial, and other vocational fields. Enrolment in these institutions stood at 862,000 in 1992, double the number in 1978, and more than one-third the 1992 enrolment level in universities.

France has created an array of upper secondary diplomas: general, technical, and vocational (*baccalauréat professionnel*). At age 15, after four years of lower secondary school, most students either continue in a three-year upper secondary programme toward a general or technical diploma, or enter a two-year vocational programme. In 1985 the vocational diploma was introduced, giving graduates of two-year vocational programmes an option to receive an upper secondary diploma after an additional two years. As of 1991–92 the number of students enrolled for the vocational diploma had grown to 114,000, compared to 707,000 preparing for general, and 290,000 for technical diplomas (Kirsch, 1994). At the post-secondary level, students holding general or technical diplomas may continue studying for higher technician diplomas or university diplomas in technology. The majority of university technology diploma recipients continue into further studies. This system thus allows students to enter a vocational programme at various ages, and to pursue occupational studies at a high level. However, once in a vocational programme, the probability of moving back into a technical or general curriculum is low.

In *Germany*, the dual system of apprenticeship is widely regarded as a successful model for initial vocational education (e.g. Hamilton, 1990). Traditionally, there was a clear separation between the pathways of apprenticeship and university: students who attended a gymnasium and received the *Abitur* diploma attended university, the others entered apprenticeship. However, in recent years a small but growing number of *Abitur*-holders are completing apprenticeships prior to entering university. Evidently they have decided that a combination of academic and vocational preparation is best. Furthermore Steedman (1993) observes:

"A relatively new phenomenon . . . , the difficulty being experienced even by the most prestigious engineering firms in recruiting trainees of the necessary high ability and aptitude. Respected commentators . . . have, as a result, diagnosed a crisis of the whole [apprenticeship] system arguing that if the high-cost high-quality training provision of the prestigious industrial companies is discontinued in favour of recruitment from higher education, then the credibility of the system as a whole will be undermined." (p. 1288)

To prevent students' demand for university education from undermining the dual system, "The social partners share the view that the transition to higher education institutions and universities should also be ensured or at least made easier for graduates of the dual system," according to a senior official in the *Bundesinstitut für Berufsbildung,* which oversees the system (Laur-Ernst, 1992, p. 40).

The *United Kingdom* is in the process of introducing a new set of vocational qualifications called General National Vocational Qualifications (GNVQs). These are intended to be the vocational equivalent of academic "A-level" examinations, which are required for entrance to university. GNVQ courses are currently offered or planned in 14 fields, including art and design, business, engineering, health and social care, leisure and tourism, manufacturing, hospitality and catering, environment, and science. The government is encouraging all institutions of higher education to accept GNVQs instead of A-levels. The 1991 White Paper on "Education and Training for the 21st Century," which inaugurated the new programme, declared, "The government wants to remove the remaining barriers to equal status between the so-called academic and vocational routes" (paragraph 4.2).

The dichotomy between vocational and academic will not disappear quickly or without struggle, since the traditional disciplines have existed for a long time, and it is still not entirely clear what will take their place. But there is pressure to create something new, in part because it is difficult to attract talented or ambitious students to traditional vocational education.

WORK-BASED LEARNING FOR STUDENTS

The new approach includes education through work, not only as an efficient method to teach knowledge and skill required on the job, but also to give students practice in using work for the purpose of learning. Examples can be found in many OECD countries:

- *Sweden* now requires students in the new three-year upper secondary programmes to spend 15 per cent of their time in workplaces. Most of these placements will be unpaid. Students use the experience to conduct study projects related to their courses (Vickers, 1994).

- *Australia* is creating "student traineeships" to allow students in years 11 and 12 "to combine their school-based studies with work experience and off-the-job training." The government will fund the purchase of off-the-job training "for up to 5,000 students by 1995–96" (Keating, 1994, p. 93).
- *France* is making greater use of *alternance* (work-based learning). While traditional apprenticeship still exists in France (mainly in the artisanal sector), and although work-based training contracts are used for unemployed young people, the involvement of students in enterprises as part of their schooling did not begin on an extensive scale until the introduction of the vocational secondary diploma (*baccalauréat professionnel*) in 1985. Vocational diploma students are required to spend at least 16 weeks in enterprises during the two-year programme. The traditional separation between formal education and employment in France has meant that these work experiences are often not closely connected with what students do in their classes. For instance, performance in the workplace has no effect on whether a student receives the diploma. Nonetheless, the fact that hundreds of thousands of vocational diploma students have in fact been placed in enterprises has encouraged the educational authorities to extend the practice of *alternance* to the two-year vocational programmes that start at age 15 and precede the vocational diploma programme. The university technical institutes are also currently in the process of adding a third year which will consist mainly of firm-based traineeships.
- The *United Kingdom* is launching an initiative to create "modern apprenticeships" for 16–17 year old school-leavers. They will receive government-funded training credits which they can cash in with employers who are able to provide the training required. Unlike traditional apprenticeships, these new arrangements will not require trainees to spend a fixed length of time in the enterprise. Instead, qualifications will be awarded when the apprentice has passed a set of performance-based requirements (National Vocational Qualifications, or NVQs, not to be confused with school-based GNVQs). Prototype programmes have been developed in 1994 in 12 sectors, including agriculture and commercial horticulture, business administration, chemicals, child care, construction engineering, information technology, and retailing. When the new system is fully up and running, there are expected to be 150,000 apprentices in training (UK Employment Department, 1994).
- *Korea* has restructured its vocational high school curriculum to include one full year in enterprises during the three-year programme. It is hoped that this will help attract more students into vocational high schools, thus reducing the perceived oversupply of students going to university. At the same time, however, the opportunities for vocational high school graduates to enter university will be expanded, also to increase the attractiveness of the vocational programme. The year of work experience for vocational high school students is intended to enhance their adaptability in actual work situations (Cho, 1994).

- In the *United States,* the 1994 School-to-Work Opportunities Act provides federal money for states and localities to design and implement new school-to-work systems, in which work-based learning is a required component. The new programmes will have their main effect on 16–19 year old students in high schools and two-year colleges. Section 103 of the Act stipulates that work-based learning must be co-ordinated with school-based learning and relevant to students' "career majors" (which integrate academic and vocational instruction and link secondary with post-secondary education). Work-based learning must also "lead to the award of skill certificates," and other federal legislation has begun the process of writing skill standards for industries and occupations, which would make it possible for "skill certificates" to be recognised by employers as actual qualifications. But Section 103 also requires work-based learning to provide "instruction in general workplace competencies, including . . . employability and participative skills, and broad instruction, to the extent practicable, in all aspects of the industry." These requirements may be met by "such activities as paid work experience, job shadowing, school-sponsored enterprises, or on-the-job training."

SCHOOL-BASED ENTERPRISE: COMBINING LEARNING AND PRODUCTION

While firms are seeking to develop methods of just-in-time learning, and schools are giving more students the opportunity to practice learning in workplaces, the emergence of the learning-intensive economy is also creating demand for hybrid organisations that combine education with production. One such hybrid is the school-based enterprise. Traditionally, many school-based enterprises have been connected to vocational programmes, in order to give students an opportunity to practice what they learn. Placements in firms may not be available, or they may not offer as much opportunity to learn as a school-based enterprise (Stern *et al.,* 1994). In addition, school enterprises are now taking on other purposes as well, including technology transfer and the development of better methods to build learning into the work process.

In the *United States,* school-based enterprise is a common feature of vocational and professional education. A 1992 survey for the National Assessment of Vocational Education found that 19 per cent of secondary schools in the United States were operating some kind of enterprise that involved students in producing goods or services for other people as part of their school activities (Stern 1992*b*). Most of these were associated with vocational programmes. For example, students in construction trades may build a house, those preparing for food service occupations may run a restaurant, classes in automotive trades often repair cars, and a child care class may provide day care for clients outside the school. Similar activities take place in two-year colleges. These school-based enterprises are analogous to teaching hospitals run by medical schools, or law review journals produced by law school students. The school enterprise provides practical experience that helps prepare students for subsequent work in a particular occupation or industry.

In *Denmark,* school-based enterprise has been used as part of the apprenticeship system, to provide productive experience for students who are waiting for training contracts with firms (Danish Ministry of Education, 1994, p. 101). Printing, retailing, and construction are examples of the activities carried out by school enterprises. Students in these programmes normally expect to stay in the industry or occupation where they receive training. There are some indications that employers prefer to have trainees work in school-based enterprises during the early part of their training, when they are less profitable for firms to hire as apprentices.

School enterprise can also be used to provide work-based learning for students who are not yet specialising in a particular occupation or industry. The Junior Achievement (JA) programme in the *United States* is one of the oldest examples. Started in 1919, JA has involved millions of students in mini-enterprises, usually on an extra-curricular basis but sometimes for course credit. JA is sponsored by the Chamber of Commerce, which recruits adult volunteers to serve as advisers, and furnishes instructional materials. During one semester or year, students start up a company by raising equity capital (typically a few hundred dollars from relatives, friends, or their own savings), electing officers, and setting up accounts. They decide on a product—often a small gift item—then buy materials, produce the goods, and sell them. At the end any profits are distributed among the stockholders.

The *United Kingdom* took mini-enterprises one step further. After an organisation called Young Enterprise, modelled on JA, had taken up the idea as an extra-curricular activity for students, the government in the 1980s promoted mini-enterprises as part of the school programme, providing start-up funds, teacher training, and curriculum materials. By the late 1980s and early 1990s, approximately 40 per cent of government-supported secondary schools were reporting that they sponsored mini-enterprises. These were seen as effective means for students to learn about work, for work, and through work (Jamieson, Miller, and Watts, 1988), though not to train for specific industries or occupations.

A different version of school-sponsored enterprise has developed in *Denmark's* production high schools. These are not part of the regular education or apprenticeship system. They serve unemployed young people who have completed compulsory schooling without obtaining a vocational qualification. They combine instruction in academic and vocational subjects with production of substantial products, for example furniture or clothing, for sale to the public (but avoiding unfair competition with commercial producers). As of 1992 there were 120 production high schools enrolling approximately 9,000 students (Danish Ministry of Education, 1994, p. 132). The spread of production high schools inspired the Danish use of school-based enterprise as part of the apprenticeship system, described above. But the production high schools are not necessarily trying to train students in a particular occupation or industry. Instead, they are attempting to strengthen basic academic skills and provide work experience while students wait for offers of regular jobs.

A particularly good example of school enterprise for the learning-based economy is the German-Singapore Institute (GSI) in *Singapore.* Founded in 1981 as a joint venture between the Economic Development Board of Singapore and the German Agency for Technical Cooperation, GSI calls itself a "teaching factory." It carries out applied development projects for local manufacturers, while preparing technicians and middle managers in the fields of advanced manufacturing technology, factory automation and robotics, plastics manufacturing technology, and (since 1992) manufacturing software. In 1994 GSI enrolled about 1,100 students, and plans to grow to 2,000 students in the next six years. Students spend most of their two or three years in laboratories equipped with state-of-the-art production equipment, much of it donated by German manufacturers. In 1991 the German Machinery and Plant Manufacturers' Association gave GSI the German Mechanical Engineering Award, with a citation that commended GSI's "project-oriented approach to training within a comprehensive and practice-oriented environment." The GSI model has been emulated in Malaysia, Brazil, and elsewhere.

The capstone experience for students at GSI is the applied project in the last semester, which engages them in "production for learning." An Industrial Project Group (IPG) contracts with local companies and takes responsibility for meeting clients' cost, performance, and delivery requirements. The full-time engineers and designers in the IPG assign students to work on these undertakings, usually in groups of four to six. Projects may involve design and construction of automated manufacturing units, for example, to assemble or package electrical components. Students take responsibility for scheduling and organization, purchase of supplies, and cost calculation. Teamwork, problem-solving, and creativity are emphasised.

GSI is organised in some ways more like a business than a school. Unlike most schools in Singapore, GSI teachers are not civil servants, but are hired by the Employment Development Board and paid at the industry scale. Faculty and students work 44 hours a week. Instead of the long holidays typical of an academic calendar, they receive only short vacations as in industry. The departments at GSI also have names that represent productive functions like tool and die making, design, and data processing, rather than academic disciplines.

Like GSI, numerous community colleges in the *United States* have assisted firms with installation of new technology, and have provided customised training for employees. University technical institutes in *France* also involve students in conducting studies for companies.

The most far-reaching, but still largely unrealised, contribution of school enterprises to the learning-based economy is their ability to experiment with methods of production that maximise learning (Stern *et al.,* 1994). Unlike firms, school enterprises have education as their primary mission; they use productive activity to accomplish it. For example, a high school on the southern coast of Alaska produced smoked salmon, packaged it, and exported it to Japan. Students used the activity to practice quality control and systematic problem solving. But once the enterprise had established itself and production had become routine, the school decided to develop new products. A commercial fish processing company in the community agreed to provide raw seafood, and the students would test new ways to prepare and package it for commercial sale. This evolution was prompted by the idea that maximum learning occurs when production workers are also involved with R&D. This idea goes beyond engaging workers in process innovation through quality circles or "total quality management." The evolution of this school enterprise may point the direction in which employment practices will change in non-school enterprises. One indication is that the highly innovative Saturn division of General Motors has involved production workers and the United Auto Workers union in designing cars and the technology to produce them. The Alaska school enterprise thus does seem to be at the forefront of contemporary practice. The fact that students and faculty participating in the school enterprise have been invited to present to meetings of corporate managers dealing with quality and related issues is an indication that their discoveries are valued by the business community.

There are other examples. A two-year vocational college in rural Ohio sponsors several enterprises, including a hotel. The director of the hospitality programme in charge of the hotel was considering the introduction of skill-based pay, which would be an innovation in the hotel industry. In a high school in suburban Virginia, the business education program runs a kiosk in a commercial shopping center. The teachers there have divided students into teams, each responsible for a different segment of merchandise. They have created a set of performance measures for each team, including profitability, service, and prevention of theft by shoppers. This experiment might offer useful lessons to commercial retailers, who have been slow to adopt the principle of team organisation that has become fairly widespread in other sectors. Whether or not they take a self-conscious leadership role, every school enterprise must find a way to blend education with production. Business might learn from watching how this is done.

Once more efficient methods to combine learning with production become known, they are available to anyone. Since it is not possible to patent or copyright such techniques, profit-seeking businesses have less incentive to invest in discovering them than in developing other ideas to which they can establish a proprietary right. If a company does find a more efficient method for employees to learn while they work, the company will try to hide this knowledge from competitors. In contrast, the school-based enterprise exists to educate students by producing goods and services for the public at large. The invention of techniques to increase learning in the context of production is potentially the most significant output of school enterprises.

FIRMS AS SCHOOLS?

All firms provide training for their regular employees. Sometimes they go so far as to create their own schools. Large, high-tech companies supply their own advanced training in facilities which they sometimes call universities. In addition, some employers sponsor workplace literacy programs (Hollenbeck, 1993).

In the context of initial education for new workers, firms participating in the German apprenticeship system have also created their own school-like structures. German apprentices in the industrial sector spend much of their time in training centres operated by individual large firms or by groups of small employers. These company schools are separate from the state-run schools where apprentices spend one or two days a week, but they are also separate from the firms' main productive activities. Though the training centres are located apart from the main production areas, apprentices may do some real work there—an application of the school-based enterprise principle inside the firm. Outside Germany, it is also possible to find company schools providing initial education and training in some large Japanese firms. Sweden's Volvo has recently created an intensive school where in three years students can complete both an apprenticeship and a regular upper-secondary diploma (Hasselberg *et al.,* 1994).

Will employers outside Germany take greater responsibility for initial education and training? As we have seen, there is a desire to offer work-based learning opportunities for students in countries where employers do not now provide it on such a large scale as in Germany. There are good reasons for wanting to do this, as we have also seen. However, training is costly. While employers are developing just-in-time learning methods to reduce the cost of training for regular employees, it is much more difficult to do this for students or young trainees who are not already part of the regular work process. Therefore, the prospects for involving employers in initial training on a large scale in other countries do not seem good, unless governments take action (Bailey, 1994).

DIRECTIONS FOR GOVERNMENT POLICY

Although many firms are trying out new methods to build learning into the production process, there has been little systematic development or testing. Accumulation of knowledge about effective practice is impeded by the natural reluctance of companies to share useful discoveries with competitors in the absence of any patents or copyrights. Government can therefore play a positive role in promoting and evaluating efforts by consortia of firms to develop techniques of learning-intensive production. Governments have already played a similar role in pooling the expertise of firms for R&D on strategic technologies (Matthews, 1994), and in encouraging the deployment of soft technologies for quality control and employee participation in problem-solving (Cole, 1989). Similar efforts could now be undertaken in support of industry groups, such as the National Centre for Manufacturing Services (1994) in the United States, which are promoting more efficient methods for human resource development. A special focus for government support might be the use of new technologies for information processing and telecommunication to create inter-firm networks of learners.

In the field of initial education and training, initiatives by governments in several countries have already been described. These are attempting to break down the barriers between the vocational and academic tracks, and to create more opportunities for students to learn through work. The reform of curriculum and instruction is within the direct jurisdiction of government, but creating more opportunities for students to learn by working in enterprises calls for the creation of new partnerships in countries that do not now have extensive apprenticeship systems. Governments must play a role in building new institutional infrastructure, which includes skill standards for industries or occupations that can guide work-based learning, and a wage system that gives both students and employers a financial incentive to invest in training (Soskice, 1994).

Governments can also promote school-based enterprises, both to provide work-based learning opportunities for students, and to serve as laboratories for experimenting with techniques to maximise learning through work. Although there have been some small initiatives by governments (notably Denmark) to encourage school-based enterprise as a form of work experience, and while the EC has sponsored youth-initiated productive projects to provide employment and training (Morin, 1992), the use of such enterprises as laboratories for improving methods of just-in-time learning has not yet been systematically attempted.

In sum, the transformation of productive and organisational methods within firms (e.g. Boyer, 1989) and the emergence of new kinds of relationships among firms (Matthews, 1994) both require faster, and continuous, learning by individuals. This implies that more learning must take place in the context of work itself, but at the same time greater instability of employment means that companies have less incentive to invest in training. Governments can help resolve this dilemma by helping to develop methods of just-in-time learning for current employees, and by ensuring that students have an opportunity to practice learning through work.

BIBLIOGRAPHY

Applebaum, E. and R. Batt (1994), *The New American Workplace: Transforming Work Systems in the United States,* ILR Press, Ithaca, NY.

Bailey, T. (1994), "Barriers to Employer Participation in School-to-Work Transition Programmes", paper prepared for a seminar on "Employer Participation in School-to-Work Transition Programmes", The Brookings Institution, Washington, DC, 4 May, Institute on Education and the Economy, Teachers College, Columbia University, New York.

Barbier, J.-M. *et al.* (1992), *Le développement de la fonction formative des situations de travail,* Centre de Recherche sur la Formation, Conservatoire National des Arts et Métiers, Paris.

Berryman, S.E. and T. Bailey (1992), *The Double Helix: Education and the Economy,* Teachers College Press, New York.

Berton, F., G. Podevin and E. Verdier (1991), "Continuing Vocational Education in France", *Training & Employment,* No. 2, Winter, CEREQ (Centre d'Études et de Recherches sur les Qualifications), Marseilles.

Boyer, R. (1989), "New Directions in Management Practices and Work Organisation", paper prepared for the OECD conference on "Technological Change as a Social Process—Society, Enterprises, and the Individual", Helsinki, 11–13 December.

Brochier, D., J.-P. Froment and A. d'Iribarne (1990), "La formation en alternance intégrée à la production", *Formation Emploi,* Vol. 30, pp. 3-19.

Brown, C., M. Reich and D. Stern (1993), "Becoming A High-Performance Work Organization: The Role of Security, Employee Involvement and Training", *International Journal of Human Resource Management,* Vol. 4, No. 2, pp. 247–275.

Cho, S.-J. (1994), "5-Year Plan For New Economy and Vocational and Technical Education System", paper prepared for the OECD seminar on "Education and Training for the Workforce", Seoul, 30 May–1 June.

Cole, R.E. (1989), *Strategies for Learning: Small Group Activities in American, Japanese and Swedish Industry,* University of California Press, Berkeley.

Committee for Economic Development (1985), *Investing in our Children,* Committee for Economic Development, New York.

Danish Ministry of Education (1994), *Danish Youth Education: Problems and Achievements,* Report to OECD, Danish Ministry of Education, Copenhagen.

Elias, P., E. Hernaes and M. Baker (1994), "Vocational Education and Training in Britain and Norway", in L.M. Lynch (ed.), *Training and the Private Sector: International Comparisons,* University of Chicago Press, Chicago.

Grubb, W.N., G. Davis, J. Plihal and J. Lum (1991), *The Cunning Hand, the Cultured Mind: Models for Integrating Vocational and Academic Education,* MDS-141B, National Centre for Research in Vocational Education, University of California, Berkeley.

Hamilton, S.F. (1990), *Apprenticeship for Adulthood: Preparing Youth for the Future,* Free Press, New York.

Hasselberg, C., R. Nordanskog and K. Sjölander (1994), "Education and Employment: Apprenticeship and 'Alternance' ", paper prepared for OECD seminar on "Apprenticeship, Alternance, Dual System: Dead Ends or Highways to the Future?", Marseilles, 12–14 April.

Hollenbeck, K. (1993), *Classrooms in the Workplace,* W.E. Upjohn Institute for Employment Research, Kalamazoo, Michigan.

Hull, D. and D. Parnell (1991), *Tech Prep Associate Degree: A Win/Win Experience,* Centre for Occupational Research and Development, Waco, Texas.

Jamieson, I., A. Miller and A.G. Watts (1988), *Mirrors of Work: Work Simulations in Schools,* Falmer Press, London.

Kearns, D.T. and D.P. Doyle (1988), *Winning the Brain Race: A Bold Plan to Make our Schools Competitive,* Institute for Contemporary Studies, San Francisco, CA.

Keating, P.J. (1994), *Working Nation: Policies and Programmes,* Australian Government Publishing Service, Canberra.

Kirsch, E. (1990), "Les CAP par unités capitalisables dans la sidérurgie : une conversion réussie", *Formation Emploi,* Vol. 32, pp. 7–18.

Kirsch, J.-L. (1994), "New Directions for Vocational Education in France?", *Training & Employment,* No. 15, Spring, CEREQ (Centre d'Études et de Recherches sur les Qualifications), Marseilles.

Koike, K. and T. Inoki (1990), *Skill Formation in Japan and South-East Asia,* University of Tokyo Press, Tokyo.

Laur-Ernst, U. (1992), "The Dual System in Germany: Advantages of Co-operative Models of Vocational Training", in Schools and Industry: Partners for a Quality Education, Proceedings of an EC/US conference held in Noordwijk, the Netherlands, Nuffic Publishers, The Hague.

Lave, J. and E. Wenger (1991), *Situated Learning: Legitimate Peripheral Participation,* Cambridge University Press, Cambridge.

Lynch, L.M. (1994), "Introduction", in L.M. Lynch (ed.), *Training and the Private Sector: International Comparisons,* University of Chicago Press, Chicago.

Matthews, J. (1994), "Organisational Foundations of the Learning Economy", paper prepared for the OECD conference on "Employment and Growth in the Knowledge-Based Economy", Copenhagen, 7–8 November.

Middleton, J., A. Ziderman and A. van Adams (1993), *Skills for Productivity: Vocational Education and Training in Developing Countries,* Oxford University Press, Oxford.

Morin, M. (1992), "PETRA Programme, Theme-based Partnership Projects, 1989–92", final report, PETRA Youth Bureau, Brussels.

National Academy of Sciences (1984), *High Schools and the Changing Workplace: The Employers' View,* report of the Panel on Secondary School Education and the Changing Workplace, National Academy Press, Washington, DC.

National Center for Manufacturing Sciences (1994), *Focus,* National Center for Manufacturing Sciences, Ann Arbor, Michigan, July.

Osterman, P. (1994), "How Common is Workplace Transformation and Who Adopts it?", *Industrial and Labor Relations Review,* Vol. 47, No. 2, pp. 173–187.

Rosenstock, L. (1991), "The Walls Come Down: The Overdue Reunification of Vocational and Academic Education", *Phi Delta Kappan,* Vol. 72, No. 6, pp. 434–436,

Seavey, D. and R. Kazis (1994), *Skills Assessment, Job Placement and Training: What Can Be Learned from the Temporary Help/Staffing Industry?,* Jobs for the Future, Boston.

Soskice, D. (1994), "Reconciling Markets and Institutions: The German Apprenticeship System", in L.M. Lynch (ed.), *Training and the Private Sector: International Comparisons,* University of Chicago Press, Chicago.

Steedman, H. (1993), "The Economics of Youth Training in Germany", *Economic Journal,* Vol. 103, No. 420, pp. 1279–1291.

Stern, D. (1992a), "Institutions and Incentives for Developing Work-Related Knowledge and Skill", in P. Adler (ed.), *Technology and the Future of Work,* Oxford University Press, New York and Oxford.

Stern, D. (1992b), "School-to-Work Programmes and Services in Secondary Schools and Two-Year Public Post-secondary Institutions", paper prepared for the National Assessment of Vocational Education, School of Education, University of California, Berkeley.

Stern, D., M. Raby and C. Dayton (1992), *Career Academies: Partnerships for Reconstructing American High School,* Jossey-Bass Publishers, San Francisco.

Stern, D. and J.M.M. Ritzen (eds.) (1991), *Market Failure in Training? New Economic Analysis and Evidence on Training of Adult Employees,* Springer-Verlag, Berlin and New York.

Stern, D., J.R. Stone, III, C. Hopkins, M. McMillion and R. Crain (1994), *School-based Enterprise: Productive Learning in American High Schools,* Jossey-Bass, San Francisco.

UK Employment Department (1994), *Modern Apprenticeships,* Young People and Work Branch, Employment Department, Sheffield.

US Congress Office of Technology Assessment (1990), *Worker Training: Competing in the New International Economy,* US Government Printing Office, Washington, DC.

Vickers, M. (1994), *Skill Standards and Skill Formation: Cross-National Perspectives on Alternative Training Strategies,* Jobs for the Future, Boston.

Womack, J.P., D.T. Jones and D. Roos (1990), *The Machine that Changed the World,* Rawson Associates, New York.

Yoshimoto, K. (1994), "Education and Training in Japan", paper prepared for the OECD seminar on "Education and Training for the Workforce", Seoul, 30 May–1 June.

Index

WITHDRAWN

XB 2564754 7